Journey through
Britain

Journey through Britain

John Hillaby

Constable London

FOR TILLY

who kept the home fires burning

First published in Great Britain 1968
by Constable and Company Ltd
3 The Lanchesters
162 Fulham Palace Road
London W6 9ER
Copyright © 1968 John Hillaby
Paperback edition 1995
ISBN 0 09 474990 6
Printed in Great Britain by
St Edmundsbury Press Ltd
Bury St Edmunds, Suffolk

A CIP catalogue record for this book
is available from the British Library

Photographs by the author

CONTENTS

ILLUSTRATIONS

BEFORE THE START

Somewhere up in the high forests between England and Wales I had been walking for hours and, not for the first time, I had lost my way. All tracks seemed to lead west when it was clear from map and compass that I should be heading north. Down in the valley an old man explained in elaborate detail how I'd strayed miles off course. In any case, he said, there wasn't much worth seeing even had I got to where I intended to spend the night. A thoroughly dispiriting old man. From time to time you meet them. I thanked him and began to move off.

'Where've you come from?' he asked. Not wishing to go into the history of a walk scarcely begun, I named the last town I had passed through. But he wasn't to be put off that easily. He wanted to know how I had got *there*? With a touch of pride, I said I had walked from Bristol. He looked adequately surprised. Had I started from Bristol?

'No', I said. Truth must out. Why not relate all? I told him I'd walked from Cornwall. He looked astonished. For the first time in days I felt rather pleased with myself.

'From Cornwall?' he said. 'Do you mean to tell me you've walked *all* the way here?'

I nodded. Shaking his head sadly, he said: 'Then all I can say is it's a pity you couldn't be doing something useful.'

You can't win. Go to deserted parts of Africa and walk round some lake or other and people say you were darned lucky to get the chance. It looks like an exotic stunt. They reckon it's just a matter of being able to raise the cash. Some point out you could have hired a Land-Rover instead of camels and got there in a tenth of the time.

If, on the other hand you decide, as I did, to walk across your own, your native land they tell you its been done many times before. Men have set off on foot, on bicycles, on tricycles. Somebody has even pushed a pram from Land's End to John o' Groats. But all that, of course, was done on the roads I tried to avoid.

For me the question wasn't whether it could be done, but whether I could do it. I'm fifty. I'm interested in biology and prehistory. They are, in fact, my business. For years I've had the notion of getting the feel of the whole country in one brisk walk: mountains and moorlands, downlands and dales. Thick as it is with history and scenic contrast, Britain is just small enough to be walked across in the springtime. It seemed an attractive idea. There was a challenge in the prospect. But to see the best of what's left I knew I should have to set off pretty soon. Each year the country in every sense of the word gets a bit smaller. Already there are caravans in some of the most improbable places. Long-distance walkers are becoming rare. You can regard what follows as the lay of one of the last.

I set off with the intention of avoiding *all* roads. I meant to keep to cross-country tracks and footpaths all the way. In places this turned out to be practically impossible for notwithstanding what's been written about the ancient by-ways, many of them are now hopelessly overgrown; others have been enclosed, ploughed up or deliberately obstructed in one way or another. As far as I know, you can't get into the Midlands from the Welsh border or cross the Lowlands of Scotland without making use of country lanes, derelict railway tracks or, in places, the towpaths of the old canals. I did my best to keep out of the public arteries, but I sometimes got squeezed into the little capillaries of transport. Otherwise I kept to the out-of-the-way places, especially the highlands and moors.

From Land's End I followed the cliff-top paths of Cornwall for sixty or seventy miles and then struck east into Devon, crossing the centre of Dartmoor and reaching Bristol by way of the airy uplands of north Somerset. Then up the Wye valley through the Forest of Dean, perhaps the most beautiful woodland in Britain. A roundabout route through the Black Mountains, Shropshire and industrial Staffordshire led me into Derbyshire and the foot of the Pennine Way. From there north a high track along the spine of England extends as far as the Scottish border. In the West Highlands I used what are called the drove roads, the old cattle-tracks that wind through the deserted glens. In all I did about 1,100 miles in fifty-five walking days. It may have been much more; it may have been a little less. The calculation is based on map-miles which means I haven't taken into account innumerable forays in wrong directions.

As for trappings, I carried the basic minimum, including a tent that eliminated the need to look for lodgings at nightfall. This gives you a comforting sense of independence. I don't mean I'm over-fond of the Spartan life. If I found a pub or a hotel at dusk, I went in, gratefully. But I had no need to rely on static shelter.

Looking back on all the stuff I bought, tried out and discarded, I don't think there's much I could have done without. I managed to reduce clothing and the contents of a rucksack to about thirty-five pounds. If I did the trip again, I should take the same gear with, perhaps, the addition of something easier to handle than a tin can to brew tea in.

Clothing is a simple matter. The trick is to wear as little as possible without becoming even a fraction too cold or too hot. The important thing is to feel comfortable throughout the whole day. I bought a light windproof anorak with a zip-fastener down the front that could be easily adjusted. I zipped it up tightly when I set off in the morning and gradually increased aeration when I began to generate my own heat. On wet days I put on one of two pairs of skin-thin bits of protective clothing, made of artificial fibre, that were supposed to be waterproof. They gradually leaked. I never got very wet and certainly never wet *and* cold, which I had been told is fatal. For this reason I covered my

3

light-weight cotton tent with an outer fly sheet made of Terylene that was wholly waterproof. When things got really bad, even during the day, I crawled inside. At night I slept in a bag quilted with what the salesman said were feathers from Chinese eider ducks. It felt like heaven, weighed three pounds and cost a lot of money.

Footwear is tricky. I treat my feet like premature twins. The moment I feel even a slight twinge of discomfort I stop and put it right. Most people advocate stout boots and thick socks. I know of nothing more uncomfortable. They give you a leaden, non-springy stride. You can't trot along in boots. I bought two pairs, broke them in and eventually threw them aside. On a trip across the desert some years ago I wore tennis shoes, but these, I found, are useless in Britain for they become sodden. After trying various kinds of shoes, I settled for an expensive Italian pair with light commando-type soles. They weighed about fifteen ounces each and, when oiled, fitted me like gloves. I had no trouble with shoes. Certainly not from blisters, although in the last stages of the journey some of my toe-nails dropped off. In places I went bare-footed through bogs, and on warm days in deserted country I sometimes wore only a pair of shorts.

The very necessary business of getting into training took about three months. I walked from Hampstead to the City each day and further at the week-ends. On these jaunts I carried weight-lifters' weights sewn high up in a flat rucksack that didn't look too odd among people making their way down to the office in the morning.

Before I set off from Cornwall I reckoned I could do about twenty-five miles a day with reasonable comfort. My pace, I discovered on a marked running track, is a fraction short of a yard and where the going's reasonably easy I walk at almost exactly four miles an hour.

Besides about forty maps, which were sent on to me in batches, I carried a camera, field-glasses, medicaments, notebooks and some works on how to identify plants and minerals. Among other books, one, an old favourite of mine on how to live the contemplative life in the desert, written by some Father of the Church in the fourth century, rather let me down in wet weather. At nightfall, alone and miles from anywhere recognizable, I found more comfort in a little Scotch and stories about wicked Roman women. For food emergencies that never arose, I stuck (until they got too sticky) to three packets of vitaminized fudge. These were eventually fed to a large dog of uncertain temper.

At this point it is usual to thank all those who helped the traveller on his way. This I do, with an enormous feeling of warmth, but there is a difficulty here, since I am indebted to so many. My brother, Joe Hillaby, an historian, suggested several ingenious ways of getting through the urban bits of the Midlands. Tom Stephenson, the self-effacing secretary of the Ramblers' Association, told me what I should be up against on the Pennine Way. In the Dales I had the brief but enormously encouraging company of Philip Hartley, a valued companion since childhood days. Donald Moir, of the Royal Scottish Geographical Society, drew thoughtful and reassuring lines across the bleak maps of Gaeldom. Two old friends and one-time colleagues, Iain Hamilton, formerly of *The Spectator*, and David Wood of *The Times* literally helped to keep me going when it came to the business of sorting out my highly-subjective notes. For the rest I wish sincerely that I could thank individually a host of folk I met. Among this very personal company are gamekeepers and church-wardens, shepherds and local naturalists, policemen, poachers, a few gypsies and a drunken priest, a bagpipe player, an eagle-spotter, several archaeologists and kindly people who just happened to be there when I turned up.

Ecstasy, I know, is an unfashionable commodity. At points on the trip when I slept out under the stars or got through the hills by means of gaps as spectacular as you can find anywhere I can only say it was a privilege to be there. To learn something about places I have never been to before, I read extensively from what I regard as reliable sources. But for the rest I shall try to relate what I saw when I set off from Land's End in the second week in April.

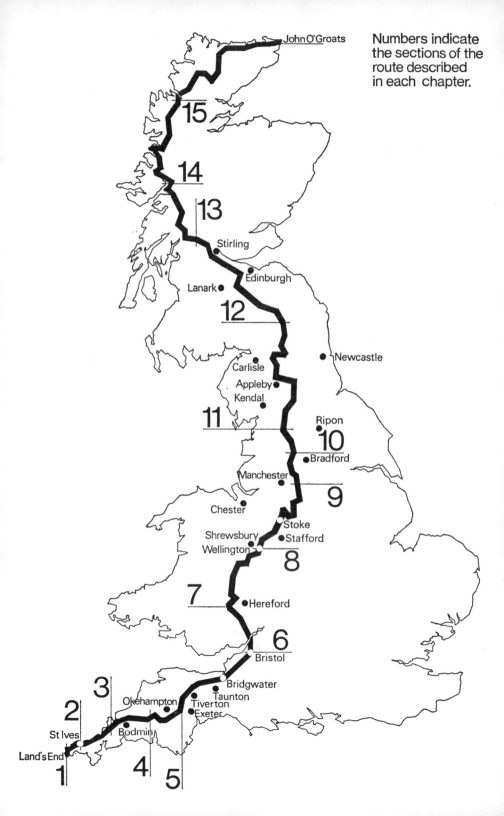

Numbers indicate
the sections of the
route described
in each chapter.

John O'Groats

15

14

13

Stirling

Edinburgh

Lanark

12

Newcastle

Carlisle

Appleby

Kendal

Ripon

11

10

Bradford

Manchester

9

Chester

Stoke

Shrewsbury

Stafford

Wellington

8

7

Hereford

6

Bristol

Bridgwater

3

Taunton

Okehampton

Tiverton

2

Exeter

St Ives

Bodmin

Land's End

1

4

5

MIST AND MEGALITH

I left at seven o'clock in the morning and I have been asked to say that my wife was there to see me off. There isn't, in fact, much else that I can say. It was misty. I couldn't see much. I could hear nothing except the twittering of invisible larks. I felt dizzy, not from the height of the cliff-tops, nor elation at the start. The feeling came from an unfamiliar breakfast of cold roast fowl and champagne. And that soon wore off.

Beyond the Land's End Hotel and the shacks of the trinket-vendors, the path that should have led to the wild blue yonder became wildly overgrown. And it was much like that for most of the way. But that I didn't know as I dodged in and out of thickets of thorn and gorse, looking for somewhere to squeeze through. The local official who assured me that, with few exceptions, I should be able to follow the coast-line as far as St. Ives and beyond had clearly not tried to get through himself, at least not for a long time. This depressed me considerably, since I had planned most of the trip on the presumptive accuracy of local information.

Here, as so often elsewhere, I can say relatively little about what preoccupied me most, that is an irrepressible, whirling stream of thoughts on which I became dependent since there appeared so little to look at: a few undistinguished plants underfoot,

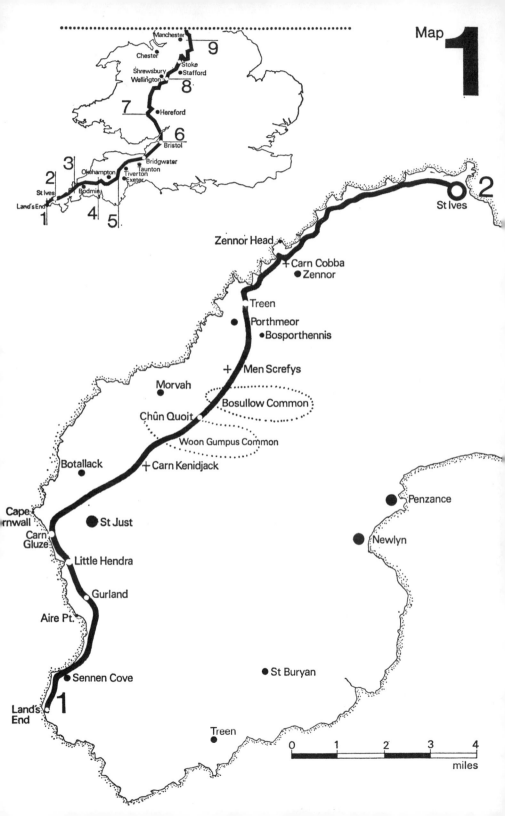

Map **1**

Manchester
Chester
9
Stoke
Shrewsbury
Wellington
Stafford
8
7
Hereford
6
Bristol
Bridgwater
Okehampton
Taunton
Tiverton
2
3
Exeter
St Ives
Bodmin
Land's End
1
4
5

2
St Ives

Zennor Head
+ Carn Cobba
Zennor
Treen
Porthmeor
Bosporthennis

+ Men Screfys

Morvah
Bosullow Common
Chûn Quoit
Woon Gumpus Common

+ Carn Kenidjack

Botallack
Penzance

Cape
rnwall
Carn
Gluze
St Just
Newlyn
Little Hendra
Gurland

Aire Pt.

St Buryan

Sennen Cove

Land's
End
1
Treen

0   1   2   3   4
miles

a mad March or, rather, April hare that turned a half-somersault and ran away, thumping the ground, some large hairy caterpillars with urgent heather deficiencies, three aerobatic jackdaws, discarded cigarette packets and, above all, a disconcerting silence. Even the invisible larks had stopped twittering. To screen off this isolation I sank deeper and deeper into thoughts about what there ought to have been rather than, visually, what there was. No chatty natives. No smugglers landing Irish whisky. Mentally, I composed a few rather clever remarks to the Cornwall Preservation Society and a rather unpleasant games master who once said I had no staying power.

In fact, I walked on, determined to stick to the top of the cliffs until I reached Cape Cornwall, a few miles north. There I hoped to find a prehistoric cemetery called Carn Gluze and much else beside. If the path disappeared entirely, as it seemed likely to, I decided from careful scrutiny of the map to strike across country to Zennor by way of Botallack, Carn Kenidjack and Woon Gumpus Common, names as strange as an incantation. I said them aloud and they sounded even more strange.

But as an incantation it seemed to work, for soon afterwards a light breeze dispersed the mist to reveal a large bay. From clouds at sea a theatrical shaft of light fell on a group of rocks which I took to be the Longships. In that eerie atmosphere it looked like a bit of the legendary land of Lyonesse.

Much of the Cornish coast-line is as desolate today as it was over five thousand years ago when strange people arrived in boats with large leather sails. They were the tomb-builders. They were peaceful men. They left no weapons behind. They came, it is thought, from the Mediterranean, perhaps Crete, although not, of course, in one stage. They established colonies on the way where they practised the cult of the dead called the Megalithic. This is the religion of the people who built the quoits or stone graves found on both sides of the Irish Sea from Cornwall to the north-west of Scotland. Like the ancient Egyptians, these priest-kings lived in order to die. Wherever they landed – in Corsica, around the Iberian Peninsula and north to Britain – they built elaborate graves.

9

Megalithic means no more than a relationship to big stones. The term is confusing since it is used often to describe circles of upright stones, such as Stonehenge. Circles mark the site of seasonal rituals, not burials. They were built by the masons of a race of warriors who arrived after the priest-kings and probably overcame them. In Cornwall there are examples of both graves and stone circles.

If any traces of these prehistoric invasions were left behind on the sea-shore, they have long since been washed beneath the waves. The sea has bitten and clawed at the granite cliffs, turning headlands into islands and grinding down the stumps into silver-white sand. In the legends Lyonesse is the land that was, the place where men said their forebears came from. It is now the floor of the sea.

I walked on, glad that the going was a bit easier, for already, after only a couple of hours, I felt a bit tired. Perhaps it was the champagne.

A Land-Rover bounced over the elastic turf. The driver, a cheerful young man in a dirty white boiler suit, pulled up and grinned. 'Thought from your pack that you were another ruddy prospector,' he said. 'The place is stiff with them. Going far?'

'Pretty far,' I said.

He was looking for tin, he told me. He and his partner had taken out a lease on an old mine. He pointed to where the chimney and a ruined engine-house stuck out above the horizon like fingers raised in an episcopal blessing. 'That's the place,' he said.

There are hopes that the industry, which has been almost dead for half a century, can be dragged to its feet. A dozen or more companies, ranging from local shoe-string operators to international giants like the Union Corporation, are probing into the granite to see what's left in the seams after thousands of years of exploitation. Cornwall once satisfied nearly a third of the world's demand for tin.

The story as most people know it is that the ancient Phoenicians came to Cornwall for tin. It seemed logical to associate the Semitic-sounding names of Marazion and Morvah with the

Mist and Megalith

people of the eastern Mediterranean, the more since the smelting-pits used to be called Jews' houses. But it looks as if the tale got somewhat mixed up in the telling.

In the first century B.C. an historian called Diodorus of Sicily put out the story that the inhabitants of Land's End, which he called Belerion, were friendly to strangers and mined a precious white metal which they shipped from an island called Iktin. This island is almost certainly St. Michael's Mount in south Cornwall.

What Diodorus failed to say was that he got his facts from the records of a remarkable voyage made three hundred years earlier by a certain Pytheas, a Greek from Marseilles, who must have been one of the first industrial spies. Tin in those days had become a strategically important metal, like uranium today. Without tin it was impossible to make bronze, the material of war. Pytheas knew that the Carthaginians, the deadly enemies of the Greeks, were getting their tin from a secret source somewhere off the Atlantic coast called the Cassiterides. When the Carthaginian ships slipped out through the Straits of Gibraltar he followed them, keeping them in sight until he had discovered two places where the tin came from.

One was Cornwall, the other a port near the mouth of the Loire. But historians mixed the stories up and added a bit of their own. They substituted Phoenicians for Carthaginians and imagined the Cassiterides were the Isles of Scilly. In fact, Cornish tin was shipped to Gaul and carried on horseback to Marseilles.

Today the abandoned workings are covered in heather. Cousin Jack, the miners' name for a Cornishman, never made much out of the industry for himself. Perhaps in the early days he was outdone by the wily Greeks. Even now, when local people talk about 'foreign' capital, they are not referring to Bibis Yukon or Rhodesian Katanga, but to non-Cornishmen in general. An old man told me that when the famous Ding-Dong mine closed down his granddad 'made a packet' with a pick and a pan of his own. I asked him how much. 'Enough to get out', he said. He took the family off to Bolivia.

In the uranium mines of north Canada I had met men called Trevithick, Tremayne and Trelawney whose first question was

II

usually about the Cornwall they had never seen. 'What's it like nowadays?' they asked me. 'What do people do?' I didn't know. One man who came originally from Redruth said he had worked within a few degrees of the Arctic Circle for nearly forty years. His father took him into Mackenzie when he was in short pants. I made a recording of his life in the camps, the long winters and the absence of women. When I asked him about women, he nodded towards a large self-possessed blonde called Betsy, who had turned up the previous day from the copper mines at the other side of the lake. 'Better ask her,' he said.

Betsy looked first at the microphone and then at me. 'Young man,' she said. 'Don't you go asking *me* any fool questions. My business is men.'

The most noticeable inhabitants of the Cornish cliff-tops these days are the hares that hung about that morning, looking for mates or rivals to scare away. Normally, hares are timid creatures, quick to scamper off. But in the spring they seem concerned only to establish the fact that they are there, alive and randy. Some reared up on their hind legs, like Lilliputian kangaroos, and sparred with their fellows, but with no great malice. These were clearly mock battles. Others sat in circles of five or six, facing each other, pretending to doze off, but in reality they were watching each other. They took very little notice of me.

As the mist rose and fell I became uncomfortably aware of the deep holes in the ground dug by Cousin Jack and his poverty-stricken friends. Most of the old workings were partly overgrown with thorn and briars and they looked deep.

Sunk in the rim of the cliffs near Cape Cornwall is a complicated excavation, a ring within a ring which, from the embankment above, looks like an enormous navel. This is Carn Gluze, an exposed Megalithic burial chamber which, I must say, is rather a disappointment. At the centre of the whorl is a shaft that probably represented the entrance to the underworld. Here was the place where the dead were inched into immortality through a narrow portal. The locals now use it as a lavatory.

Carn Gluze was excavated about a hundred years ago by a gang of miners directed by the famous Copeland Borlase, an antiquarian who opened up barrows with the confidence of a surgeon lancing a boil. Among what he describes as 'greasy mould', the remains of someone, he found an amulet. Elsewhere his men discovered a bit of pottery and the bones of a lamb, perhaps a final sacrifice. Nothing else. Somebody had evidently got in before him.

The cairn stands within fifty yards of the edge of the cliff. A mile out to sea the Atlantic rollers throw a lace-work of foam against the jagged Brison Rocks. Whatever may have happened there in the days of the priest-kings, the impression now is one of utter desolation. The old gods are not so much forgotten as dug up and left horribly exposed. They ought to cover up that entrance hole. I left the cliff-top and headed inland, in search of Kenidjack Carn.

Carn or carneth means a pile of rocks. At Carnac in Brittany, which is closely related to Cornwall in its prehistoric cultures, there are many rock tombs. What Kenidjack means I don't know. It sounds like something from a manual of witchcraft. The local people call it the Hooting Carn. The rocks are a natural formation, an outcrop of granite. Nobody, as far as I know, is buried there. But from the top of the hill I heard a low moaning noise. It came, I am bound to admit, from far out at sea, where the captains of coasters chugging round the Brisons in the mist were trying to get a signal from the coastguard station on the Cape.

Local legend says that many, many years ago two miners crossed the heath at dusk and heard a strange hooting noise. Among the rocks they saw wild-looking men watching a wrestling match in the presence of the Devil himself. At length one of the contestants lifted his adversary high in the air and dashed him to the ground with the sound of thunder. The giants crowded round the victor, making a hooting noise, disregarding the defeated man, who lay on the ground, apparently dying. The miners hurried to his aid and one of them, they say, knelt down and spoke some words of Christian comfort. Instantly the earth shook and the demons vanished in darkness. What can be made of this rugged stuff?

It may well contain echoes of the arrival of the first Christian missionaries.

In the sixth century the Blessed St. Samson and his followers landed at Padstow from south Wales with a waggon-load of books and holy vessels. The good fathers immediately tried to put an end to pagan customs. They saw people wrestling, dancing in the open air and 'worshipping fearful idols'. They are said to have remonstrated with the heathens and cut Christian crosses on the huge upright stones. Perhaps this evoked the hoots and cries perpetuated in folklore. In the mist I saw only the base of the Kenidjack rocks and though the hooting persisted the sound came unmistakably from the sea.

Beyond the carn the moor is scarred by the ruins of innumerable barrows or earth-mounds, each one an ancient grave. The majority were ransacked centuries ago by men in search of treasure. I intended to poke about among them myself but, to my dismay, after only five hours of walking my feet felt tired. I bathed them by walking bare-footed in a refreshing patch of cold, wet grass. This done, I slept for twenty minutes, adjusted the pack and went on to the cairns and quoits.

Cairn, like 'carn', means a heap of rocks; a quoit by definition is a flat disc of stone or metal, a word used also to describe the roof of a Megalithic grave. There are more of these bits of prehistoric scaffolding around Woon Gumpus Common than anywhere else in Britain. To walk alone among them as I did on that first morning out of Land's End was a strange experience – strange and frustrating. Monuments are mute witnesses. Great circles are for miracles to happen. They are not to be walked through in cold indifference. I make no apology for this preoccupation with the past. It seems amply worthwhile to learn something about where our ancestors came from and how they lived and what experiences lead to fear of the dark, reverence for the dead and interests beyond the merely utilitarian. From the number of sites marked in Gothic lettering on the map you might expect to find the ground littered with graves. This is not so.

They are there to be found, but they have to be looked for and identified and it's far from easy to see what they were used for.

Chûn quoit lived up to all expectations. It loomed up over the horizon like a huge stone mushroom, an impression heightened at close quarters by the roughly circular capstone which, like a shallow inverted bowl, overhung a stalk of supporting uprights. I walked up to it and fingered the rough granite. I tried to squeeze into the little cell beneath the flat stone roof, but gave up lest I got trapped like a squirrel in a cage. Quoits are very odd affairs.

Lanyon, an example lower down the valley, is an almost perfect smooth-topped table on granite legs so high that originally a man on horse-back could ride underneath without ducking his head. After it fell in Waterloo year some romantic antiquarians put the broken slabs together in such a way that it now looks like any film director's concept of a Druid altar for human sacrifice.

Zennor, another one higher up the coast, has a sloping capstone and a portal like the doors of a little cathedral. Trethevy is blocked by a huge piece of granite, a stone door that leads nowhere.

All the stone is local stuff, but the slabs are so big that the people who built the tombs must have laboured for years prising the sections out of the parent rock and smoothing them down with mauls. The biggest stone of all, the capstone, is always balanced delicately on the top of a quadrangle of slabs arranged so that they lean against each other like a house of cards. Originally, the burial chambers were covered by a large mound of earth. What remains above ground today are merely the supports of the innermost chamber.

Three centuries ago, John Norden described Trethevy as a *casa gigantis*, '. . . a howse raysed of mightie stones, standing on a little hill within a fielde'. The 'little hill', as he calls it, is what remains of the mound that once covered the inner chamber. In Megalithic times west Cornwall must have been dotted with tombs. It was the great necropolis of the Megalithic. Most of them have been dismantled to make sheep-pens or gate-posts. Yet the men who cut out the slabs of rock must have thought that, like the Pyramids, they would last for ever. From the size of the stone doors that lead only into the chambers of the dead, it looks as if the fear was not so much that strangers might get in as that the spirits of the dead would get out. The priest-kings went to extraordinary lengths to ensure only one-way traffic on the journey to immortality.

Cornwall is badly served by those who ought to be looking after this treasure. In the three-mile walk from Lanyon quoit to the coast you move in and out of hut circles, settlements, burial mounds, Iron Age forts and Celtic stones, but, apart from advertisements for ice-cream and Pepsi-Cola, there isn't a notice-board or signpost in this layer cake of prehistory. The monuments are tucked away in corners of fields; they lie on hill-tops, where they are largely defaced or partly obscured by rank vegetation. For this the Ministry of Public Building and Works is largely to blame. They have either turned their back on the relics or dressed them up with bits of imported turf, making them look like putting greens.

Chûn Castle, for instance, was built to guard the tin mines at the time when Pytheas was shadowing the Carthaginian merchantmen. At first glance it looks like an enormous bomb crater. A walled depression about sixty paces in diameter encloses three clusters of courtyard houses. Here were the homes and workshops of the old Celtic tin-smelters, but there is nothing to indicate who they were or what they did. What is intriguing about the place is that the deep passage-way through the main gate turns sharply to the left, so that bowmen inside the walls could shoot at the unshielded right-hand side of anyone who tried to get in at them. Pytheas would have got it in the neck.

Not far away is Mên-an-tol, a stone that resembles a cart-wheel standing upright on its rim. This is the entrance to yet another type of Megalithic tomb. Children used to be pushed through the hole to be cured of rickets and arthritis and, just to be on the safe side, for I felt a bit stiff, I crawled through myself.

Moving down to Bosporthennis, a mile from the coast, you come to a stump of rock called Mên Scryfs. This is a memorial stone to an unknown Celtic chief, Rialobranus. He must have lived towards the end of the Roman occupation, for the inscription is in bad Latin. Perhaps it was cut into the stone by one of his proud descendants, a man who remembered the day the legions marched away. Did he recall the officers in their billowing red cloaks, the Red Devils as they called them in the south-west? They marched off saying they would return. Britain would always be part of their empire, the Romans told them. But something must have happened to those lines of marching men, for no one saw them again. They never came back.

Here on the hills between Kenidjack and Zennor you are among the first instalments of history: Megalithic, Bronze Age, Iron Age and Roman: some clear, some shadowy, all for speculation. In a walk across those downs you can't escape the relics of past occupations. They crowd in on you. And of all their monuments the most distinctive are the Megalithic, the works of a solemn and heavy hand.

Why a people whose culture seems to come from the eastern Mediterranean should have brought their religion to the windblown shores of Britain is a mystery. They may have been tempted to practise their priest-craft in a landscape that put them in mind of home. Cornwall looks like southern Greece. In appearance at least, it might be the Peloponnese. A hill above Mên Scryfs would provide a good setting for the opening scene of the *Agamemnon*. They built their graves above Zennor, a place so poverty-stricken that years ago a cow is said to have eaten the bell-rope of the church.

On the cliffs there I lay on my back listening to the yelp of the jackdaws. With growing concern I watched a group of youngsters from the climbing school haul themselves up a vertical stack with a rope. One after another they reached the little plateau at the top until they all squatted there, shoulder to shoulder, like nesting gulls. At Hor Point the thickets of thorn at the edge of the cliff became wholly intolerable and I had to make more and more detours inland.

At six o'clock that night, foot-sore and extremely dirty after a walk of twenty-four miles, I trudged down to St. Ives. You can't wash in the town. The explanation is that if they installed public facilities they would only be crowded out by the dirty beatniks. St. Ives seemed curiously concerned about the long-haired youngsters who either strolled about minding their own business or sat on the beach, talking and strumming their guitars.

'A dirty lot,' said the car-park attendant, looking, I thought, at my knees. 'And no good for business,' added a man who sold candy-floss at scandalous prices.

The picturesque little town still harbours a few artists, but for the most part the local people live on boarding visitors and selling trinkets. The middle-aged and the elderly buy pictures of flaming sunsets whilst the young walk up and down, looking for something to do. There is an undeclared state of war between the young and the old.

The patron of St. Ives, the gentle St. Ia, a virgin of noble Irish birth, is renowned as the saint who missed the boat. She and her companions agreed to set sail for Cornwall, but she came down to the shore too late. The galley had left. Anselm says that in her grief she knelt down on the beach and prayed, long and earnestly, whereupon God wafted her across the Channel on a leaf, so that she reached her destination before the others. These Celtic stories come from medieval manuscripts, but they embody ideas of earlier times. A common theme is of young people who came from across the sea and returned to the Isles of the Blessed before they grew old. There are tales of islands of young girls; of the beautiful Deirdre, who beguiled a sailor into her boat simply that she might look once more on the face of ardent youth.

In St. Ives today the fishermen are less romantic. One told me he had seen a beatnik, a young girl, bathing naked at dusk. 'Not a bloody stitch on her,' he said, his voice rising in indignation. 'She got out and dried her hair on her pullover. I saw her, I tell you. Bold as brass. I should like to have given her a damned good hiding.'

INTO WEST BARBARY

I left St. Ives at dawn, but not alone. The constable who woke me up insisted on accompanying me to the edge of the borough, explaining as we trudged along that the Vagrancy Act would apply equally forcibly in the next town. I tried to argue, pointing out that by camping on a vacant lot between the bathing huts and the esplanade I relieved pressure on the official site at the top of the hill. The man poked about in my rucksack; he showed a certain amount of interest in books on the birds of Britain and the archaeology of Cornwall, but conceded, reluctantly, that they were not evidence of evil intent.

All very humiliating, the more since I had planned to get up in a leisurely fashion, wash, feed and wave goodbye to the sleeping town. As it was, I limped towards Carbis Bay, hungry and burning with indignation. I got a shred of satisfaction from recalling that in 1870 the Vicar of St. Ives confessed to the Reverend Francis Kilvert, the diarist, that the stink of fish in the town was sometimes so terrific it stopped the church clock.

In outline the south-westernmost tip of Cornwall resembles the head of a snake. The head was originally an island related to the Isles of Scilly with a narrow strip of water between what is now St. Ives Bay and Mount's Bay on the south coast. The strip is now a dry valley, but to get from one side to the other I had

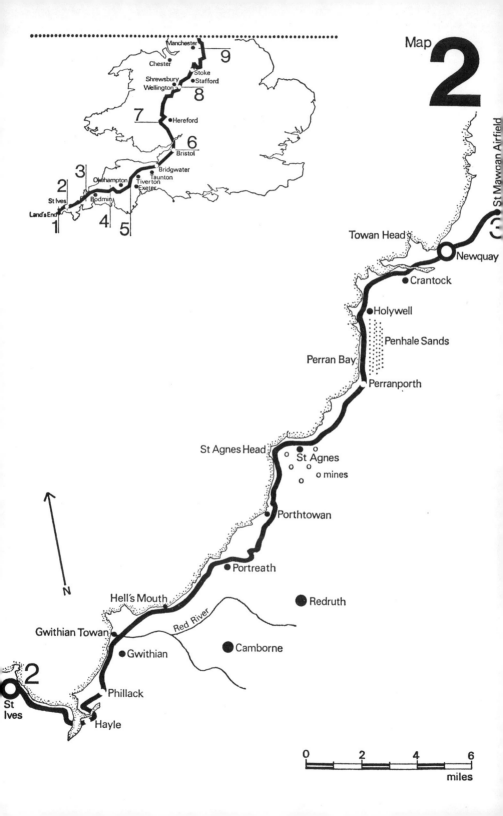

Map
2

St Mawgan Airfield

Towan Head

Newquay

Crantock

Holywell

Penhale Sands

Perran Bay

Perranporth

St Agnes Head

St Agnes

o mines

Porthtowan

Portreath

Redruth

Hell's Mouth

Red River

Gwithian Towan

Gwithian

Camborne

Phillack

St Ives

Hayle

N

0   2   4   6
miles

Manchester
Chester
Stoke
Shrewsbury   Stafford
Wellington
9
8
Hereford
7
Bristol
6
Bridgwater
Okehampton   Taunton
Tiverton
St Ives   Exeter
Bodmin
Land's End
1   4   5
2   3

either to make a long detour inland or take a chance and wade across the mud of the Hayle estuary. I took a chance and waded in.

A stupid decision. Gulls yelped. Clouds of sandpipers flew off, piping derisively. Halfway across the confounded slime I went in up to my crotch. Momentary panic. Much sploshing. Here it was that John Wesley had to be rescued from the fast-rising tide. Holding my shoe strings between my teeth, I tried to keep to a few firm patches of sand, but found they were separated by channels of deep water. A man shouted from the far bank. He seemed to be pointing upstream. I waded in that direction, cautiously, testing each slobbery footfall. I recall thinking that if I slipped in, my pack would probably sink and that for the time being would be the end of the trip. I eventually clambered out under the walls of a big engineering works and sat there, scraping the mud off my legs, using a twig like an old-fashioned razor. Still as muddy as a rat, I set off for the first hotel I could find, not caring what impression I made on bourgeois respectability. I felt cold and fed-up. The fact that I had been kicked out of my first bed in the open air had dampened my enthusiasm for the care-free vagrant life.

Things soon improved. I got a splendid breakfast. I chanced on a hospitable place where the landlord asked if I wanted a bath without implying I badly needed one. A Cousin Jack of sorts, he had spent a lot of time abroad, running canteens in mining camps, but had come back to Hayle, hoping that the town would regain some of its former prosperity. In the old days it supplied the world with rock-drills and pumping machinery.

'Go into any engine-house in north America in the old days,' he said, 'and you'd see the name of your home town on the pumps.' I nodded. I know almost nothing about plumbing. He seemed shocked that I hadn't heard of Harvey's engines. 'Not the monster?' I shook my head. But he was such a warm, enthusiastic man that I was glad to take a short course in hydraulics over breakfast.

Hayle is proud of its great engineers, the Harveys and the Trevithicks. You get the impression that Cornishmen are still indignant that their patents were stolen and ideas exploited.

Trevithick of Illogan, probably the greatest of them all, died penniless although his engine carried the first passengers ever to be conveyed by steam power. As my host put it, he was up against 'the foreigners', as, indeed, they all were. Trevithick made a pump that helped to make deep mining possible; he designed dredgers, rock-boring and crushing equipment, even agricultural machinery. But after years abroad, seeking work in the traditional manner of Cousin Jack, the old man came home to find Parliament had turned down his petition for a modest pension.

In 1840 the Harveys of Hayle got an order for what was then by far the biggest engine in the world. The Dutch ordered the monster for a draining operation in the Haarlem Zee. To make the twelve-foot cylinder they calculated that twenty-five tons of iron had to be melted in less than six minutes, a feat which most engineers at that time considered impossible. The engine was made and shipped to Holland, where it was reckoned a great success. Orders began to flow in for more of the famous fire engines. But Hayle's fortunes were largely tied to Cornish mining, and first tin and then copper went prodigiously bust. As my host put it: 'They sucked us dry and then went somewhere else.' *They* were the foreigners, the exploiters from the east of the Tamar. In London in the last century they referred to Cornwall as West Barbary.

I walked through the deserted streets of the town, towards the sand-hills, where the going proved slippery but more direct than a tortuous path inland. It remained dry for most of the day, but I had the impression that at any moment I might be swept up by a hurricane. The sky turned from sickly yellow to apple green and from far out to sea a line of billowy white clouds began to roll in like a mounting wave. The B.B.C., I learnt later, had been putting out gale warnings at hourly intervals. They reported snow in the hills and ice on most of the principal motorways. It was, they said, the worst April for years. An incoming stream of moist, warm, water-vapour from the Atlantic had collided with an enormous pond of cold air over Britain. As I recall that ominous line of cloud over the sea, my impression is that without knowing it I walked into at least the eye-brows of the storm and, perhaps for that reason, nothing phenomenal happened. At intervals the wind rose until it blew like an express train, but it died down and there was no sound except the gentle breathing of the sea. Some rain fell, but as a seasoned walker across an often wet island I am used to rain. Pipits cheeped among the marram grass. From far back in Hayle came the growl of a dredger; for the rest a silence fit for saying office in the open air.

I came by Gwithian Towan, a strange little sea-shore settlement of bungalows and home-painted shacks, each with a fenced-off garden bright with sea-pinks and lavender and each, to judge from the names, the home of retired people. The man planting onions at the 'End of the Rainbow' told me that he and his next-door neighbour from 'Journey's End' had, in fact, that morning lent a couple of spades to a party of archaeologists who were digging into the dunes above a wooden chalet called 'At Last Ours'. I found the diggers: five brisk women in tweeds and wellington boots, trenching deep for relics of Bronze Age farmers who scratched out a living in Gwithian Towan at the time when Paris laid siege to Helen. A woman with a pronounced Scottish accent asked me if I had come to dig. I said no; I had come to learn. She told me to sit down with such an air of authority that I sat down there and then and accepted a Woodbine. The sand-hills are distinguished for their traces of ancient cultures, but it needs a lot of imagination to get any sort of mental picture of what went on there. An additional problem is that some of the best stuff is still probably buried under the foundations of 'At Last Ours' and the 'End of the Rainbow'.

Gwithian lies near the mouth of the Red River, a stream that washes down the colourful spoil of the mining town of Camborne. Long before the Megalithic tomb-builders arrived in Cornwall, the coastal regions were populated by wandering food-gatherers, a people who hadn't learnt how to grow food or domesticate animals. They hunted animals, speared fish and seized on anything edible washed up by the tide. They were the poor relatives of the Old Stone Age hunters who painted fantastic pictures on the walls of caves in the Dordogne and the

Pyrenees. Nothing in Britain can match this outburst of French art. Archaeologists have found a bit of scratched bone, a few dabs of red ochre; at Gwithian a handful of tiny flint blades called 'microliths'. Life in Palaeolithic Cornwall must have been pretty tough.

Conditions were different in south-western France. It was warmer than Britain. The hunters lay in wait for herds of migratory animals to appear and, in between times, they created an unsurpassed art form. The pictures, archaeologists say, can be interpreted in terms of magical invocation, especially fertility. You can see all the classical symbols: the phallus, the circle, the inguinal triangle, the wheat grain and the cowrie shell. But after looking at some of the French caves I am inclined to think that here is the prehistoric equivalent of the television set. They painted the highlights of the times on the uneven surfaces of dark caves. In flickering torchlight the herds of bison and horses and the bulgy women probably looked as if they were moving.

My Scottish friend told me of the little socketed axes they had found and of the first traces of the ploughs used by farmers who settled in Gwithian long after the Palaeolithic hunters were dead. She came, she said, from Caithness, and was interested in ancient farmers and pastoralists. At some point in the conversation I referred to her fellow-countrymen as Scots.

'Scots?' she said. 'Good heavens! In Caithness we're not Scots. We're Vikings.'

From the sand-hills I went north-east, briskly, cutting across the Godrevy Peninsula to a gash in the cliffs called Hell's Mouth, making for Portreath beyond Samphire Island. At times the wind blew hard and carried rain in from the sea, but it was April rain from the west and hurt no one. No shacks nor billboards here. A strip of good walking country between the road and the sea has been providentially snatched up by the National Trust. Cars pulled up at intervals. The occupants got out, stretched themselves, and when they felt the wind they got in again to eat their lunch. Most of them lowered their windows as I walked up; they waved and smiled. Two of them hospitably offered me cups of tea. They said it was good to get out into the air and suggested that I might care to get in.

Jogging along, alone, I began to wonder what couldn't be seen from the front seat of a car. Perhaps not much that morning: a few newly-arrived swallows. They fluttered about on the telephone wires, desperately tired, scarcely able to fly against the wind. In the hollows between the gorse bushes were cowslips and violets, the first of the year, and innumerable large snails coupled tightly in a bubble-bath of ecstasy. Little else. Yet without these diversions, a glimpse of spring's stirring and mixing, I might have been more concerned about the rain or an occasional twinge in the small of the back. It was, in fact, due to an intrusive tent-peg in a rucksack packed hastily under police supervision.

Beyond Portreath, a little harbour tucked away in a crack of the coastline, you are obliged to make an elaborate detour to avoid heavily-fenced off military installations, which both look and sound pretty ominous. When I eventually got back to the cliffs the moorland was riddled with holes like an old Gruyère cheese. These are the remains of the old copper-mining industry. Boards saying 'Danger' leaned erratically over some of the biggest depressions; above them stand tall brick chimneys and roofless engine-houses. Wheal Charlotte has collapsed, Wheal Friendly is a hollow shell and there is not much left of Wheal Music, Wheal Liberty and a score of others. 'Wheal' means workplace - a place, that is, where men used to work.

At the bottom of these mines naked men stood up to their knees in water for about twelve shillings a week. Women and children received far less and, when the price of wheat rose to seventy shillings a quarter, families were obliged to spend at least half of their combined wages on food. James Watt, the inventor, said it turned his stomach to see men scraping the grease off his engines and eating it, yet before the coming of steam power conditions were far worse.

The water at the bottom of the deep workings had to be soaked up by an endless chain to which were tied strips of rag and leather an arm's length apart. These crude sponges were squeezed out by gangs of men standing one above the other in recesses at the top of the shaft. To reach the surface after a day's work in the heat of the galleries, they had to climb up hundreds of feet of ladders before walking home, wet and cold. The funeral registers tell their own story. The average age of 600 people buried at St. Just in the middle of the last century was under twenty-six. Apart from starvation, disease and the squalor of living in a one-room hovel that often had to be built in a few days, the new-fangled steam engines were overworked and dangerous. Wheal Rock had a record output of copper, but the boiler blew up twice in three years. The opening lines of a contemporary broadsheet recall that:

> *Down Wheal Rock, the boiler brock*
> *. . . and eight poor souls was killed*

Most of the miners were warming their hands by the side of the boiler when it exploded. They were blown to bits.

Copper contributed far more to the economy of Cornwall than tin, the better-known, older industry. The copper mines were richer, more numerous and they went down far deeper than those that produced the white metal. The tragedy was that after providing abundant work for miners left unemployed by the slump in tin, copper-mining collapsed about a century later. Competition from abroad killed it stone-dead and in one year, 1866, 12,000 miners roamed the country, looking for something to eat. Philanthropists visiting distressed families say that in a little room in Redruth they found a poor sick woman in bed, her married daughter and five grandchildren. None of them had tasted a morsel of food that day. They had supped the evening before on a little soup without bread. Everything left over had been baked into two pasties for the husband and his brother to carry to work, and even they went underground without breakfast.

Thousands of families in West Barbary were on the verge of starvation. Cousin Jack sought work abroad and sent home whatever he could. As John Rowe, the historian of the period, puts it: 'Before long there were to be as many Cornishmen in Butte City and Johannesburg as there were in Redruth and St. Just. They could not live without the mines and many of them

26

felt that without mining they were not living. So with reason it came to be said that wherever there was a pit in the world, a Cornishman would be found at the bottom of it, digging away. . . .'

Late that night in St. Agnes I quartered about in the moonlight, looking for a place to put my tent up. I found a wind-free hollow in the lee of the wreck of Wheal Kitty. Sleep came slow on the hard, ore-laden ground, and I tried to remember the names of the other ghostly mines: Great Pratt, Wheal Squidler, Wheal Prosper, Turnavore, Balnoon, Seal Hole and Puckerell, most of them long since dead.

I got up without any assistance from the police, washed in a horse-trough and looked at my young beard in a steel mirror. It looked pretty dreadful. After a swig of coffee and a sandwich bought the evening before, I packed and strode off towards Perranporth, the first stage of what promised to be a long day. For the first ten days my equilibrium depended to a great extent on the weather. A bit of sunshine in the early hours of the morning and I could endure hours of rain later on. Conversely, it took me a long time to throw off the depressing effect of a shower as I set off. That morning it began to pour down within ten minutes of starting and it kept it up for a couple of hours. I ran to a barn, the only building in sight, and found that it sheltered a bull. I ran on, stopping only to pull on some allegedly waterproof trousers. I say I ran; more accurately I jogged along. It's not easy to run when you're carrying a heavy rucksack. It was apparent, too, that neither trousers nor jacket made of a light synthetic material were impervious to a heavy downpour. They began to leak in several places. Wet and perspiring, I reached the deserted streets of the little town of Perranporth, determined if need be to stay there all day.

For an hour I stood in the bus station, gently steaming, drinking tea, brooding, wondering if the whole trip wasn't a mistake. I stood because if I sat down I had some difficulty in getting up again; knee and calf muscles unused to vigorous exercise tended to lock, rigid and painful. There wasn't really much that I could do. The pubs were closed and small provincial hotels are equipped

Chûn quoit

for travellers who want little more than a television set and an electric fire at night. In the morning they are expected to pay their bills and go away. I could take a bus to Newquay, where I intended to spend the night. But if there, why not go further on? Why walk at all? Pretending that it was all part of a carefully thought-out plan, I paid for three cups of tea and walked out, not only into the rain, but the quite unexpected splendour of the Penhale Sands.

The arc of tawny sand extends for miles - dead flat and firm underfoot. Nobody in sight that morning. Better still, it grew brighter and stopped raining. A few gulls hung in the wind. No sound except the sea. Bustling along, I raced the tide to a little promontory, knowing that if the waves cut me off I could scramble up the low cliffs. To crown all, the sun burst out, turning the tawny sand to crocus yellow. I sang as loud as a man can sing on his own. A dismal dawn turned into a great morning. I like Penhale.

Somewhere inland, according to fable, lies the buried city of Langarrow, once the capital of western Cornwall. It was renowned for its churches and noble buildings, built out of granite. The citizens grew rich on the products of their mines. They employed gangs of criminals underground, scouring the countryside for these wretches, so that in time a slave community sprang up with its own customs and, as the citizens discovered too late, its own vices. The story is that young girls, the daughters of the nobility, grew tired of their lonely life on the edge of the sea. On the pretext of keeping an eye on the work underground, they gave themselves to the lusty criminals, indulging in orgies of such an extravagant kind that, like the cities of the plain, Langarrow perished overnight in the storm. The sea rose and threw mounds of sand over the scenes of infamy. Today only St. Piran's cell remains.

It may well be that the fable of Langarrow embodies something that had to do with the end of communal fertility rites. The Cornish saints were dead against the lusts of the flesh. Two lovers who imprudently embraced on the tomb of a venerable bishop were 'unable to release themselves' until St. Gwinear turned up with a powerful prayer. On another occasion a group of disbelievers stole his sacristan's bull for a pagan sacrifice, but as the animal stood there in the dawn light, awaiting the fatal blow, the assembled mob were amazed to see its horns glow with a holy light. They promptly returned the beast and made amends for their theft.

It is commonly said that Cornishmen are not English. Robert Louis Stevenson could make nothing of the inhabitants. He said not even Red Indians seemed more foreign in his eyes. The population is supposed to be in part Phoenician, improbably supplemented by survivors from the wrecks of the Spanish Armada. It is, in fact, Celtic and the language once commonly spoken is related to Welsh and Breton. The landscape certainly looks strange. The sand dunes and the gritty soils are the products of weathered granite. They are loaded in places with arsenic. They have nothing in common with the milky shires of Saxon England, yet in sheltered localities there are growths of exotic fuchsia, myrtle, tamarisk and rare heaths and clovers. The coast is warmed by the Gulf Stream, although not, I felt, whilst I was there. The place names are very curious:

> *By Tre, Ros, Pol, Lan, Car and Pen*
> *Shall ye know most Cornishmen.*

'Tre' is a village or house. By doggedly following the ins and outs of the cliff tops, I got to Holywell Bay. The air of saintliness implicit in the name is not immediately evident in the character of the local farmers who tried often to turn me back, arguing that there is no such thing as a coast track and as long as they're landowners there won't be one. I swung inland, trying to distinguish between the names of hamlets that sounded like galloping horses: Treago, Trevella, Trevethick, Trevamper, Trethellan and Trenance. To make Newquay by way of Trenance, I waded across the Gannel estuary, an incoming which I recommend to nobody. Once again I got wet at the point where it felt most cold. I pitched down in one of the biggest caravan sites I have seen and went off to whoop it up in Newquay.

Not my favourite town. Thousands of boarding-houses and

unattractive little shops and restaurants radiate from the ghost of a harbour. There is nothing else - unless you count the listless visitors looking for something to do. No trouble with the beatniks in Newquay, a policeman assured me. By blocking two roads they could isolate the town and, as he put it, 'let the dogs loose among 'em for a bit of fun'.

Back in my little tent among the caravans I slept uneasily, my head on a lumpy rucksack pillowed with a towel and some underwear. It rained hard and at one point it rained in. At dawn the vehicles around me were almost totally enveloped in mist, and in that dispiriting atmosphere I packed a sodden tent and set off without breakfast, hoping to get something in St. Mawgan a few miles inland. I had had enough of the Cornish coast.

No colour anywhere. The grey-white town dribbled away into misty, monotonic country without either shape or perspective. I tramped on, trying to think of something to think about. The hamlet of St. Columb Minor was still fast asleep. Tregenna might have died years ago. Not a sound, not even from a farm where the lowing of cattle would have been a comfort. Still in a dank mist I came to the outskirts of a military airfield. Notice-boards warned me to keep out, but as there was nobody about I decided to cut across a corner of the runways.

From a point of no return in the middle of the first stretch of tarmac I heard the sound of a distant plane. Until the drone changed to an aggressive roar it hadn't occurred to me that the pilot was trying to land. Although it was almost impossible to determine where the sound came from, I started to run. Events thereafter became somewhat confused. A horse galloped out of the mist, neighing wildly. The plane zoomed overhead. Two more horses galloped past, followed by a man, shouting and swearing. He saw me and ran away. The plane swung round and flew off, apparently unable to land. I found a gap in the fence and slipped through, puffing like an engine. What farmer, I wondered, had been fool enough to graze his horses on an airfield.

The animals were owned by gypsies. Almost out of sight behind a hedge were two brightly-painted caravans. 'Thought you was a ruddy gavver,' said an old man comforting a steaming horse with a mixture of affection and blasphemy. 'Gavver' apparently meant authority, especially the police.

He explained that when the plane swooped down they had been up to their usual trick of poovin' the grays. A 'gray' is a horse. To poove it is to put it in a field at night without permission and retrieve it early the next morning. They had banked on having the airfield to themselves until the mist lifted, but the blanking plane had spoilt the blanking best poove they had struck that week. 'And nearly done this ole blanker in, too,' he said, stroking the nose of what must have been the oldest gray in Cornwall.

We parted convivially. He advised me to keep clear of Tiverton and Bridgwater, where they had no time for travellers. They even keep us out of the pubs, he said. He mentioned, too, that the gavvers of St. Columb Major were a set of bastards, although the Vicar was always good for a touch.

ACROSS THE TAMAR

During the remainder of that day and for the two days that followed I covered in all about seventy miles. I met nobody who comes immediately to mind except an intemperate priest and a very sober publican. In planning the walk, it had not occurred to me that by taking to the hills and the fields I should be cut off from company along the way. This sometimes made the going wearisome, especially between Newquay and Bodmin, where the country is for the most part undistinguished, bounded to the south by a range of dazzling white dunes, the waste from china clay works. To the north the downs of Denzell and St. Breoch looked good, but when I tried to get among them the land turned out to be enclosed, the pastures walled and the little valleys soggy and impassable. Thus it was I loped along, taking a likely footpath here and there, cutting across fields wherever I could, but finding only too often that road-builders knew more about short-cuts than I did.

On the roads, even in the little lanes between the villages, the number of wild animals found dead, run down by cars, seemed out of all proportion to the weight of traffic encountered. Why, I wondered, had three hares died so close to each other? Were they fighting or playing or chasing a female? And was it an instinct for the soft and familiar that enabled a badger with a

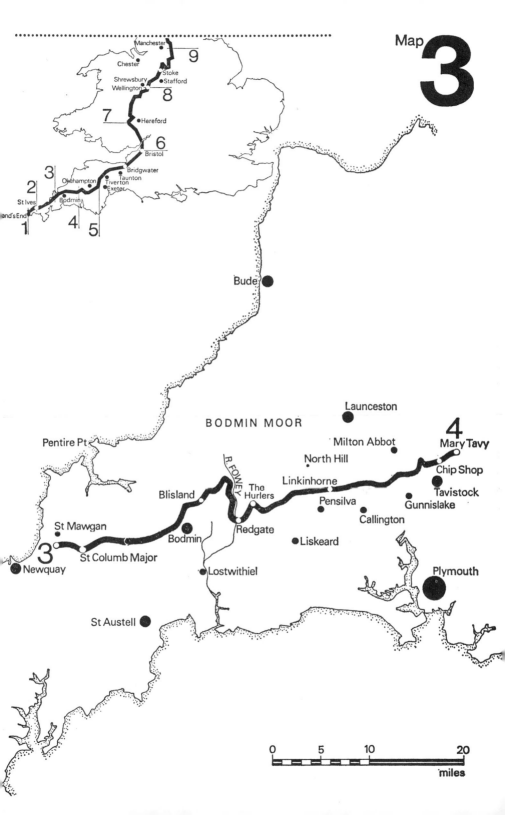

Map **3**

Manchester
Chester
Stoke
Shrewsbury Stafford
Wellington
9
8
Hereford
7
6
Bristol
3 Bridgwater
2 Okehampton Taunton
Tiverton
St Ives Bodmin Exeter
and's End 4 5
1

Bude

BODMIN MOOR

Launceston

Pentire Pt

Milton Abbot
North Hill
R. FOWEY
The
Hurlers
Blisland
Linkinhorne
Redgate
Pensilva
Callington
Liskeard

St Mawgan
3
St Columb Major
Newquay
Bodmin
Lostwithiel

4
Mary Tavy
Chip Shop
Tavistock
Gunnislake

Plymouth

St Austell

0   5   10   20
                                  miles

broken back to drag himself on to a bed of stitchwort before it died?

During brief sunshine the voices of birds, especially the newly-arrived warblers, made up to some extent for the conversation I lacked. I tried to put the outpourings of robins, the indignation of wrens and prim songs of big bosomy chaffinches in the context of a village street with the scold, the housewife and the bawd all shouting, singing and crying their small wares at the same time. But the spring tide had been held back by that wall of cold air from the north and even with most eager eyes and ears there wasn't really much to be seen or heard.

A curious feature of the Cornish lane is the unexpected appearance of Wesleyan chapels in places without apparent congregation. They seem deserted today, but from the number of these barn-like buildings it is evident that in the eighteenth century all the lightly buried religious fervour of the Celt rose to the evangelists who came to save their souls. John Wesley was persecuted in many places; riots followed a meeting in St. Ives, but in less than a century the movement was in full swing. Much of this can be put to the credit of Billy Bray, the miner of Twelveheads, a superb orator whose impetuous manner and sense of humour endeared him to the common people. When he heard of the conversion of an obdurate clergyman, he carried that embarrassed man around the parish in his arms as a mother might show off her new-born child.

His simple criticism of the use of tobacco is typical of his style. 'I don't believe our Father meant for men to smoke,' he once declared. 'If He did, He'd have put a hole in the top of their heads, for 'tisn't no heavenly architect that'd leave the smoke go out by the front door.'

To save a few miles I tried to ford the River Camel in the late afternoon, but it proved deep and bitterly cold. I crossed the bridge at Nanstallon. Then up through the larch woods of Dunsmere to Merry Meeting and simple comfort at a pub in Blisland on the edge of Bodmin Moor. For the walker the majority of pubs are far from what the 'Come to Britain' advertisements make them out to be. In this house they promptly aired a bed. By the time I had eaten a meal my tent and sleeping-bag, still wet from the previous night in Newquay, had been spread over the back of the cider barrels to dry.

The locals sat round chatting, spitting into the fire, speaking slowly, but with such a heavy burr that, heard from a distance, it might have been a foreign language punctuated with only a few familiar words. It sounds rather Russian. That curious *zh* consonant you normally hear in pleasure and leisure is used at the beginning of such words as 'zsheep' and 'zshearing'. The letter *f* frequently becomes a *v*. 'Varmer Brown's got vorrty zsheep,' they say and the *r* in the middle of certain 'wurrds' buzz like bandsaws. It all sounds very pleasant.

Here, as in other isolated pubs in the West Country, the landlady mothered the company, entering into their affairs with easy familiarity. Nobody seemed surprised when an old man who had some difficulty in bending down said it was about time she cut his toe-nails again. Another with a bad cough was given a couple of aspirins and told to take them that night with a glass of hot milk.

Although they knew very well what I was up to, nobody asked me where I came from or where I was going. But they all said 'Good night' as they dutifully filed out at halfpast ten and one, in an unexpected burst of confidence, added that if I tried to cross the moor the next day he reckoned I'd go right in up to my arse.

He was wrong. I got a bit wet. I couldn't avoid it. The moor had soaked up a great deal of snow melt. It rained, too, but not for long. A shepherd plodding along with a new-born lamb under each arm nodded and said it looked 'a bit mousy-like'. That sounded good. Better by far than black or leaden. I looked up at the towering clouds and decided that with a bit of imagination they might be described as oyster-coloured or dove-grey. In time there was even a glint of silver here and there.

Between Blisland and the famous 'Jamaica Inn', the moor abounds in barrows and big stones. Some of them have been dragged there for ritualistic purposes. Others are natural formations, the product of weathering. A particularly large one loomed up over the horizon, looking so grotesque that I swung off course by half a mile to look at it. It turned out to be an example of what is grandly called the pseudo-architecture of Cornish granite. A flat slab of rock weighing several tons had been undercut by the wind and the rain to such an extent that it wobbled on a point of balance. These formations are known locally as logans or rocking stones. I gave it a shove. It moved very slightly and by pushing rhythmically I found that I could move it about two or three inches, backwards and forwards.

The most famous logan in Cornwall was pushed over the cliffs at the beginning of the last century. This was at Gwennap, near Land's End. It started a row that involved the Lords of the Admiralty. Before the affair, the stone was neither more nor less famous than any of the others. Tradition said a giant had put it there and only a giant could push it over. This was regarded as a challenge by a certain Lieutenant Goldsmith, a nephew of the poet. At the time of the Gwennap affair he was in charge of a local coastguard cutter.

With half a dozen of his men, he scrambled up the cliffs and after a great deal of heaving and ho-ing they managed to push it over. The local inhabitants were highly indignant; they had lost their only claim to distinction, but the power of the Navy being what it was in those days it didn't look as if they could do much about it. However, when a letter appeared in the Press accusing the Admiralty of vandalism in good rolling nineteenth-century prose the dignity of the Sea Lords was upset.

They summoned Goldsmith to Whitehall, ticked him off and gave him unpaid leave to put the stone back at his own expense, a considerable task, since it weighed nearly seventy tons. Undaunted, the young lieutenant took the stage to Devonport, where he borrowed the strongest chains and the biggest blocks and capstans available in the dockyard. Within a month the cliff-tops at Gwennap Head were festooned with ropes and scaffolding. Hundreds of locals were employed at a shilling a head to stand by the hauls. On the great day when the logan stone was finally inched up the cliffs, the scene was described by a Fellow of the Royal Society who had come along, as he put it, to see fair play. He wrote that: 'In the presence of thousands, amidst ladies waving their handkerchiefs and universal shouts, Mr. Goldsmith had the glory of placing the immense rock in its natural position, uninjured in its discriminatory proportions.'

I made good progress that morning, keeping to the contours, making elaborate detours to avoid the worst of the bogs and walking sometimes on the tops of walls. I seemed to be gaining momentum. Only an unusual sight, a flock of golden plover or a stone circle, enticed me off course. Beyond Carbilly Tor the gorse bushes were hung about like cotton-wool on Christmas trees, with pathetic wisps of wind-blown wool from dead lambs. The little corpses lay in the hollows. Chilled at birth by the bitterly cold wind, they had died, a shepherd told me, before they could struggle to their feet for their first suck of milk. The ringlets of wool on the bushes had been scattered by the buzzards and the crows that flew down to feed on them.

It is noticeable that the barrows and stone circles are invariably located where there are no pastures worth the name nor land fit to plough. It looks as if those who built them chose places as remote in Bronze Age times as they are today. But what might have been learnt from the graves has for the most part been lost. The practice of tomb-robbing began as soon as it became customary to arrange articles of value around the dead. Ancestor-hunting became particularly fashionable in the eighteenth century when barrow-surgeons like Lord Conyngham could boast of how many they had despoiled in one day. Seven or eight was by no means unusual. Labourers removed the earth from the top of the mound, whereupon the excavator-in-chief, 'suitably attired in an exploring costume', had the privilege of breaking into the central chamber.

Bodmin Moor is bisected by the old coach road that ran to London by Launceston. It is now a busy highway, but once across it at Bolventor there are miles of open moorland to the south. For company I chose one of the most enchanting little streams in Cornwall, the head-water of the River Fowey. The rivulet ran ahead of me for hours, prattling away about nothing in particular and agreeing with whatever I thought about. I like company of this kind.

Among the patches of celandine and wood anemone, it pleased me that morning to think of the stream as a young girl. She skipped over the little waterfalls, ran round the edge of high rocks and admired herself in deep pools overhung with tresses of birch and willow. At Harrowbridge she lost some of her charm; she became more retiring, conscious perhaps that Liskeard Fishing Club had the right to sport with her. 'Fly Only' it said on the trees. At Redgate we parted company, she to the south, to Lostwithiel and the sailors at Fowey. I mooched off to a Celtic cross below Commonmoor for no better reason than that King Doniert's memorial is marked on the map. In front of this stone a clergyman knelt, but not, as I saw it, for the good of his soul. Intent as he was on the inscription, he had clearly drunk too much and had some difficulty in standing.

Pointing to the scarcely decipherable words, he said: 'Doniert didn't die here. He got drowned somewhere.' He paused, searching for the exact words. '*Mersus est.*' King Doniert died in the ninth century. Very little seems to be known about him except the manner of his death and a last request (*Doniert rogavit*) that for the sake of his soul (*pro anima*) a stone should be raised to his memory for all time.

The clergyman thought that Doniert, like Tristan, was related to King Mark of Cornwall and perhaps also to Arthur of Camelot, occupying, he thought, the traditional position of the nephew. In most of the Celtic cycles the hero is the son of the sister of the reigning monarch. Thus Gawain is nephew to Arthur, Cuchullin to Concochober and Diarmid to Finn. Doniert, he believed, was doomed to die by water, a ritual calculated to restore the fertility of the waste land.

'And who are you?' he asked, looking me up and down. Trying to enter into the spirit of the occasion, I said, 'The Green Man.' At least I wore a jacket and trousers of that colour. He shook his head, unconvinced. Green Men didn't carry rucksacks or ask questions about what they should have known. He talked of his interest in antiquities and how he came down to Cornwall each year. He described himself as a pilgrim 'and something of a refugee'. But from what I never learned.

Acting on his advice to spend some time in the strange company of the Hurlers, a famous ring of stones above the village of Minion, I trudged up an obscure track wondering, as I so often did, why on earth the authority responsible for these mighty monuments doesn't do something about even trying to explain what they are.

The Hurlers look like the abandoned ring of a travelling circus: flattened turf bounded by large stones, the mute witnesses of whatever happened there long ago. Like all primitive things, the impression is great and simple. There are, in fact, three circles, two of them marked by granite uprights, the third by stones that have collapsed. They are about forty paces in diameter. As usual, Christian tradition says the uprights are men transformed to stone for the abominable practice of playing the Cornish game of hurling on the Sabbath.

For me the wonder of the stone circles has been enormously enhanced by recent theories that they were not designed merely for ceremonial parades. There are good reasons for believing that they are examples of Bronze Age geometry, a record in stone of outstanding achievements in mathematics. Many of the circles can be regarded as calendars, as the predictors of future eclipses. The men who built them sought to capture time, for the return of time and the season for special ceremonies must have been for them the only safe prophecy, showing order and symmetry in Nature.

Unlike their predecessors, the Megalithic tomb-makers, the overlords of the architects of the stone circles, were far from peaceful men. They were the round-headed Beaker Folk, a race of warrior pastoralists who landed in the south and the east and very soon overran the whole country. They were armed with bows and arrows and daggers, and when they were buried a clay beaker thought to be a drinking pot was usually buried with them.

Such was the might and mobility of the Beaker Folk that

Britain was united for the first time in one distinctive culture. The round-headed men introduced luxury goods: buttons, pins and jewellery made of greenstone and jet, copper and gold. They traded with Irish smiths. It looks as if they were a relatively small governing class, always on the move, searching for good grazing. Settlement sites are hardly known. But in between their wandering they established sanctuaries, culminating in Stonehenge and Avebury, which are now among the architectural wonders of the world. These can be regarded as Bronze Age cathedrals. Elsewhere, their architects built circles that seem to have been designed on the apparent movements of the sun and the moon. Perhaps they were linked up like modern meteorological stations. To build them they used mathematical concepts only slightly less sophisticated than discoveries made more than a thousand years later by Euclid and Pythagoras.

Circles can be drawn with a piece of rope attached to a stake, but in order to describe complicated ellipses and egg-shaped figures, the ancient engineers must have understood the properties of triangles and how to measure the length of subtle curves. This can't be done with rope.

The mathematical significance of Bronze Age circles has been obscured for centuries by romantic notions of Druids and sacrificial altars. It seems more reasonable to assume that people who were almost wholly dependent on the seasons would try to discover exactly when the seasons changed. They could do this by recording on part of a circle of fixed stones the point at which the sun rose each morning. They would notice it rose more and more towards the north in the summer and the south in the winter. Those outside the priesthood might be able to keep track of the date by putting stones in a bag or arranging them in a pattern on the ground, adding one or subtracting one for each day in the lunar month or solar year. But who defined the inconstant days in a year? It would be less trouble, certainly more enjoyable, to leave the calculations to an *élite* and celebrate seasonal changes with a public orgy. The next problem would be to work out cycles of several years in terms of eclipses.

Astronomers and mathematicians who have studied the plan of

Stonehenge think that by periodically altering markers or sighting stones in a ring of holes, the monument could have been used to keep track of the moon's complicated motions. Some archaeologists doubt this, arguing that the people who built the great circles were barbarous and illiterate. But were they? There are distinct cultural links between Bronze Age Britain and the descendants of the Cretans or Minoans, who were far from illiterate. What seems to be the Cretan sign of the labrys, or double axe, has been found on the uprights of Stonehenge and a variety of beautiful Mycenaean necklets, amulets and chalices made of amber and gold are known from British Bronze Age graves.

One of the most famous pieces of Bronze Art treasure, a little cup of gold with a finely chased handle, was discovered in a burial chamber near the Hurlers. I looked at the grave. What's left of it looks bleak. Yet the story of how the cup of a warrior-prince came to be used as a shaving mug by King George V is a testimony to the age-old association between royalty and gold.

When the Rillaton barrow was opened during the nineteenth century the gold cup, according to custom, became treasure trove, the property of Queen Victoria, the reigning monarch. Years later, when archaeologists heard of the discovery of very similar objects in the shaft graves at Mycenae, they wondered what had become of the treasure. The old Queen had died. Many of her priceless relics had been scattered among the innumerable branches of her family. The Royal Librarian made some discreet enquiries at Windsor. Queen Mary recalled that before her husband came to the throne he had kept just such a cup on the table of what is politely described as his dressing-room. The little vessel is now in the British Museum.

I heard the story at Linkinhorne, where for the second night in succession I sought the comfort of a pub. I felt too tired to put up a tent, too tired almost to eat. I had covered about a hundred and twenty-five miles in five days. My ankles were rather swollen. This, I think, came not so much from the mileage as my inability to get some rest during the day, especially my normal sleep after lunch. It usually rained too hard to lie down in the open. On one occasion when I stretched out by the roadside under a waterproof, an anxious, kindly motorist pulled up in a hurry. He thought I had died.

I hoped to reach Bristol by the end of the following week. With an ominous date with a bank manager to think about, I couldn't devote more than about three months for the whole trip, and that meant keeping to an average of about twenty-five miles a day. I had kept up with the schedule for the better part of a week, but I had walked for the most part on reasonably well-defined tracks. I didn't know what I could do in rough country. Dartmoor loomed ahead. I proposed to cross the central portion, keeping to the line of tors between the Tavy and Chagford. But, as I heard on the radio that night, at least part of the moor was still under snow. Cars were being dug out of drifts. It looked as if the gaunt line of clouds that had hung over me on the coast had shifted to north Devon.

By ten o'clock the next morning I had crossed the flooded Tamar at Horse Ferry and entered Devon. The river is something more than a county boundary, the source of all the jokes about the dividing line between barbarians and courtiers. It flows from the north of Cornwall to the south, and but for a bit of land between the source of the river and Parson Hawker's famous parish of Morwenstow, the division would be complete. Cornwall is almost an island. As it is, there is no spot in the whole county where the sea is more than twenty miles away.

Parson Hawker, the nineteenth-century recorder of Cornish eccentricities, was perhaps the most notable eccentric of them all. His parishioners once saw him sitting on a rock, pretending to be a mermaid, with a seaweed wig over his head and an oilskin wrap over his legs, 'flashing the beams from a hand-mirror and singing in a strident falsetto'.

'Care for a lift?'

I thanked the farmer who had pulled up and said, 'No'. Ten minutes later another offer, this time from a district nurse in a

Logans or rocking stones

mini-car. 'Are you *quite* sure?' she asked. I stress the cordiality of these offers in Devon, for many drivers make it abundantly clear that they know all about the hiking business. Some never spoke. They pulled up, stared straight ahead, merely pointing to the spare seat.

I thanked my courteous Samaritans. I said I liked walking and tried to remember the name of the next town in answer to the inevitable question about where I was going. I had sworn to myself to say nothing about my destination until I got at least halfway there.

At noon I settled down in the peaceful obscurity of a pub, the 'Hare and Hounds' at Chipshop, determined for once to doze for half an hour. The locals chattered like starlings, started quiet arguments, broke them off to play darts. For no particular reason that I can recall, a man who had been sitting near me, reading the local newspaper, put it down and began to sing a well-known hymn, softly, yet with no self-consciousness.

To my surprise, the rest of the company joined in, harmonizing the refrain with mounting volume until the little bar shook with the noise. This sounds maudlin, a tribute more to Devon cider than anything else. In fact, it said quite a lot for the character of the landlord, who told me later that he knew people liked to sing and the tunes they knew best were usually hymn tunes. He encouraged them by humming them now and again, but not ostentatiously. Sometimes they sang them on Sunday nights for about half an hour. On one famous occasion, when the company supplemented the local church choir, there were, as he put it, 'only six vacant seats left that night and a good time was had by all, including, I imagine, the Lord'. An extraordinarily nice man.

THE DIRE MOOR

To the east of a dreary little village called Mary Tavy the rolling landscape of Devon rears up and disappears into what an ancient charter describes as 'our forest of Dertymoor', an almost circular expanse of bog, heather and bracken, broken only by outcrops of granite tors. The impression that gloomy evening was of those purgatories where damned souls have the choice of going back or going on. I felt something inimical, almost terrifying in the prospect ahead. The urge was to run, to get out into more wholesome air. In the middle of the moor, Baring Gould said he had known a horse stand still and sweat with fear.

All that I have to say about Dartmoor is watered down by the weather, which was, to say the least, dank. I was also very hungry, and Mary Tavy is not particularly interested in hungry pedestrians. It lies on a hill where the traffic tears up and down between Tavistock and Okehampton. For about an hour I went from place to place in search of food and information about how to get across the moor.

At the mention of food the woman at the first pub said, predictably, that they didn't do meals nowadays. Another soul referred me to a guest-house, which turned out to be closed. Neither the Vicar nor the village constable were at home, but the charitable woman who runs the village store fried up an enormous

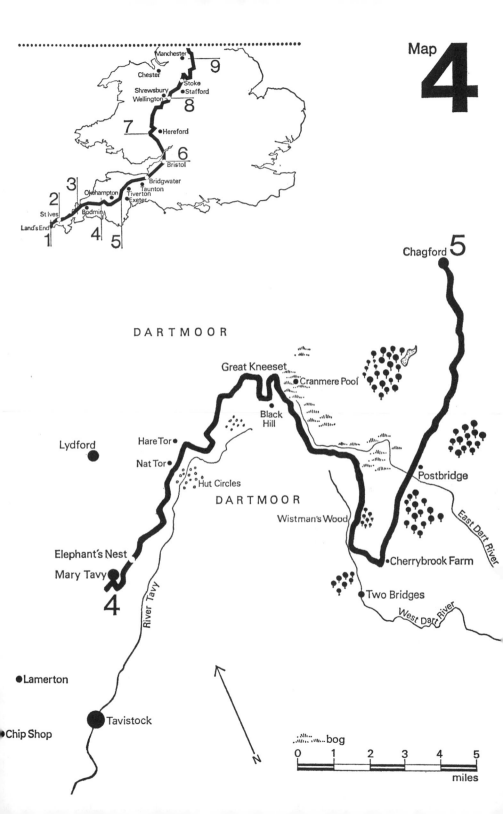

Map

4

9

Manchester
Chester
Stoke
Shrewsbury • Stafford
Wellington
8

7
• Hereford

6
Bristol

3
Bridgwater
Okehampton Taunton
2 Tiverton
Exeter
St Ives
Bodmin
1
4 5
Land's End

Chagford 5

D A R T M O O R

Great Kneeset
• Cranmere Pool

Black
Hill

Lydford
Hare Tor •

Nat Tor •
Postbridge

Hut Circles

D A R T M O O R

Wistman's Wood
East Dart River

Elephant's Nest
• Cherrybrook Farm

Mary Tavy

4
Two Bridges

River Tavy
West Dart River

• Lamerton

N

Chip Shop
Tavistock

bog

0   1   2   3   4   5

miles

plate of bacon and eggs and prepared enough sandwiches to last two days. She also put me in touch with the landlord of the 'Buller's Arms', who, she said, had something to do with the business of rescuing people who got lost.

That plain-speaking man said that if the mist came down and I wasn't prepared to stay where I was until it lifted it would save them all a lot of trouble if I didn't start.

'Fine,' I said. But what could I expect?

He 'phoned up somewhere or other and got a noncommittal prediction of changeability.

Did I want to chance it or not? I'd chance it I said.

To reach Chagford on the diametrically opposite side of the moor he advised me to make my way up to one of the sources of the River Tavy, which, he thought, would be easy enough to find. There, he told me to strike out for Great Kneeset, which was supposed to be a big, easily recognizable tor. From there onwards he reckoned I ought to be able to make my way from one tor to another until I struck a tributary of the Teign that led to Chagford.

It sounded reasonable. He gave me compass directions, and from his back door he pointed out peaks disappearing in the half light. I looked at them with no particular enthusiasm. It was agreed that I should keep to the route he suggested on the practical if somewhat disconcerting grounds that if I failed to telephone him within thirty-six hours they would at least know where to come out and look for me. He didn't even mention a pool called Cranmere that nearly did me in, but I don't suppose he thought that anyone in their right senses would even go near it.

On the banks of the Tavy, on the very edge of the moor, there is a cheerful little pub with the improbable name of the 'Elephant's Nest'. There I had been advised to look for a Mr. Lillicrap, a local farmer in whose field I proposed to spend the night. For good historical reasons, you have to be very careful about where you squat down among the in-farmers of Dartmoor. By occupying a bit of land you can, under certain conditions, lay claim to it.

I remember the almost paralyzing din from the juke-box.

'Can't do without it these days,' said the landlady, pouring out a bright green intoxicant for a girl in jeans who looked about fourteen. Around her the young lads of Devon snapped their fingers and waggled their bottoms to the Beatles' version of 'I Wanna Hold Your Hand'.

Mr. Lillicrap said if I really wanted to sleep in that field of his he'd no objection, like, though he hoped them old cows wouldn't mind, because they didn't really take to strangers, they didn't, a remark which had them rolling round the bar. Mr. Lillicrap accepted a drink with dignity. It wasn't necessary at all, he said. We shook hands and I went out into a field which was not only dark and lumpy and full of cows, but distinctly damp. For various reasons, I didn't get to sleep until long past midnight.

Something kept scratching on the outside of the tent. I wouldn't have thought much about it if I hadn't recently seen a ridiculously melodramatic film on television in which a monster tried to get into its victim's bedroom by incessantly scratching at the door. A stupid fantasy, but it kept coming back, ruining sleep. When a cry rang out across the moor I crawled out to see what it was all about.

In a small tent this is less easy than it sounds. After extricating yourself from a cocoon-like sleeping-bag, you have to fumble with the zip-fasteners of the tent from a kneeling position.

Outside all seemed in order. The scratching noise came from clumps of spiky rushes intermittently blown by the wind against the canvas. The only explanation I have for the eerie cries is that overhead may have passed a migratory flock of stone curlews, birds which make a diabolical noise.

The moon was the colour of a corpse. Uncomforted, I crept back into the tent.

Dawn was pretty dreary, too. Flocks of drifting clouds had settled down low on the horizon, jostling each other, uneasily, like sheep undecided what to do next. Hoping fervently they would push off, I packed up and walked on, taking the left bank of the River Tavy, looking for its junction with the tributary that led to Great Kneeset. Nattor Down loomed up where it should have been, but another apparently unmapped hill popped up on the opposite side of the torrent, rather spoiling my simple conception of the landscape.

The going became difficult, for a great deal of stuff they call clitter, the rubble from the outcrops of granite, had fallen down into the gorge. But the compass confirmed the heading and I scrambled along as fast as I could in weather that seemed to be worsening. I decided to make for some high place where I could look around and see whether it looked safe to go on.

On both sides of the stream are circles of stone blocks about two feet in height and some three or four paces in diameter. They are the overgrown foundations of places where men of the Bronze and Iron Age lived. There are about a thousand of these circles on the moor. The entrance of each hut is usually marked by a pair of upright stones, or jambs, that face south or south-west to afford the occupants some protection against the bitterly cold winds that must have swept down on them in winter. The huts are generally grouped in clusters, representing formless villages or hamlets, sometimes protected by an enclosing wall.

The oldest were built about three or four thousand years ago – that is, they date back to Beaker Folk times, but the majority, especially the compound variety, are the home of Iron Age farmers who were there when the Romans arrived. They lived on in snug isolation for centuries after the legions left, undisturbed because scarcely anyone knew they were there. Even time seems to have passed them by. They must have been primitive even by the standards of the Iron Age.

With six or seven families and their animals in a patch of ground about the size of a tennis court, it is likely that, in those days, conditions were both smelly and untidy on the banks of the upper Tavy. But very companionable. Certainly nobody could keep a family secret, a pregnancy, a quarrel or the discovery of something to eat for themselves for long.

Poking about among the stones, I found a slate-coloured ball about the size of a grapefruit. I touched it cautiously with my toe. To my intense surprise, the mass slowly expanded and then uncoiled. Three snakes glided away. They were adders.

Two were brightly-coloured with a black zigzag stripe on their olive-coloured backs. The third, which I took to be a female, was somewhat smaller and more drably marked. They seemed largely oblivious to my presence, for after what seemed to be a limbering-up exercise they rushed backwards and forwards, brushing against the female in a state of excitement.

She appeared completely unmoved by this passionate display and coiled up as if to sleep. First one and then the other glided up, rapidly weaving from side to side, quivering as they touched her. I expected to see them fight, but they showed no sign of aggression, awaiting their turn as if in a ritualized dance. At a point where their ardour might have been rewarded I took an incautious step forward and frightened them. The males plunged into the heather and the female followed, more slowly, but with a purposiveness that suggested she had no intention of losing her suitors.

I walked on, wondering if they had been coupled when I came across them or if, alternatively, they had been wrapped up in a winter-long sleep. Adders are beautiful creatures and more harmless than most people imagine. Only seven or eight people are known to have died from a bite in the last half-century.

Still climbing, I reached Watern Oke, where the river opened out into the emptiness of the moor; still hopeful about the weather, I followed a tributary, the Amicomb, that trickled down from the heights of Great Kneeset. At worst I could follow the stream back to the bridge below the 'Elephant's Nest', and at best I should get across the moor that day. To be on the safe side, I took a back bearing on the point where the two streams united and poured down into the crop. Towards Lydford the sky looked bright, but elsewhere, especially to the north-east, the tors were veiled in mist.

After an hour of squelchy progress, a rain squall drove me into a narrow crack in the rocks. By using the outer fly of the tent as a roof, I made as good a shelter as I managed to find that day. I munched a sandwich and looked round. From the hewn face of the rock I had apparently strayed into an old tin-working. In the peat the skull of a sheep leered at me and around it, bright green with verdigris, were three or four empty bullet cases, the remains of an army exercise.

Dartmoor is a military training ground. During firing practice the public are kept out of the most attractive parts of this much-abused National Park. The region is also an enormous sheep range. The inhabitants of about twenty-five villages on the edge of the moor exercise ancient rights of 'common and turbary' that enable them to graze sheep, usually, these days, without a shepherd. In bad weather the animals die in thousands. But Commoners have the right to do what they like, including the privilege of setting fire to the heather.

Nobody has actually lived on the moor since the Iron Age farmers gave up the struggle against the poor soil, the wind and the winter weather. But down the centuries the place has been the Tom Tiddler's ground of squatters, tin-miners, speculators and, more recently, the military and the Government Forestry Department.

The old tin-miners bartered or sold the metal direct to foreign traders or collecting agents, just as blueberry-pickers nowadays sell their wares to fruit-dealers. In time the Crown established stannaries, or tin centres, in the towns of Lydford, Tavistock, Chagford, Ashburton and Plympton, but the local tinners turned the stannary system into an extremely powerful trade union, perhaps the first example of a closed shop.

In the sixteenth century the tinners began to make their own laws. They upheld the right to invade private property, even to the extent of pulling down houses that stood on real or imaginary seams. They declared that no man with property worth more than £10 could dig for tin except on his own freehold. There was no appeal against the judgment of the Stannary Courts. The victims were thrown into the dungeons of Lydford Castle, where

> *In the morn they hang and draw*
> *And sit in judgement after....*

Water began to trickle round my feet, but before it became more than a nuisance the rain ceased. I decided to leave the guidance of the stream and walk up to the summit of Great

Kneeset. It looked quite close and quite deceptive, since before I got more than halfway to the top, the mist came down again, enveloping me completely. Dartmoor seemed to have drifted away. The feeling was as if the whole planet had plunged into a cloud, leaving only a little circle of uncomfortable reality in which I alone survived. There is no sound that I know of more fearful than the sound of silence.

Writing this down after the event, I am trying to recall precisely what I felt at the time. I felt pretty depressed. I could see for no more than about ten yards. The slope was too steep to put the tent down, but if I climbed upwards I reckoned I ought to be able to reach the top of the tor, where I proposed to stop until the mist lifted. I carried half a bottle of Scotch and enough food, including the vitaminized fudge, to last a day or two. More than anything else, I could have kicked myself for parting company with that stream at a time when I could have done with both guidance and company.

The crown of the tor was surrounded by little bogs and depressions, filled in some places with deep drifts of snow. Keeping an eye on the compass, I tried to work my way between them, prodding the ground with a stick, determined if need be to walk round to the back of the slope in an effort to get to the top.

From somewhere in the murk above I heard a succession of deep barks that might have come from a wolf-hound. The barks were followed by high-pitched yelps. I thought momentarily of the Hooting Carn of Kenidjack or, worse, that a rescue party had come to look for me with a pack of dogs.

The noise, in fact, came from the air above, where two or three ravens were being mobbed by a host of jackdaws that were apparently trying to drive them away. When the sound subsided to an occasional uneasy yelp I realized that the birds had settled and that, instead of lying immediately above me, the summit rose away to the left. No wonder I had run into bogs. I had been trying to cross the flat top of a projecting spur. Taking a rough bearing on the source of the noise, I made off in quite a different direction and very soon got to the top.

A disappointing place. No caves, no deep cracks nor protective overhangs. Almost no shelter. As far as I could see, the cliff of granite had collapsed, leaving only a jumble of tightly-packed rocks. I stayed there for about a couple of hours, squatting under the flysheet. This became boring, irksome and, eventually, intolerable. When it looked a bit brighter I took a swig of Scotch and squelched down the side of the hill. Although I didn't expect to get off the moor that day, there was no advantage I could see in clinging to Great Kneeset when with luck I might find something better. The man back in Mary Tavy had told me to make for Hangman's Hill, another tor, about two miles away.

I never got there. The marvel is that in the mist I got anywhere.

It hung about all day, sometimes so thickly that I couldn't see for more than a few paces. When that happened I hung about, wriggling my toes and stamping my feet like a restive horse. But for most of the time the visibility veered between twenty and forty yards. During what can be euphemistically described as bright intervals, I moved on as fast as I could on a bearing of seventy degrees.

To do this I took a sight on the most distant object I could see, usually a tuft of grass or a vaguely distinguishable hunk of peat, and made for it, counting the paces on the way. The counting didn't amount to much, navigation-wise, but it gave me something to do. All this became a childish ritual, like hopping over paving-stones, sloping arms or taking part in a square dance.

One, two, three, four . . . keeping my eyes on the marker tuft, with only an occasional glance down to avoid the worst of the wet patches, I muttered the numbers aloud . . . *seven, eight, nine, ten* . . . who cared a damn about the big bad mist? Play it cool, man. Nobody who tackles a problem scientifically gets hurt . . . kids' stuff, this . . . *thirteen, fourteen, fifteen* . . . seemed to be getting brighter. A lot brighter. I could see beyond the tuft. Maybe twenty yards . . . *seventeen, eighteen, nineteen* . . . and then a splosh as I went into two feet of water.

Optimism vanished as I looked round for something more

substantial to walk on. Couldn't see the marker when I got going again. Chose something else in what I took to be the right direction . . . *twenty-two, twenty-three, twenty-four* . . . only a few paces to go. Mental censor asked if I wasn't feeling *just* a bit tired? Nonsense! Never felt better in my life. Mist is good for you. Like Guinness. But it really wasn't. I knew it wasn't . . . *twenty-nine, thirty.*

In thirty sodden steps, in fifty seconds, in less time than it takes to relate this, I usually swung, unpredictably, between elation and depression. Little fantasies, some comforting, some frightful, flickered on and off like a series of projected slides, leaving only for the most part that feeling of damp, rather miserable ordinariness. In this way I suppose I must have covered several miles. In the scenic, the seeing-something-ahead, sense I saw very little.

Towards noon I hustled down a long slope and, at a point where the murk seemed unusually thick, I went in up to the bottom of my jacket. Done for, I thought. I got out by leaning backwards and lifting one foot out slowly, and then the other, and then looked around. Nothing comforting. The bog stretched out as far as I could see. In the cold air, the surface steamed slightly, like a pudding. I chucked a piece of turf in. It quivered. From the map it looked as if I had walked into Cranmere Pool.

I cannot explain how I managed to stray so far off course. The Confucian explanation, no doubt, is that small errors multiplied lead, inevitably, to pronounced unhappiness. The immediate problem was how to get round the pool. Or even out of it, since I had apparently walked out on to a little promontory with the bog on both sides. Somewhere out in the mist a frog croaked, but not, I felt, as a harbinger of spring. I felt as Pharaoh must have felt. Or Job.

In the face of physical obstacles I am neither courageous nor particularly resourceful. But I have a pronounced sense of in-destructability which has proved serviceable on several occasions, especially that afternoon, when I went in about a dozen times. The fact that I got into the mess in the first place is due to stupidity. The fact that I went on is less foolhardy than it sounds. I tended to sink in if I stood still. I found a stick and by prodding and poking I got back to what seemed to be the west side of the bog. And then I went on, step by step, slowly.

No counting here. I kept my eyes down, looking for a sign of that pea-green, wee-green, greener-than-green green bog, the sloppy stuff that really scared me. For company: thoughts. Mostly unpleasant thoughts. The brain unoccupied seems to get up to some mischief of its own. I waded about in thought streams or what J. B. Priestley has called the skull cinema.

The odd thing about these performances is that you can't choose the programme. Think of something to think about and whatever it is that controls fantasies changes the spool. Or alters the focus, almost imperceptibly.

I tried hard to be philosophical about Cranmere Pool. An *interesting* bog, I thought. But before I could decide whether it was wet dissected peat with liverworts or the classic blanket variety with sphagnum moss in between the heather and the cotton-grass, the skull cinema operator snapped on a hideous one-reeler about stepping into the stuff and going down with a plop.

I didn't, of course, die, not even in my imagination. At the point where I was in up to my armpits and the rescue party from the 'Buller's Arms' were looking for me with military helicopters, I thought things had gone too far and changed the film. But I couldn't keep off bogs: the Bog of Allan and that misty place where the hound of the Baskervilles roamed. What was it called? Grimpen Mire?

I went back to Africa where, years ago, I had clambered over the Ruwenzori, the Mountains of the Moon. Now there were some real bogs for you. You get into them at twelve thousand feet, above the bamboos, not far from the snow-line. There you find a belt of giant heathers, *les bruyères arborescentes* which are about forty feet in height.

'*Dans toutes ces régions,*' said my companion, a Belgian geologist, '*le leopard est commun.*' And by God he was right. The giant cats sat up in the giant heathers, dozing, waiting. More cats than you could find in a Venetian slum. Below the heathers and the leopards were the giant bogs - bogs that engulfed the little forest elephants, the ones with round ears. The Wanande, who knew all about cannibalism - *Yam-yam* they called it - said that the bits of a man they didn't want could be pushed in, too. The bogs were far deeper than Cranmere Pool. Or so I thought until I put my foot into a particularly wet patch.

I kept on squelching south until an array of tufts, a tussocky kind of grass known as negro-head, popped out of the mist and it looked as if I had got to the lower end of the pool. More probing, a few tumbles and I found a little gulley in the peat with a trickle of water at the bottom. As the opposite bank looked too sodden to risk a jump, I followed the rivulet for about a quarter of a mile, where to my inexpressible delight it appeared to drop into the stream I had been looking for.

Young streams, especially moorland streams, have a certain waywardness, an indisposition to flow straight for more than a few yards. This one ran east, but it seemed to be trying to get back from wherever it had come from. After meandering about in a scrics of loops and whorls, it swung round completely. I seemed to be walking backwards and forwards along the banks of a series of parallel rivulets. When it eventually curved south and stayed that way it became miserably clear that I had struck the south-bound Dart and not the Teign, which flowed east, towards Chagford, my destination that night. But I didn't particularly mind where it went if it kept me out of the bogs.

Dartmoor is a dome. From a distance it looks like an enormous teacake with a flat top and rounded sides. In the centre of the moor, as I had discovered, there is a great deal of moss that quickly becomes overloaded with water. This huge sponge is the source of about half a dozen big rivers and a lot of little streams. They radiate in all directions. I had set off from the western rim of the dome, reached a point north of centre, and must have been about halfway across the opposite side when I struck the wrong river. This, I knew, would add at least another five miles to the day's total. I reckoned I had done about twenty, but at least I knew where I was.

The day never really came to an end. It fizzled out, damply, like a squib that refused to burn. Stopping only to cheer myself up with a little Scotch and Dart water, I jogged on, mile after mile, playing the usual game of partly contrived thoughts. In time these become the iron rations of the intellect.

By five o'clock the river had become a noisy torrent, pouring over a series of waterfalls, hurrying along, too deep to be forded anywhere. At six o'clock I reached a point where it spilt over into a bog. With solid map references to work on, I struck out for another tributary, the West Dart. More hut circles, rings and an avenue of stones. I scarcely gave them a glance. Wistman's Wood, a freak forest of dwarf oak trees, hove up through the mist and disappeared again. My mind wasn't on the wonders of Nature.

At seven o'clock I got onto the road at Cherrybrook Farm, to find that Chagford was still eight miles away. There isn't much that I really care to recall about any part of that day.

WEST-COUNTRY DAYS

Chagford is a cheerful little off-beat place with two or three pubs around a mini-market square. The pubs, I assumed, were looking for business. I am warmly disposed towards the landlord of the second house I went in to. He took me in and did all that he could at a time when, heaven knows, I needed a bit of care and attention. I looked pretty dreadful. But the manager of the first place I tried more or less told me to go away. I grant him I didn't look like the sort of custom calculated to attract Cadillacs and Jaguars.

It was nine o'clock. I said I had been on the moor since a quarter past five. I had got into a bit of trouble; I needed a meal, anything he could put on. And a bed. Could he provide them? He said he was full, and he said it firmly.

No room at all? In the interval of waiting I had glanced at the visitors' book. Unless they were reduced to two rooms, they were far from full. Full, he said, unless by any chance I cared to take what appeared to be their royal suite. He named an exhorbitant sum. I protested. I said ... but what does it matter what I said? I went next-door.

The curious, the embarrassing, the totally-unexpected sequel to this little incident is that back in London, months later, I telephoned what I took to be the landlord of the first house and

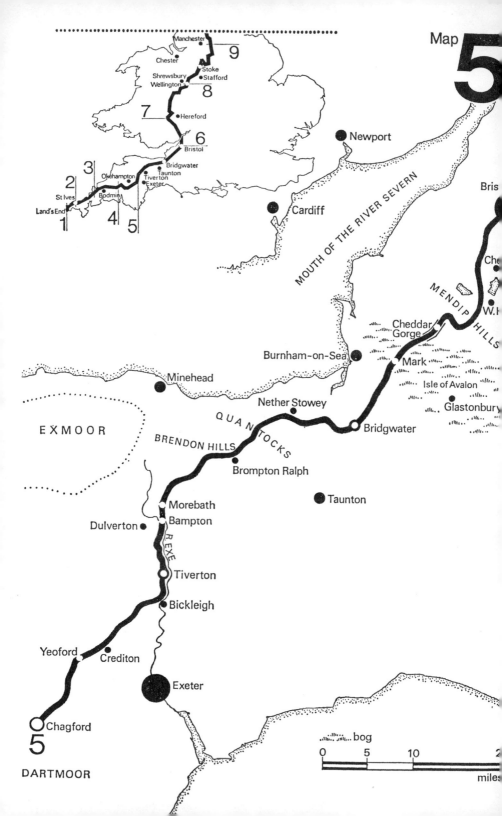

Map

5

Manchester

Chester

Stoke
Shrewsbury Stafford
Wellington
8

7 ● Hereford

6
Bristol
Bridgwater
Okehampton Taunton
Tiverton
Exeter
St Ives
Land's End Bodmin

1 2 3 4 5

Newport

Bris

MOUTH OF THE RIVER SEVERN

Cardiff

Che

MENDIP HILLS

W.H

Cheddar
Gorge

Burnham-on-Sea Mark

Isle of Avalon

Glastonbury

Minehead

EXMOOR

Nether Stowey

QUANTOCKS

BRENDON HILLS

Bridgwater

Brompton Ralph

Taunton

Morebath

Dulverton Bampton

R. EXE

Tiverton

Bickleigh

Yeoford Crediton

Exeter

Chagford

5

DARTMOOR

bog

0 5 10 2

miles

asked him what he normally charged for his most expensive rooms. When he told me something approximately a third of the sum I recall, I indulged in a minute's worth of long-bottled-up indignation.

'But,' he said, 'we did all we could for you, didn't we? You did say you were comfortable here.' May dear God and Chagford forgive me. I had telephoned the wrong house.

After three days of rain, Devon that morning stood knee-deep in water. The Dart, they said, had cut the Tavistock road in several places; the Tavy had become a torrent and for miles downstream the villagers were anxiously watching the rising level of the Taw and the Teign. From time to time I thought of the wilderness from which all that water came, that enormous sponge around High Kneeset, and hastened on, glad to know that it lay far behind to the west, where the hills were still under cloud.

Time smooths all things. Today, whenever I hear the name of Dartmouth, Teignmouth or Tavistock, I think affectionately of those turbulent streams. There is much to be said for getting a row over and done with in one day. The Teign, certainly, is a river of considerable charm.

I followed its meanderings across meadows where the glassy blue eyes of forget-me-nots looked out from far beneath the water. In profusion on the banks were primroses and balsams, wild orchids, willow-herb and a curious plant called water-pepper or arse-smart because, as an old herbalist says, 'if it toucheth the taile or other bare skinne, it maketh it smart, as often it doth, being laid unto the bed greene to kill flease'. Overhead, the birds sang their heads off.

It's unfashionable, I know, to talk about jubilation. Any suggestion that thrushes are glad to be alive on a bright spring morning is romantic old-hat. Bird-song, the ornithologists tell you, is strictly purposive. The poor creatures are up to their throats in the estate business. They are trying to get a little place of their own in the country. The phrase is territory-establishment. The thrush says: *Keep away, Keep-away, This-is-mine, This-is-mine.* And so on. And so on. But I must say that on the banks of the Teign that morning the old notion of creatures being glad to be alive was nicer to think about. And nearer the heart.

From somewhere near Drewsteignton I looked back on the misty outlines of the moor with a certain amount of satisfaction. I had grappled with the old monster, and there it lay, flat on its back: not perhaps defeated, maybe waiting until I came back another time.

Dartmoor is the hard core of Devon. The famous red soil and the sandstones are no more than the remains of the roof that used to protect the ancient foundations of granite. This roof was raised many years ago when lava bubbled up towards the softer rocks at the surface. Instead of cracking open, the roof bulged like a blister or dome. The bottled-up lava cooled under tremendous pressure. It became granite and took its shape from the mould that held it down. Over the years much of the dome got washed away, leaving behind the ridge of intractable rock that stretches from Dartmoor south-west to Land's End. This is the stuff on which I had been walking for a week.

There is a roundabout track leading from Dartmoor to Exmoor, a path that dodges in and out of bits of common land, but I couldn't locate it on the one-inch map and, still tired from the previous day's bog-hopping, I preferred to keep to the little lanes. I had one distinct advantage over the motorists that morning. I could at least wade through the floods.

At Yeoford the River Trony gurgled into the bar of the 'Station Hotel' and gurgled out again through the door marked 'Gents'. It washed in a sad assortment of plastic dolls, tomato-boxes and dead chickens, the flotsam of flooded farmsteads far up stream.

'Crediton?' said the landlady, vainly trying to stem the flood with her husband's underpants wrapped round the bottom of a broom. 'It's *that* way,' and she pointed to where the river all too plainly ran along the road.

Near Crediton you strike the famous red-earth country, a colour as distinctly Devonian as the slate-grey cliffs and dazzle-white clay heaps of Cornwall. Everywhere a rich brown, cocoa-brown landscape of cows, earth and water. The local folk were

busy cutting ditches, looking for lambs, hanging their mattresses
out to dry. They waved and got on with the job of trying to
repel the cocoa-brown water.

It is noticeable that the men talk deliberately, the women fast.
With an accent of my own that some people regard as quaint, I
am diffident about apeing other people's phonetic peculiarities.
The idiom of this part of Devon is full of colour and the voice
warm with a built-in burr. Old men claim that the way of
speaking hasn't changed much in three hundred years and quote
a set of dialect verses written in 1625 in which a countryman who
has seen the wonders of the sea at Plymouth rebukes a neighbour
who has never left the moor:

> *Thou voole, that never water zaw'st*
> *But think-a in the moor-a,*
> *To zee the zea would'st be a-'ghast,*
> *It doth zoo rage and roar-a.*

The people of Devonshire are courtly, correct; they can
rarely be faulted on a point of etiquette or manners. For centuries they have lived well in a warm climate and assume that
other folk like to be comfortable, too. They are also surprisingly
matter-of-fact. Mention the superstitions, the pixies and all that
stuff about Uncle Tom Cobleigh and they smile apologetically.
Many of them live on the tourist trade, and they know very well
that visitors like to hear about Drake's drum, Lady Howard's
phantom coach, and, as I heard afterwards, an unmentionable
creature that lives in Cranmere Pool. As one of them put it, if a
dog howls at midnight a Devon farmer doesn't put salt on the
doorstep and ask himself who's going to be next in the cemetery.
He throws a brick at the animal and assumes that his own bitch
is on heat again.

As for the moor-men, or the in-country farmers, as they
call them, they are reckoned to be zummat on their own, a
community apart. Calculating, penny-saving, often down-right
mean, they have remained very much a law unto themselves
since the days of the tinners.

The landlord of a pub at Cadleigh gave me an elaborate wink

when one of these gnarled old men walked in and began to ask the price of everything in sight: cigarettes, liquor, the different brands of bottled brew. The ancient settled, eventually, for half a pint of bitter, which he paid for in pennies extracted, slowly, one by one from a leather purse. It took him half an hour to drink it. After the door closed the landlord, a Northerner, said he knew him well.

'Worth about thirty thousand quid, that chap,' he said. 'But you won't get anything out of *him*. Ask him the time and he'll give you ten minutes less.'

For two days I dodged the worst of the floods, walking in gym shoes across meadows that were often knee-deep in water. From the panoramic top of the Raddon Hills you could see hundreds of little pools and rivulets that drained into the tumultuous Exe. Most of the traffic in the valley had been diverted. I headed for Tiverton and Bampton, where they sell the little Exmoor ponies. I could have taken drier tracks, but I wanted to see the valley of the Exe, which is the natural high road north.

Devon is a big county, ranking third in size after Yorkshire and Lincolnshire, but it can boast only of one great painter, Reynolds, and a poet, Coleridge. Herrick, an immigrant, thought the place was rude and the people beastly. It is, perhaps, too rich and too beautiful for that class of artists who, in order to turn out anything good, need to be dissatisfied with their lot. The enormous churches of pale pink stone are a testimony to the fortunes made out of sheep. The old wool barons rebuilt them in Perpendicular Gothic. Those who paid for the stone-work still lie in the aisles in effigy or in brass, their feet resting as cosily on a wool-pack as any knight with his hound or lady with her lap-dog. Flocks of tourists have now largely replaced the sheep as a staple. Even on a wet spring afternoon in Tiverton they were queuing up for bric-a-brac, pixie bowls, plaster casts of Tom Cobleigh and jars and jars and jars of yellow clotted cream.

With vast quantities of rich milk to spare, it struck me as curious that Devon has never managed to make a notable cheese. But the cream is on sale everywhere. They put dollops of it on pastries, on fruit, on tea-cakes, even on bread and butter. After two helpings of roast lamb and at least a quart of cider that night, I walked out of Bampton, stuporous, intent only on somewhere to lie down.

All that I can recall of the barn is that it smelt strongly of fish manure and the wind rattled the galvanized iron with a noise like stage thunder. I do, however, remember that, the next morning, during a highly inconvenient moment when I was clad only in a shirt, a large dog walked in. Before it could utter more than a couple of half-hearted wuffles I got it hooked on vitaminized fudge. Dog and I ate breakfast together. It polished off about two days' supplies. By the time I had packed up the animal was still champing noisily and trying to get the lead foil off its palate by standing on the roof of its mouth.

Above Bampton the road rises like a funicular to the country of *Lorna Doone*. At the top of the rise, breathless, I sat down on a heap of turnips and looked round, marvelling at the hills that rolled away in all directions: the Brendons, the Quantocks, Winsford and Dunkery. Far behind, the Exe trailed back into Devon, for me now a county in the past tense, since somewhere on the climb up between Brockhole and Withywine I had passed imperceptibly into Somerset. In front lay the road to Minehead and the Bristol Channel; another ran east towards Bridgwater and a third, a mere track, trickled away until it became lost in the clear, inviting expanse of Exmoor.

Although I saw little of the moor at close quarters, it seemed to have none of that environmental hostility I felt at Mary Tavy. The heather-clad hills are gently rounded; they invoke, they don't repel the thought of exploration. The moor is freely channelled by little coombes or valleys, tree-lined and cared for. Or so it seemed from a distance. No doubt the windy-bright morning accounts for this opinion.

The situation is that although Exmoor and Dartmoor are both National Parks, both are being slowly destroyed. On Dartmoor the problems are overstocking and excessive land-burning by the Commoners, the planting of conifers, the development of water undertakings and military exercises. On Exmoor the problems are different.

The walker is being fenced out. The land is being developed by private owners and Government foresters. This is not to say that the place should be allowed to become an overgrown wilderness. The unique character of the country lies in a delicate and tried system of farming in which the stock on the unimproved uplands was balanced by the more intensive use of the 'inbye' land lower down in the valleys. On Exmoor there is also the problem of deer.

The largest herd of red deer in England can be seen within a ten-mile radius of Dunkery Beacon. They are neither aliens nor re-introductions. They are natives - animals who were here before the Beaker Folk. They are probably our oldest inhabitants of unbroken line of descent. And if they weren't hunted as they have been, for hundreds of years, the argument is that they would be soon wiped out.

This is an inflammable subject. Mention stag-hunting and temperatures immediately start to rise. As I have never followed a hunt, I am relying on the opinions of a forestry officer who quite clearly knew a lot about the habits of deer and the local farmers. He said, in effect, that whatever it may look like to the outsider, Exmoor farmers lead a hard life. The sheep that graze the moor in summer have to be fed during the winter on whatever can be grown in their little rocky fields.

On one October morning he recalled seeing a farmer with a horse and cart, picking up swedes damaged by a party of stags the previous night. The man had collected more than a ton. Each root had just one bite taken out of it. The stag has no teeth in the front of its upper jaw and to get a mouthful it bites with its lower incisors and then twists the mouthful, a movement that usually wrenches the swede out of the ground. It then bites another one. The deer spoil far more than they eat, and one night's attack can ruin an acre or more of crops, for roots bitten in this way quickly rot and can't be stored for winter feed.

Exmoor farmers are fond of hunting, and for the sake of the sport they are prepared to overlook a certain amount of raiding. If hunting were stopped they would have no compunction in shooting the animals that stray on to their land, as they are entitled to do. The ethics of the sport aside, on Exmoor it comes down to the simple proposition that if there were no hunting there would soon be no deer. They can't be driven away, for there is nowhere else they can go.

Between the Brendons and the side of the Quantocks I made about thirty miles in a long day's walk, feeling in every sense on top of the world. The curb of bad weather and frustration had been cast off; only the cloud shadows raced ahead. I scuttled along, taking the hills as a challenge and the views from the top as a reward. Near Rayleigh Cross the sea crawled far below in Blue Anchor Bay, a glimpse only of the Bristol Channel, but a spur to be in that town within three days.

On the uplands of Rayleigh are several dark-looking, fenced-off holes in the ground. A notice-board announced that they were not only dangerous, but private, and they had all been sold. Who on earth, I wondered, bought holes in the ground? An old man with a scythe over his shoulder told me they were the abandoned shafts of iron mines, the relics of an industry that came to an end about eighty years ago. Somebody with a good nose for business had bought them for next to nothing and would, I suppose, make a fortune. A survey had shown that they were extraordinarily deep and capacious enough to hold the combined municipal garbage of the neighbouring towns, including Bristol, for years to come. The buyer had apparently already sold the concession.

We sat down together, the old man and I, and put the world right for about half an hour. Before we parted I asked him a few personal questions. Did he drink? As much as he could get, he said. But it didn't come easily these days, not the price it was. Cider? I enquired. Not that stuff, he said. All right for young chaps, but it went through you like a dose of salts. He preferred beer. Where was he raised? He came, he said, from Exebridge on the border of Devon and Somerset. Reckoned he was a bit of both. Sort of mixed up like.

I asked him whether, in his opinion, there was any particular difference between Devon and Somerset. Didn't think there was, he said, although on the whole he preferred Somerset. Why? I asked.

'Oh, I dunno,' he said. 'I reckon the women are easier.'

The impression you get is that these people of west Somerset are Celts. Tucked away in their drawling responses to questions were little flashes of unexpected directness, rarely matched in Devon and alien to the general character of Saxon England. I asked a verger what his church was famous for, expecting to hear something about the bells or the rood screen. 'The Vicar's wife,' said the man. 'She drinks fair *turrible*.'

In Somerset there are words and phrases that for me were entirely new. Trees are never felled, they are thrown; afterwards they are barked and rinded. Hounds have feet and sterns, not paws or tails. And as for that Lorna Doone, the woman in charge of the village store told me, she was just somebody in an old tale. Nobody *really* believed in her nowadays.

The Brendons are the outermost ramparts of Exmoor; they are about the same height and they have the same rolling gait, but they are more compact and, on the whole, they are better dressed. There is old oak in the coombes and the villages are attractive incorporations of cob and honey-coloured stone. Cob is curious stuff. The daub is made out of mud mixed with almost anything, from gravel to straw and hen feathers. They slap it on the outside walls, carefully rounding the edges to stop it cracking. All that cob needs, they will tell you, is a good hat and a good pair of shoes, meaning a tight thatch and durable foundations. In bright sunlight a newly-whitewashed cob house hurts the eyes. There are dazzling examples in the sleepy village of Stogumber, where Sir Francis Drake went courting and the six bells of the parish church of Our Lady St. Mary speak in the accent of Somerset, inscribed as they are with the words: 'When oil call in God rejoice all.'

It grew dark. Some distance ahead, on the lonely track up into the Quantocks, a young maid hurried ahead, alone, intent on her own business. For a fast walker this is always something of a tricky situation since to slacken speed, with a destination in mind, is irksome. If, on the other hand, you keep up your pace you put yourself in the unwelcome position of a pursuer. I recall occasions when girls ahead almost broke into a run when they became aware that they were being overtaken by a crop-haired bearded stranger. This is particularly noticeable in the vicinity of towns.

The creature ahead of me that evening began to dally, and when she put her basket down and I had no time for more than a formal 'good evening' as I hurried on, I became more than usually aware of the drawbacks to a long, fast walk.

Years ago, on a wide, muddy river called the Congo, I had seen slim, completely naked women pole their simple pirogues across the mirror-like surface of the water, and I know of few sights more beautiful. They gave the impression that those of their sex were but the more delicately-built, graceful members of the species. But if from the decks of the stern-wheeler that chugs up and down that stream you approached a mission station, the women on the banks became more and more voluminuously clothed, mincing along like street walkers. Quite what parallel there is in this to the attitude of town and country women towards strangers I'm not quite sure.

On the brow of the Quantocks that night I settled down on a little platform of heather where the coast of Wales could be seen across the splendour of Bridgwater Bay. The light turned from gilt to rust and hovered between those colours associated with bishops' robes and impure prose. An owl rolled a call through the pine trees; swifts screamed and hinds grazed in the dingle below. For a little time there seemed to be no time that I could recall with greater pleasure. I slept for nine hours. In default of water for bathing, the next morning I tried for the first and last time the Spartan practice of rolling about in the dewy vegetation. With teeth chattering, I brisked on to Bridgwater for breakfast. This briskness, as I have said, is in part due to my nature, to my pattern of walking. I like to get on, to peel off the miles. There is a dragon-slaying feeling in distance done.

I often regretted that I hadn't time to spare, to wander about and talk to more people than I did, but it came down to a simple choice between a little of the more populous parts of the country seen leisurely or a large amount of the lonely places viewed at speed. I had another reason for walking briskly that morning: I knew from twinges in my calves that unless I got somewhere and holed up for a day or two the walk would soon come to a full stop. Bristol seemed to be the best place to head for. It stood between England and Wales. And so I brisked on.

The walker's way down from the Quantocks is by Nether Stowey, once the home of Samuel Taylor Coleridge. He and the Wordsworths – that is, William and his sister Dorothy – who rented a house nearby, walked hundreds of miles together, arguing, discussing what they intended to write. 'Three persons and one soul,' said Coleridge.

Wordsworth was a prodigious walker. De Quincey calculated that by the age of sixty-five, fifteen years before his death, he had covered little short of 180,000 miles. Hazlitt, the essayist, went for a walk with Coleridge 'like running footman by a state coach'. Rather churlishly – since he was an enthusiastic accompanist and thoroughly enjoyed the torrent of talk from his distinguished companion – he wrote afterwards that he couldn't see the wit of walking and talking at the same time. 'I like solitude', he said:

> the soul of a journey is liberty, perfect liberty to think, feel, do just as one pleases. We go on a journey chiefly to be free of all impediments and of all inconveniences; to leave ourselves behind, much more to get rid of others. It is because I want a little breathing space to muse on indifferent matters . . . that I absent myself from the town for a while. . . . Give me the clear blue sky over my head, and the green turf beneath my feet, a winding road before me, and three hours' march to dinner – and then to thinking. . . . I laugh, I run, I leap, I sing for joy.

All this you can find in a splendid little book called *Shanks's Pony*, by Morris Marples. But I wonder, sometimes, whether Hazlitt would have laughed and sung for joy had he got into a mist on Dartmoor. In the eighteenth century they kept to well-defined tracks which, for the most part, no longer exist today.

Thanks to Marples, I discovered the writings of A. H. Sidgwick, a classical scholar who held that walking alone is, as he put it, 'on a much lower moral plane' than walking in company:

> Talking requires a definite activity of mind; walking demands passivity. Talking tends to make men aware of their differences; walking rests on their identity. Talking may be the same on a fine day or on a wet day, in spring or autumn, on Snowdon or Leith Hill; walking varies according to each and every one of these conditions.

Somerset offers the walker more than almost any other county I know of, and it is at least appropriate that one of the first literary pedestrians was a Somerset man. He is Thomas Coryate, son of the Vicar of Odcombe, who, in 1608, crossed the Alps on his way to Venice and returned home, walking most of the way. Describing himself as the 'Odcombian Legge-stretcher', he wrote a book entitled *Coryate's Crudities Hastily Gobbled Up in Five Months Travels in France, Italy, &c.* His purpose, he said, was 'to animate the learned to travel into outlandish regions'.

Coryate could be something of a clown when it suited his purpose. He hung about the court of James I, where Ben Jonson described him as 'tongue-major to the company'. And yet with his enthusiasm, scholarship and lively ability to describe 'Beautifull Cities, Kings and Princes Courts, Castles, Fortresses, Towers', Coryate gave a picture of Europe to those who knew virtually nothing of what lay beyond the Channel. As Marples puts it, where he led the way, Baedeker in due course followed.

The shoes of the 'Legge-stretcher' hung for over a century in Odcombe parish church. Their owner died of drink and dysentery on a journey to India.

In that robust age Coryate was matched by John Taylor of Gloucester, a Thames waterman who was pressed into the Navy. For his profusion of verse and prose about his travels he was hailed as the Water Poet before he died. Despite a lame leg, he walked to Scotland and Wales and made a number of stunt voyages to satisfy his patrons, who presumably took side bets on the outcome. In one remarkable adventure he declared his intention of rowing round part of the Kentish coast 'in a brown-paper boat with two stock fish tied to canes to serve as oars'. This perilous trip was actually accomplished, although the craft all but foundered before he made land.

In *Wanderings to See the Wonders of the West* Taylor described how at the age of seventy he limped from London to Land's End and back, a distance of nearly six hundred miles. After cutting his name four inches deep in the turf at Land's End he walked on to Nether Stowey, where in lodgings he says he fought a battle with an 'Ethiopian army of fleas'. Near Bridgwater he tore his britches on a fence and was obliged to hasten into the town for modesty's sake.

Bridgwater still looks like an old port, a bit of Bruges or Antwerp, especially down on the West Quay, where the muddy River Parrett winds round the walls of tall brick granaries. But they are mostly locked up and empty. There is nothing inside them, even for sparrows. Employment today is centred on British Cellophane, brewing, the manufacture of brassières and little things that go into radio sets. For the farmers who come down from the Quantocks and Mendips to the famous St. Matthew's Fair the principal attraction these days are the nude shows held in a tent, where for a shilling the men of Somerset can watch girls take their clothes off.

For a town with at least eight restaurants, including the Italian, the Parisian, Chinese, Indian and Pakistani, breakfast is hard to get. I settled in a pub with a note in the front window saying 'No Gypsies'. Remembering my Romany friends on the airfield at Newquay, I asked the landlord what he had against the travellers.

'They spit,' he said. 'And if they ain't spittin' they're fightin'. And if they ain't doing *noither* they're a-trying to sell you something. Or pinch the clock.'

Outside the pub the docks owned by British Railways looked sadly deserted. A collier had come in from the Baltic. The merchantman with 'Liverpool' on its rusty stern might have been there for years. Children played hopscotch on the cobblestones and leapfrogged over the bollards. There wasn't a sign of life on the ships and yet, only a few years ago - 'just before the Kaiser's war', the watchman said - Bridgwater had been one of the busiest ports in the West Country.

I asked the watchman what he watched these days and was told, for my impertinence, that it was mostly the telly.

In a modest way Bridgwater is beginning to sell slices of its history which is as thick as the local accent. The Conqueror gave the town-site to one of his knights called Walter de Douay. Hence *Brigge-Walter*. The name has nothing to do with the tides that lift ships thirty-six feet at high springs. Outside the town there is a noticeboard saying 'To the Battlefield', which is Sedgmoor, one of the last fought on English soil.

Here in the Civil War Colonel Wyndham surrendered the town to Fairfax after both sides had raked each other for two days with red-hot balls. When the firing had all but ceased, the Colonel's militant wife nearly restored the Stuarts with one brisk shot. Looking round the battlefields for something to do, as a woman might, she pooped off a cannon herself. The ball is said to have whizzed over Cromwell's head when he was busy drawing up some document about the terms of surrender.

The morning I got there the talk was of King Arthur and Camelot and whether the new discovery out on the moor would bring the tourists in.

Across the marsh, not far from Bridgwater as the heron flies, is the Isle of Avalon. At nearby Cadbury archaeologists had found remains of a Celtic chief who might, they thought, have been King Arthur. Was Cadbury Camelot? The only evidence that the perfect king and his adulterous wife had lived there - assuming they were both flesh-and-blood people - is pretty thin. It rests on a statement by John Leland, the sixteenth-century antiquarian, who said the place was known to local folk as Camelot 'and they have heard say that King Arthur much resorted there'. Modern historians can add substantially nothing to this fragment of gossip, but for all that I decided to have a look at the place.

This is far from easy. Beyond the town bridge you strike the marsh that lies between the Quantocks and the more northerly

Mendips. This is what locals call the Moors and geologists the great plain of Somerset. Avalon and the other mounds in the marsh used to be islands in a shallow sea. In contrast to the rolling downs of the day before, the landscape seemed curiously Dutch-like and two-dimensional, a waste-land criss-crossed with canals and willow-fringed roads.

On the town dump, opposite British Cellophane, some hundreds of gulls fought hard for foul things periodically tipped by municipal garbage trucks. The wailing noise sounded wonderful. Of all birds the herring gull has a melodious voice and a richer vocabulary than most. It mews and whines. It trumpets *keeeee-ow*, *kee-ow*, *kee-ow* and when alarmed it laughs nervously *hahahaha*.

Through glasses I looked at one of the creatures in close-up. Very smooth: white front, grey mantle, yellow beak and the cold blue eyes of a successful general or a cruel blonde.

At the noise of an engine whistle the whole flock rose as one bird. Up they went, whirling like snowflakes. And, taking advantage of an airy uplift, they drifted away, slowly, towards the Isle of Avalon. And on the mere the wailing died away.

I followed them without success. The marsh is almost impassable and the raised embankment arranged in inconvenient squares. After chasing up and down the polders for hours I became painfully aware of my feet and calf muscles. They were beginning to seize up. I felt the only chance I had of reaching Bristol the next day was to head straight - or as straight as you can go in those marshes - for Cheddar Gorge. Through field-glasses from the highest point I could find, a deserted windmill, I looked at far-away Avalon. It looked as misty and as insubstantial as the legend.

Did Arthur really exist?

At Cadbury, the Press said, the archaeologists were burrowing into not one but four or five layers of human occupation. This is what might be expected from one of the few defensible sites in an extensive swamp. They had found flint axes, bronze goods and Iron Age pottery.

'Avlon' means apples. Were those the mystic apples that gave eternal youth to the faltering? Was the juice the original Somerset cider? Did Sir Bedivere throw Excalibur into one of the lakes on the marsh? There are no answers to these questions. There never will be. But deep inside this strange story, the most durable of English legends, there are, I believe, the echo and counter-echoes of profound changes in religious belief as it has been related and interpreted by a succession of chroniclers.

The central theme of the Arthurian legend is of a search, a quest for something which, in the earliest known form of the story, is never explicitly defined. It is enough for the knights to know that something is wrong with the land and that questions need to be asked and something needs to be done to put it right. The quest for the Holy Grail seems to be an addition to the story, something added later, connected, perhaps, with rival claims between monasteries such as nearby Glastonbury for the exclusive possession of holy relics, especially a bit of the shroud, which attracted pilgrims from all over the Christian world.

In the early versions of the story the questor roams through a land the desolation of which is associated in some mysterious way with a stricken but once powerful king. He visits a lonely chapel on a sea-shore; during a storm he seeks refuge in a chapel where, on a bier, he sees a dead body, the identity of which is never revealed.

All these incidents, the death of a good man, the ensuing misfortunes of the unimplicated and their eternal salvation through sacrifice are to be found in mythologies of the eastern Mediterranean, including Christianity. The cup, or grail, and the lance are commonplace sexual symbols, whilst the release, the freeing of the waters may be interpreted as fertility invocations.

At the time when Arthur is supposed to have sat among his knights the land was possibly in the grip of chronic famine. Or attack from Germans romantically described as Anglo-Saxon. It may symbolize the replacement of Celtic paganism by Christianity. Or perhaps the fact that at various times Britain was laid under a papal interdict when Mass, the consolation that comes from the grail or cup, could not be legitimately celebrated. The story recounts how on his way to the Grail Castle Sir Gawain is overtaken by a terrible storm and takes refuge in a chapel. The altar, it says, is bare except for a burning candle in a golden candle-stick. Behind the altar is a window and even as Gawain kneels to pray 'a hand black and hideous' comes through the window and extinguishes the taper. . . .

Romanized Christianity came to Britain in the wake of the legions; it came in through Kent and the Thames. When Julius Caesar attacked Britain, London didn't exist. Much of Britain's trade was conducted through the Bristol Channel, through Bridgwater and what is now Bristol and Glastonbury. Along that south-western coast, the coast where the Megalithic tomb-builders had landed 2000 years earlier, the local chieftains were acquainted with Celtic Christianity in the 2nd century B.C. It had come to them from south Wales and Ireland, perhaps originally from the Levant. The Jewish God from Galilee had begun to replace Epona and Tammuz, Attis and Adonis, the old gods who had been imported earlier. Missionaries said the great stones the chiefs had hewn and the circles they built were the works of the devil. That's why they were in trouble. All this must have made for conflicts of faith and a quest for truth of which, there is reason to think, Arthur is the legendary survival.

On a marsh track about two miles from that great uplift of lime-stone called the Mendips, the tight strings in my calf muscles twitched painfully. I stopped then and there and went to sleep in a ditch for about four hours.

> *April 21:* Awoke to find pin-points of light shining ahead in Cheddar Gorge. Imagined they were welcoming fires lit by womenfolk of Palaeolithic hunters who lived there. Slunk on feeling, and probably looking, a bit Palaeolithic myself. Gorge is immense cleft in a cliff which was once a cave, the roof of which collapsed. Place buzzing with tourists, coach parties. Lines of little shops, neon-lit grottos. Famous cheese rather tasteless. Feel pretty well done in. Am apprehensive about 22 miles slog into Bristol tomorrow.

It began to pour down as I climbed up through the deathly-grey gorge early the next morning. The impression is of Wall

Street on Sunday. Putting a towel round my neck and dressed only in shorts and shoes, I set off for the first place in big type on the map I could find, the undistinguished village of Ubley. Thence by the reservoirs of Blagdon to Bristol.

Dogs barked at me. I had become used to this. In the distorted, hunched-up shape of a man carrying a rucksack there is something that upsets dogs. The *Rigoletto* syndrome. Perhaps I reminded them of the postman. But when, halfway across a field, two horses ran away, neighing wildly, I began to think there was something seriously wrong with my appearance and gait.

THE BARDIC BORDER

In a Bristol hotel the next morning I thought the walk had come to an end. Overworked calf muscles seemed to have gone on strike. They had seized up. Despite hot baths and amateurish attempts at massage, I could scarcely walk for more than a few paces without wincing.

A long-distance telephone call to an old friend in the medical business confirmed what I knew: that I needed rest; that I should take things easy. I would be advised, he said, to get some professional attention, locally. It could be serious. I shouldn't fool around with myself. And so on.

All very well, this, but though my legs were in poor shape, somewhere else inside a hound still leaped, barking, anxious to get off the chain. Still, if I had to rest . . . I lay back on the bed and rang for the Manager, determined to squeeze the last star of luxury out of that hotel.

The Manager recommended the personal attention of his chef and offered to send up Paddy, the head porter, who at one time had apparently been something of what is called a professor in the boxing game. He reckoned that if anyone could get a man to his feet it was Paddy.

The consultation had about it the atmosphere of almost forgotten visits to the regimental medical officer. No formality. No

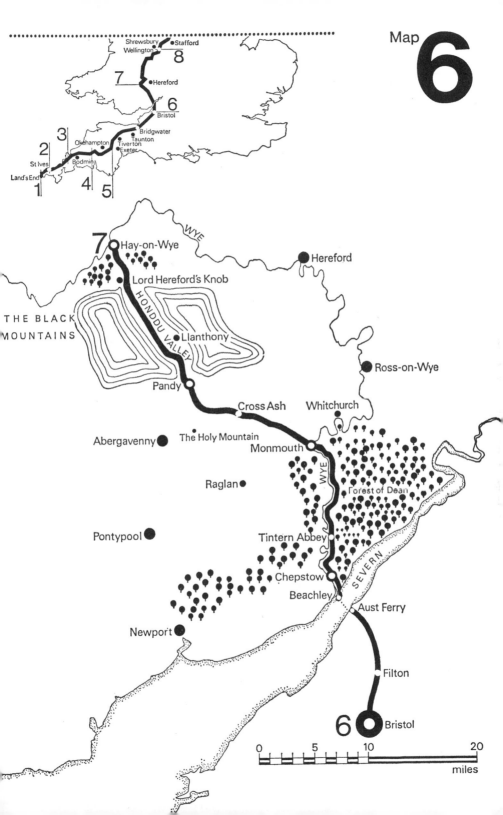

Map

6

Shrewsbury • Stafford
Wellington **8**

7 • Hereford

6
Bristol

Bridgwater
Okehampton • Taunton
Tiverton
3 Bodmin • Exeter
2
St Ives
Land's End
1 **4** **5**

WYE

7 ○ Hay-on-Wye

● Hereford

• Lord Hereford's Knob

THE BLACK
MOUNTAINS

HONDDU VALLEY

• Llanthony

● Ross-on-Wye

Pandy ○

Cross Ash ○

Whitchurch

Abergavenny ● • The Holy Mountain

Monmouth ○

WYE

Raglan ●

Forest of Dean

Pontypool ●

Tintern Abbey •

Chepstow ○

SEVERN

Beachley ○

Newport ●

Aust Ferry ○

Filton ○

6 ◎ Bristol

0   5   10   20

miles

speeches. A brief examination and then an almost oracular pronouncement.

Paddy looked me up and down. With something near affection he stroked the pink, swollen muscles with his forefinger, and sighed. Was he, I wondered, about to recommend a masseur, faradic baths, an ambulance? Not a bit of it.

'What you want, sir,' he said, 'is *exercise*.'

For two days I took short, painful walks saying, resolutely, that they were doing me good. The first was both painful and embarrassing, for, without saying who he was, a local reporter watched me hobble out of the lift with a stick and asked me, respectfully, if I were the person who intended to walk to John o' Groats. We talked for about half an hour and, perhaps, fortunately, I never saw what, if anything, he wrote.

Call it Irish insight, skill or sheer bluff, the fact is that Paddy's suggestion worked. On the Monday morning, when the early breakfasts were paying their bills, he stood near the revolving doors, holding up my loaded rucksack, high, respectfully as if it had been a space-suit, as if it weighed nothing at all. I backed into the proffered straps, gingerly, like a horse between shafts.

'Now take it easy, sir,' he said. And off I went.

Even better, on the road north out of Bristol I discovered that the supercharger still worked. On long walks, as every walker knows, there comes a point when the conscious effort of shoving one foot in front of the other disappears. This is the change from ambulatory neutral to normal cruising speed. But above that point and infinitely superior to it the walker finds that on good days he has slipped almost imperceptibly into a supercharged form of motion. He can tackle hills or go faster with the confidence of a driver of a powerful car who knows that by a mere touch on the accelerator he can pass almost anything. This doesn't mean, necessarily, that the walker increases speed. What counts is the consciousness of being able to do so without effort. My legs had not only rejoined the expedition; I knew that, despite a slight leaden feeling around the ankles, I could still slip into top gear. Remembering Paddy's advice, I dropped down to a rolling gait, a notch or two below normal.

At this speed I fell in with a tramp, or, rather, he with me, since he shuffled up and clung on, mile after mile until, tiring of his whine, I dissolved the partnership with half a crown. He carried two armfuls of old newspapers, among which he slept, and a parcel of fish-heads, his stock-in-trade.

It seems that he usually chose a pitch in a town where there were both a lot of cats and a lot of passers-by, ideally a food warehouse in a busy street. The cats came round for the bits of fish and whenever this contrived philanthropy seemed likely to attract attention and bring in a coin or two he fed the animals and stroked them, tenderly. On the face of it, a harmless stratagem of benefit both to indigent cats and man. But he complained there was next to nothing in it these days and I had the feeling that at heart he hated cats.

I took what turned out to be his wholly impractical advice to keep to the main road until I reached the unfinished England-to-Wales motorway, the M4. There, he said, I should be able to walk among the construction gangs, towards the huge new bridge over the Severn at Aust Ferry.

A miserable morning. After a fortnight on my own in the country I was wholly unprepared for the almost unbearable noise of the traffic, the testing of Bristol aircraft engines at Filton and the pile-drivers and pneumatic drills on the last length of the super-highway. Worse still, at the point where the road begins to run over the estuary, suspended on ferro-concrete stilts, I came to an unspanned gap of several hundred feet. Cursing the tramp, I walked back until I could get down and slosh across the fields towards the wide expanse of the River Severn. At Aust Ferry, predictably, I missed the ferry boat by minutes and had to wait for two hours.

Aust is the place where St. Augustine crossed into Wales during his unsuccessful effort to bring the Celtic bishops into line with the different rituals of Rome. Among geologists Aust is even more renowned for a thin grey layer of smashed-up fossils in the muddy little cliffs immediately below the first arch of the new bridge. You can see the layer clearly. Students in wellington boots were chipping into it that morning. This, technically, is a relic of the Rhaetic, a period of about 400 million years ago, when a shallow sea surrounded islands now known as the Mendips, the Quantocks and the Cleveland Hills. On one of those former islands geologists found the remains of one of the first-known British mammals, a little rat-like creature that sniffed about among the eggs of dinosaurs. Not perhaps in itself a handsome animal, but distinguished as one of the earliest ancestors of us all.

For a shilling I chugged across an estuary of liquid chocolate in the company of twelve cars and a furniture van.

'A lovely day, aye?' they say as they help you ashore at Beachley. The landscape looks much like Gloucestershire, but the accent here is littered with the little question-marks that characterize the speech of Wales.

'To Chepstow? But *that* way? Can you see the signpost *over* there?'

Grey, crumbly, friendly, castle-dominated Chepstow ('Cheap' means 'merchant', as in Cheapside) is remarkable for its narrow, twisting, up-hill-and-down-again main street, and for its baffling, its quite mind-bewildering noise.. The traffic is forced into a single line between ancient, echoing walls and squeezed out through the Town Gate that looks much like a keyhole in an enormous door. Between the gate and the town bridge, a place where little boys gather to spit on the bargemen below, there is about a quarter of a mile of sonic hell. I sought tea and refuge in a country hotel where visitors, a notice said, are 'Forbidden to wash underwear in the bedroom basins'.

At this the skull cinema operator snapped on a bit of comedy relief about a reporter (myself) who, years ago, had been told by an Editor to report the All-England Angling Championship at Newark-on-Trent. Scenically it was dull; statistically superb. Six hundred fishermen spread along eight miles of river. Twenty bookmakers, men who, on these occasions, offer enormous odds on all but a well-known few. A hundred and forty gallons of maggots for bait. The worms unweighable. Beer ditto.

In a pub that night I recall a contestant from Nottingham

holding a piece of his favourite bait, baked wasp grub, up to his ear and squeezing it, much as a man might test a good cigar. Another sat there with his mouth full of gut, softening it. He looked like Fu Manchu with a transparent moustache. A notice in the bar said 'Anglers must *not* wet their worms in the bath'. But they sub-edited the phrase out of what I wrote. They said it sounded improbable and rather indecent.

The Wye is a noble river. It rises within a mile or two of the source of the Severn at Plynlimmon and winds about, trying to get through cracks in the limestone by such devious ways that the Romans called her Vaga, the wanderer. In the loops of the lower reaches there are floods. At Chepstow the tide has been known to rise forty feet, putting brackish water into the town's indifferent beer.

I went up into the woods that night, hoping to find somewhere to sleep on Piercefield Racecourse, but from the deep yodelling barks in different keys it became apparent that the buildings were guarded. The country bed-seeker soon learns to distinguish between yap and yowl, the noise of cur and hound and that gurgling, conversational almost human voice of the Alsatian.

After an apprehensive moment in the fading light on the edge of a cliff, I remembered something the tramp had told me and gently kicked a cow to her feet. The animal rose from the dew-wet grasses, rumbling indignantly, leaving a warm, dry patch, just about the size of a groundsheet. I put the tent down there and slept like a child.

Here in the spring you wake up among soft-green beech and curiously golden oak. This is Forestry Commission country, the Forest of Dean, perhaps the most beautiful assembly of trees in Britain. From Norman times onwards the woodlands were held by a succession of great families: the de Clares, Strongbows, Marshals, Warennes, Bigods and then, until the Crown took over the property at the turn of the century, by the Earls of Worcester and Dukes of Beaufort. Their names, now, are perpetuated most noticeably on signboards of the local pubs and their timber, hewn originally for the ribs and skin of naval galleons, is chopped up for poles and pit-props.

From among the wind-flowers on Chapel Hill that morning I looked down on the grey shell of Tintern Abbey, so delicate, so beautiful, it looked as though a breath of wind might bring it down. The impression is of stone lace-work marvellously upheld on paper-thin walls. Walter de Clare built the Abbey for the Cistercians; the Bigods helped to raise the nave, but the wealth of the foundation lay in its beauty, not in its coffers. When Richard Wych, the last abbot, handed over the keys to the destructive bailiffs of Henry VIII at the time of the dissolution of the monasteries the books showed an annual income of about £192.

No breakfast at the 'Beaufort'. They were still abed. But I munched a left-over sandwich from the day before and saw what I could of the west front of the Abbey through locked gates.

Apart from the dog-like howl of the mechanical wood-cutting saws, the Wye Valley is probably more peaceful today than it has been for some hundreds of years. Until the end of the nineteenth century there used to be iron-works here, pouring out smoke, and many barges on the river carrying cider to the Severn and coal upstream. Local records tell of bow-hauling – that is, of gangs of up to thirty men who pulled the heavy craft up through the rapids, harnessed to ropes by chest-bands. To make any progress against the spring floods, they were often obliged to crawl on all fours. The river is strongly tidal:

> There twice a day the Severn fills
> The salt sea water passes by
> And hushes half the babbling Wye
> And makes a silence in the hills.

To bring down the rich iron-ore from the hills without using the turbulent river, the eighteenth-century industrialists built the Monmouthshire Canal. This ran from the sea at Newport to Pontypool. It crossed the Usk Valley and worked its way up into the Brecon Hills. It was linked to a series of horse-drawn tramroads like fingers to an outstretched hand. I had reason to be grateful for these tracks when I got into the hills. But that morning I kept to the forest rides until far past Tintern, where I switched to a disused railway and reached Monmouth in time for lunch.

In the 'Queen's Head' there they refer to Monmouthshire as Gwent. It is, they say, a *cantref* (or portion) of Morganwg and Wentllwg, the one being the western industrial valleys and the other a strip of the coast where the isolated people are reckoned to have something in common with the in-country farmers of Dartmoor.

Monmouth has a traffic problem no less than Chepstow. A furniture van that morning had knocked a chunk off the 'Queen's Head'. And in cobbled Agincourt Square a host of little cars hooted and squealed as they tried to get out. All this takes place under a commemorative statue to that maker of almost silent engines, Charles Stewart Rolls of Rolls-Royce who, with his head on one side, seems to be wincing at the noise.

High above him, in a niche, stands Monmouth's noblest son, Henry V, victor of Agincourt. Born in the town castle, he brought a fine set of French bells back to his birthplace. The story is that when he set sail for England after the Siege of Calais the citizens celebrated his departure somewhat prematurely by a mighty peal of bells. On the deck of his galleon the impetuous Harry heard the noise, turned back and removed the bells which now hang in the local church of St. Mary's.

Two rivers flow into the Wye at Monmouth, the Monnow and the Trothy, and the country between them is as fair as any in the whole of Gwent. I set off with the intention of looking at the Norman castles at Grosmont and Skenfrith, but on the way fell in with some likeable students and went bird-watching instead.

They told me that a pair of red kites had been sighted nearby and suspected they were breeding in the oaks beneath a little mountain called the Skirrid. This handsome fork-tailed bird is now a great rarity in Britain. A few pairs, the sole survivors of a once great company of scavengers, are confined to a valley in another part of Wales. I never saw them that day, but I was glad of the company of the three who were looking for them.

Dai studied botany at Aberystwyth. There, I suppose, they

taught him about transpiration and photosynthesis, but he thought most about minstrels, ash trees and scansion. He was an authority on Welsh poetry, which is very curious and very beautiful stuff. His two friends, a young theologian and a tough little engineer with red hair, were ardent bird-watchers.

Seeing my field-glasses, they hailed me enthusiastically, but mistakenly, since I had been looking at that moment not for birds, but for a pub. I knew nothing about the kites. At Newcastle – Castell Meirch, the castle of the war horses, they said – we lunched together under a sacred oak somewhat blighted by an official notice about swine fever. There they marked my maps to Cross Ash and the gateway to the Black Mountains and tried to teach me how to pronounce Welsh words.

There are, as far as I can see, no counterparts for the *dd* and the *ff* in the English alphabet. This, together with the fact that the *w* and the *y* are pronounced as vowels, makes a number of little everyday words such as *dyffryn* (valley), *ynys* (island), *myndd* (mountain), *ffrwd* (stream) and *llwch* (lake) look more strange than they sound. For thick-tongued Saxons the difficulty lies with the letters *ch* and *ll*. The former is pronounced as in the Scottish loch but with rather more venom. For the *ll* the trick is to touch the back of the teeth with the tongue and hiss like a goose, blowing the air out sideways into the cheeks. If properly done, this makes Llanvihangel Crucorney sound like a toy train scampering over points.

We parted, warmly, they for likely haunts of kite beside the Skirrid and I to the hills between Gwent and Herefordshire. In this border country the folk are friendly. England and all she stands for is no longer an alien thing. The policeman at Cross Ash sounded Welsh – at least, he did to me – but, as somebody nicely put it, a blackbird singing where the boundaries meet sounds the same from either side.

Much lies in the manner of greeting these border people. My impression is that in their dealings with outsiders the Welsh seldom speak first. And for good reason. They have been attacked since Caractacus fought the Romans. To mark the boundary between Celt and Saxon, Offa, King of the Mercians, built the dyke that bears his name. William gave his Norman lords as much land as they could hold as a cheap and effective method of subduing the borderers. The Lords of the Marches had absolute authority. They were land-grabbers. The Welsh were hounded into the hills. They expected hostility from those who came from the east.

When Pope Gregory sent Augustine to Britain to enlist the support of the Celtic Church the Welsh bishops were at a loss how to treat the great emissary from Rome. Had he come to treat them as equals? Or were they expected to listen meekly to what he had to say? The Welsh deserved to be respected. Glastonbury was a great Celtic church and Wales still held much of the West Country. The bishops decided they would be guided by their visitor's response at the first meeting. If he rose to his feet they would embrace him as their brother-in-God. If not, it would go hard with him, even though he came from the throne of the Fisherman.

Augustus is reported to have remained in his seat, lifting no more than two fingers at the approach of the bishops. They, in turn, promptly sat down, and the talks, conducted largely between emissaries in stiff ecclesiastical Latin, were a failure.

Some hundreds of years later Gruffudd Llewelyn, a Welsh prince who held sway at the time of Edward the Confessor, agreed to negotiate with the English King. Both sides were encamped on opposite sides of the Severn, but neither was prepared to cross first, lest it were reckoned an admission of inferiority. Edward is said to have got fed-up with this formality. He called for a boat and his men began to row him across. This gesture brought a great shout from Gruffudd. He threw off his sword belt; he waded out into the water, embraced the King like a child and carried him ashore on his own back.

Beyond Cross Ash you can see the Skirrid-fawr, the Holy Mountain, an oddly shaped dune with a little lump behind. The pair form a saddle in which the Ark is said to have rested. Another belief is that the peaks were split by the earthquake that followed the Crucifixion. Local farmers used to sprinkle the soil on their land.

'Not a worm, not a snail, for 'tis a haunted place and spell beset.'

'A *treadful* superstition,' said the woman who looked after the trim Wesleyan chapel. Her opinion was that St. David probably preached on the mound, which is, in fact, an out-lier of the Black Mountains.

In matters of hospitality the Welsh have qualities in common with what I know of desert-dwellers: those who come among them honourably are reckoned to be guests of Fate who should not go away dissatisfied. Guests, too, are a great source of information in outlying parts.

'So there you are now,' said the old man at the gate of his cottage. 'Your friends from college they told me to tell you they are down by the stream. Very comfortable, too, I think they are. But first, perhaps you will take a cup of tea?'

As I sipped it, gratefully, he asked me about the new road through Monmouth and whether I had seen the Highland cattle at Llidiart-y-fran. The great bridge now, the one at Beachley, wasn't that a gi-ant? Did I know it? They would soon be in Bristol in no time at all. How could one get along nowadays without a car? By a series of indirect questions, I got the impression as we shook hands that he had learnt more about what I was up to than anyone else I had met. The Welsh have a great gift for this sort of thing.

Dai and his two friends had not said anything about their proposal to camp where I should be most likely to find them. Beside a stream they had put up a tent and lit a fire. They greeted me with comfortable familiarity. With our combined resources of food and a little drink, we talked and sang and put literature in its place until, for a few hours at least, a number of conflicting matters became as simple as the noise of the stream.

For people like myself who know almost nothing about Celtic literature, the first impact of Welsh poetry is a staggering experience. Here you feel is a strangely beautiful choir with a voice of its own. By means of word-play, repetitions and an atmosphere that seems to disappear as soon as you touch it, the Celt gets near to describing the indescribable.

Dai talked of poets I had not heard about: of Aneirin and Llywarch Hen, Myrddin or Merlin and Taliessen. Sometimes, especially in Taliessen, you catch the ruthless note of the saga, of the ravens screaming shrilly over the sword-feasts. But for the most part, as Dai related this treasure, the music lay in transmuting everyday life:

> *I shall make if I am met*
> *psalms of the kisses of love.*

The stress here is on that word 'psalms'. In Wales there was conflict between the court bards, the *Gogynfeird* and the wandering minstrels who spoke more nearly from the heart. The bards never told a story. They were pledged to avoid what the Church called 'untruth', that dangerous exercise in poetic imagination. The minstrels refused court patronage. They wandered about, keeping alive the ancient literary tradition, mostly in the form of popular tales.

Into this clash of singers came Daffyd ap Gwilym, the darling both of the courts and the lonely, one of the greatest poets of medieval times. He struck at the fetters of the Church. The story is that he also tried to persuade a nun on whom his passion fell to break out of her cloister. 'God,' he said, 'is not so cruel as the old men say . . . better a woodland than a nun's calling. Thy religion, lovely maid, is treason to love.'

> *I shall make if I am met*
> *psalms of the kisses of love*
> *seven kisses from a girl*
> *seven birch trees over the grave*
> *seven vespers seven masses*
> *seven sermons of the thrush*
> *seven litanies under the leaves*
> *seven nightingales seven rods*
> *seven accents of free delight*
> *seven diadems seven odes*
> *seven odes to slim Morfudd*
> *sprightly of body and seventy more*
> *thus she'll no more lock up*
> *the rent that's due to love.*

The next day I tackled the Black Mountains, which are not so much black as grey, and on a wet day they are very grey indeed. There was something leaden and unlovable about the dripping, slate-grey roofs, the sprawling rocks and the overhanging Fwddog Ridge, a place ready-made for violence and brigandage. Here, a certain Tebris is reputed to have had captains under him who levied toll on travellers.

Coxe, the nineteenth-century traveller, warned the timid to give the valley a wide berth, for, as he put it, 'in the whole course of my travels I seldom met with one more inconvenient or unsafe'. The Reverend Francis Kilvert, one of the country's great diary-writers, a man who lived at Clyro on the far side of the mountains, said that in winter the locals 'were obliged to keep their putrifying dead in cottages for weeks before they could carry them to Llanaigin for burial'.

For all that, the going is easy and I kept up a steady four miles an hour. There are three roads through the mountains. I chose the track that follows the Honddu River. It gets progressively steeper towards what is indelicately called Lord Hereford's Knob, but for most of the way you could drive up there in a bus. I walked fast because I wanted to get over the ridge by nightfall and sleep near Hay-on-Wye. Behind the Skirrid Inn the little road climbs through a cleft carved out by foam-white water. For mile after mile, mounting steadily, the track runs between hedges of hazel and holly trimmed like a fashionable hair-do.

A young shepherd to whom I mentioned the rain looked up surprised, as if he hadn't noticed it before, although he had left his jacket folded up under a tree, to keep it dry. He had been up on the tops looking at the leaf and 'kicking that *treadful* bracken to bits'.

The leaf is blueberry. The sheep, he told me, love blueberry. As soon as it begins to sprout in the spring, the custom is to drive the flocks up into the hills from the valley foldings, knowing they will be very comfortable there and less likely to stray down again.

As for the bracken, they kick off the snake-headed sprouts until, exhausted by constantly drawing on its roots, the pest curls up and dies, leaving a little room for more digestible fodder.

The lad asked me where I came from. I said London, and he said that from all he'd heard it was a very, very busy place. He had no ambition to go there for, as he saw it, there would be nothing at all for him to do.

The principal attraction of the Honddu Valley is the high-arched ruin of Llanthony Priory, which stands on a ledge, aloof, spectacular even in the rain. The guide tells you in lyrical Welshified English that it was 'the blessed St. David who first made holy this ground'. The saint's name (Dewi) is perpetuated in scores of local shrines and wells.

A notice in the bar of the modern refectory (for tourists) says that originally two hermits, one of them a kinsman of William Rufus, lived there. Their successors, a little band of monks, are said to have been very happy, for when they looked up 'they beheld the tops of the mountains touching, as it were, the heavens and herds of wild deer feeding on the summits'. They prayed for divine support. To their consternation, riches began to pour in. Two rich landowners, William and Hugh de Lacy, financed the building of the great Priory. It was adopted by the Black Canons of the Order of St. Augustine. Llanthony became an ecclesiastical centre and hundreds of people came to savour the solitude which their coming destroyed.

But Providence, working in its inscrutable way, diverted most of the wealth to a daughter church in Gloucestershire, and until the dissolution of the monasteries the brotherhood lapsed into what one of their recorders describes as a laudable state of mediocrity.

In the oak-panelled gloom of the lodge next to the refectory I approached what I took to be a robed brother, only to find, when she turned round, that I was addressing a young handmaid of God.

'Is that where the Brothers meditated?' I asked, pointing to some outworks that might have been a cloister.

'No,' she said, smiling. 'That's where they washed their clothes'.

Before I could ask more about the meditative way of life, a company of naval commandos swarmed in, wet, boisterous and thirsty after a two days' exercise in the hills.

One of them blew a bugle blast that put all the rooks into the air, chattering. The trees seemed to explode in black fragments. Another for no reason that I can think of fired off a thunderflash behind the refectory. Llanthony suddenly became fearfully alive.

The men sat around, eating sandwiches and drinking bottled beer. The Sister moved through them, nodding and smiling so pleasantly that when one of them quietly wolf-whistled he was told violently to shut up.

Beyond Llanthony the Honddu runs faster. The valley becomes more steep, more constricted, the crags more overhanging and oppressive. Here, you feel, is the Glencoe of the Welsh border, a place marked indelibly by conflict. Long after the border feuds were over and done with, a succession of world-escapers came here and went away again. Or died, defeated.

For £20,000, a prodigious sum in 1807, Walter Savage Landor, the poet, bought an estate that landed him in remarkable trouble with his neighbours. He left, hating the Black Mountains and all they stood for. Nearby, at Capel-y-Ffyn, a farmhouse chapel which is now a Youth Hostel, Joseph Leycester Lyne, better known as Father Ignatius, founded a British Order of Benedictines. No glib phrases can sum up, briefly, what this passionate, dedicated, much-loved man did or left undone. It is a fact that when he died his Order died with him.

Eric Gill, the sculptor, took over the estate, saying that the surroundings would compensate anybody for anything. But he, too, moved on, incapable of coping with the oppressive, almost indefinable down-pressing atmosphere of the Fwddog.

Opposite the entrance to the long drive into Capel-y-Ffyn there is a place on the map called 'The Vision' where the Brothers of Father Ignatius caught a glimpse of the Blessed Virgin Mary. That afternoon the commandos I had met at Llanthony were assembled there, ready to march down into Hay-on-Wye and I fell in with them.

Together we swung up towards the Knob, the highest point in the range, where the track leaps over a hillside and glides down into the valley of the Wye.

A thoroughly enjoyable afternoon. We marched in step, singing. Bugles tooted. It could have been that occasion, centuries ago, when Gerald of Wales - Giraldus Cambrensis as they call him - rode down that self-same track in the company of the Knights of the True Cross, a noble band, heaven-bent on recruiting for the Third Crusade.

A splendid cavalcade as it has been described: gentry in full armour with liveried retainers and priests carrying tall wooden crucifixes. In his *Itinerary*, Gerald says one miracle followed another.

Lakes turned to blood; the sick were healed, heretics blinded and, most marvellous of all, after the severe pains of a woman in labour, a soldier called Hagernal voided a calf 'in the presence of many people'. Old Gerald is cautious about explaining the event. It may have been, he thinks, something to do with divine revelation or, as he puts it, possibly the punishment attendant on some abominable crime.

WYE TO TRENT

In trying to relate what happened that night when the cat moved into the light of the log-cabin fire I am forgetting, perhaps, that enchantment has its own time and season. I am not at all sure now whether I can recapture the sight of splintered moonlight on the river, the sheer beauty of the place, the sense of peace. Perhaps Rosamunda, the gentle paramour of the King, had something to do with the occasion for she lived at nearby Clifford Castle. And Clifford is under a double spell. It is in Kilvert country, near Clyro, the home of that clergyman-diarist who found life such 'a curious and wonderful thing' that he could not bear to let it go unrecorded. I have kept the notes I made that evening and fragments of them may serve to show that among all the hustle, the urge to get on, there came times of great contentment.

In all I had tramped that day, I suppose, about twenty-six miles, most of it through the mountains. I parted company with the commandos at Hay, and after dining there, handsomely, I struck out along a derelict railway track that follows the generous curves of the River Wye. At dusk, near Clifford, I came across a disused plate-layer's cabin, clean and serviceable, with a fire grate, and decided to spend the night there. On impulse, I lit the fire.

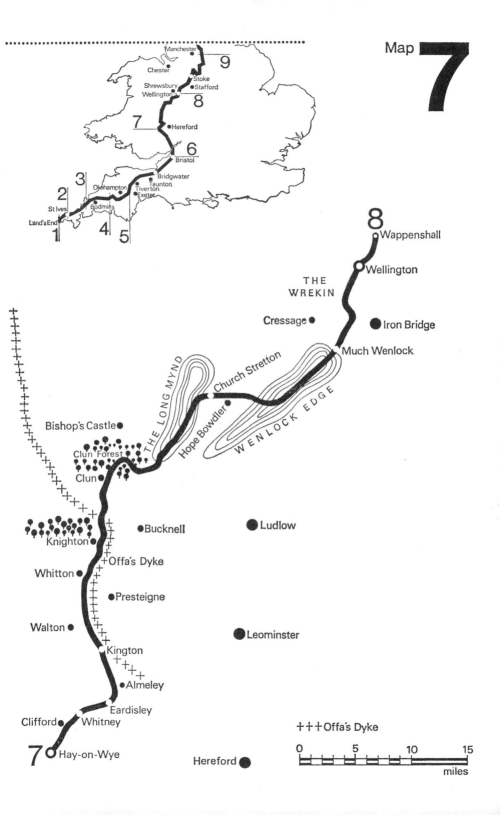

Map

7

Manchester
Chester
9
Stoke
Shrewsbury ● Stafford
Wellington 8
7 ● Hereford
6
Bristol
Bridgwater
Taunton
Okehampton Tiverton
St Ives Exeter
Land's End Bodmin
2
3
1
4 5

8
○ Wappenshall

○ Wellington

THE
WREKIN

Cressage ●
● Iron Bridge

Much Wenlock

THE LONG MYND
Church Stretton
Hope Bowdler
WENLOCK EDGE

Bishop's Castle ●

Clun Forest
Clun ●

● Bucknell
● Ludlow

Knighton ●

Offa's Dyke

Whitton ●
● Presteigne

● Leominster

Walton ●

Kington

● Almeley

Eardisley
Clifford ● Whitney

7 ○ Hay-on-Wye

+++ Offa's Dyke

0   5   10   15

Hereford ●   miles

The wooden chocks that clench the rails burn wonderfully well. They are bituminous and dry as a bone. Immediately the spell began to work as surely had I touched the sorcerer's wand. In the amber-coloured light the hut became the log cabin of everyone's dreams.

At a moment when I could not have been more grateful for company a ginger cat walked in from some neighbouring farm-stead. It walked round, delicately, tail high, exploring the place and then started to play. In time it grew tired of pouncing on flickering shadows and looked to me for amusement. I gave the animal a fragment of corned beef and, with promise of more to come, the two of us sat down outside and looked down on the river.

Where the old castle lies in the dark is of no account. Enough to know that Lord Clifford's daughter, the maid immortalized by troubadours, lived there. They say she was still under the instruction of nuns when Henry II, out hunting, caught a glimpse of a face with the complexion of a rose. In the manner of the times, he sent for her.

Henry had married Queen Eleanor, that proud woman who bore the rose of Aquitaine on her device, but he loved his mistress more. He called her not just rose, but Rosamunda, the rose of all the world and installed her in a bower at Woodstock.

> *. . . most secret and inviolate Rose*
> *Enfold me in my hour of hours.*

William Longspee, Earl of Salisbury, is reputed to have been their bastard son. What the Queen did to the girl of shining loveliness is not known. Chroniclers saw the tomb inscribed *Tumba Rosamundae* in the nunnery at Godstow. It was covered with a pall of silk and set about with wax lights, 'a pity beyond telling'.

I sat there, thinking about the story, weaving it into fantasies until it grew chill, and cat and I went back into the glow of the fire. Before I wriggled into my sleeping-bag I wrote an affection-ate line or two about the cat. An extraordinarily nice animal, gentle but not possessive.

The affair didn't last. For breakfast the wretched creature

brought in a decapitated goldfinch. I couldn't even pretend it was
a gift. She crouched over the little bag of feathers, growling like
a dog. I shooed her out and tried to ignore the stain on the
floor as I munched a sandwich.

As you look across the Wye into Kilvert country the hills
rise above fields of buttercups which, on that fresh morning,
seemed more golden than green. There are mountains to the
north and the west, but otherwise little to distinguish the in-
dividual character of Brecon, Radnor and Hereford, the three
counties that converge on Hay-on-Wye. They used to call the
place *The* Hay much as today we say The Hague.

On the opposite side of the river stands Clyro, where for seven
years (1865–72) the Reverend Robert Francis Kilvert served as
curate and began to write the diaries that brought fame to the
parish*. As it says on his tombstone at Breadwardine: 'He being
dead, yet speaketh.' And he was only thirty-eight when he died.

Kilvert had a keen eye and a passion for gossip, for the bizarre,
for sentiment, for beauty and, quite clearly, for little girls lightly
dressed. He makes no bones about it. 'I stroked back her fair soft
curls,' he wrote. 'Her arms tightened round my neck and she
pressed her face closer and closer to mine, kissing me again and
again. . . . Time was of no account. An hour flew like a few
seconds. I was in heaven.'

The curate is nicely uncensorious about what the no-good boys
are up to on parish picnic parties. Or lovers in lanes. He *loves*
love. And life. 'What is it? What is it?' he asks. 'What do they
all mean? It is a strange and terrible gift, this power of stealing
hearts and exciting such love.'

In a way that would get him into much undeserved trouble
today, he writes ecstatically about where beams of sunlight are
likely to fall in little girl's bedrooms. In his own parish simple
people and children took him very seriously and with them he
was at his best. 'I had the happiness', he says, 'to have the poor
people all to myself. None of the grand people were at church
because of the snow, so of course I could speak much better and

*Kilvert's Diary in three volumes, edited by William Plomer and published
by Jonathan Cape.

more freely.' For all that, he deals conventionally with conventional morality :

> 'That liar and thief of the world Sarah Thomas, Mrs. Chaloner's servant, is gone. The evening she went no one knew what had become of her all the early part of the night. Probably she passed it under some hedge and not alone. At a quarter before midnight she asked for a bed which Mrs. Price very properly refused. I hope she has cleared out of this village. Beast.'

> 'This morning Edward Morgan of Cwmpelved Green brought his concubine to Church and married her. She was a girl of 19, rather nice-looking and seemed quiet and modest. She had a pretty bridesmaid and they were both nicely prettily dressed in lilac and white. After the ceremony I saw the stout dwarf Anne Beaven pinning on bright nosegays.'

These are isolated fragments from the Kilvert diaries. In between terrible stories of the man who committed suicide by self-decapitation, of the child found dead in the water closet; there are heart-touching accounts of dressing the church for Eastertide and harvest-home at Clyro when 'the air blew sweet from the mountains'. There is much wry humour, too.

A woman called Mrs. H., he says, 'has two pet toads which live together in a deep hole in the bottom of a stump of an old tree. She feeds them with breadcrumbs when they are at home and they make a funny little plaintive squeaking noise when she calls them. Sometimes they are from home, especially in the evenings. . . .'

To get to Knighton, about thirty miles away, I took to the old railway track that runs between Hay and Whitney and beyond. This is a relic of one of the old horse-drawn truck systems. Financiers called Adventurers built the truck-road at the beginning of the nineteenth century. They used it to bring coal and coke into the valley from the new canal at Brecon. Trucking must have been a leisurely business.

The drivers were given elaborate instructions about what to do when they met each other head-on. It also turned out to be an unprofitable business, for the Adventurers were apparently deaf to the sound of the little puffing engines in the adjacent valleys. They became mechanized too late to recoup much on their original investment. The track has never been a busy one, even in the days of steam, and it began to sprout weeds a few years ago.

The problem about walking on an old railway track is that the wooden sleepers are about six inches short of a normal stride. You can't get into the swing of the thing without constantly looking down. It's like trying to walk rapidly on stepping-stones across a river. Exasperated by the motion, I took to the cinders on the outskirts of the rails. There the innocent-looking clumps of over-hanging grass concealed the sharp, wire-like tendrils of briars that tore at my ankles and tripped me up. Worse, I misread the name of one of the derelict stations, overshot a junction and found myself among the half-timbered houses of Eardisley, miles beyond where I should have taken to the hills.

After a miserable detour of five miles on a main road I reached Kington, grateful for the light, almost champagne-like cider they sell there.

A word about drink. I drank two or three pints at lunch-time and a similar amount at night, sometimes more to slake a prodigious, metabolic need for liquids. I not only drank a fair amount; I ate more than I have ever eaten before. I started at dawn on coffee and sandwiches. This kept me going until I found someone prepared, ideally, to cook bacon and three or four eggs. Walkers need a lot of liquids and a lot of fat. In time I learnt to avoid places with a set menu, especially those half-timbered cafés and genteel guest-houses on the fringes of country towns where the guests speak in whispers, terrified, I suppose, of the retired soldiers on half-pay who usually run them.

The trick is studiously to avoid the middle of the catering spectrum. I rarely failed to get substantial meals in cottages, transport cafés, small pubs and big hotels – the bigger the better. The hospitality of cottages is something I cannot easily describe, nor praise sufficiently. The difficulty often was to pay something in fair relation to the amount of food I ate.

Kington is a little, squashed-up, narrow-streeted market town ca the Welsh frontier where they sell cartridges and sheep dip, fertilizer and men's flannel underwear. A town for farmers. Everything feminine or fripperish comes from Hereford, about fifteen miles away. Even on the fitted carpets of the best pub in town there were snuff-coloured fragments of what the company had recently been walking on.

'Offa's Dyke?' said the landlord obligingly. 'Why, yes, now. I'll ask George. He's lived here all his life.'

The shrimp-pink, toothless George - 'nigh on ninety,' he told me, twice - reckoned I should strike it most easy if I went by Herrock Hill - that is, if I went down below, like, where you couldn't see the old ditch, anyhow. He brought in Thomas for a second opinion, but Thomas didn't favour that way at all.

He rattled off two or three names which, I discovered later, were hidden farmsteads, but all were in the direction of a village everyone talked of, a place called Evenjobb.

'Must be wonderful fond of scenery, you are,' said Thomas as I prepared to go. '*Wonderful* fond, you must be. Now I'm an old never-sweat I am, for don't you see I *can't* hurry no more, like.'

On paper - that is, from a guide-book and a skimpy little line marked on the corner of the map - I thought I should be able to walk along a clearly-marked dyke. It extends, inter-mittently - I had read - for about a hundred and forty miles - that is, from the point where I crossed the Severn at Beachley to the south of the Dee in the north. What I found (when I eventually did find it) was a ditch with raised banks, only slightly distinguishable from other ditches.

The Romans conquered the whole of Wales, but they failed to Romanize anything more than the southern plain and the fringe of the mountains. In the eighth century A.D., long after the Romans had left, Offa, King of the Middle Kingdom of Mercia, decided to contain what he had conquered by a boundary rather than a frontier. The descendant of the great Penda and Wulfhere decreed that anyone carrying arms on the wrong side of the ditch could expect to be put to death, summarily.

As George predicted, I struck the Dyke on Herrock Hill on what I took to be the present boundary of England and Wales. To get there you strike west out of Kington and turn up Dunfield Lane between hedges eight feet high.

The afternoon promised well: the sky blue and billowy with friendly clouds. Cuckoos called, lambs skipped. I saw a great deal of that part of Radnorshire, but very little of the Dyke.

My impression is that it switched off into a country lane. In other places it looked as if the raised bank had been bulldozed flat by somebody working off old scores against the English. The few locals I spoke to were subtly and sometimes suspiciously evasive.

Now that old Dyke, they said, it was difficult to explain *just* where it went to someone coming in fresh from outside, *like*. Everywhere you hear that slightly distrustful, border-conscious, evasive 'like'. It 'could be' in that direction. But on the other hand they would have started off from somewhere else if they had a mind to look at it themselves. The rabbits, one of them told me, had done it in, proper. They had burrowed into the banks, so now the Dyke wasn't there at all. Like.

It took me some time to catch on to the fact that the ditch invariably lies on the west flank of the hills - that is, in places where Offa's Mercians could look down on enemy territory. With an occasional glance at the compass, I edged round Gilfach Hill and tried to get back to a little road I had left, reluctantly, some time earlier that afternoon.

Despite thick, mature woods and rolling downland, Radnorshire is a strangely lonely, nobody-about place, the most sparsely populated county in England and Wales. The inhabitants are not at all sure, most of them, whether they are English or Welsh and the majority, fortunately, don't seem to care. At the last count, only a handful of families said they preferred to speak Welsh. Most of the people you meet know only a few words related to place-names, such as *Gil-fach*, the little retreat, *Fron-las*, the green bank, *Pen-y-bont*, the head of the bridge, and *Sais*, which is Englishman.

What catches the ear is not so much the extraordinarily

variable accent, as the inversions and idioms which come through from the Welsh. They say 'Good evening' in the afternoon. They tend to speak demonstratively: 'Stay you there now and I'll ask him.' Pronouns are tossed about indiscriminately. 'So him told I you was looking for Herrock.' A Radnorshire tombstone is inscribed:

> *Him as was has gone from we;*
> *Us as is must go to he.*

Weather is usually the first topic of conversation and fields are sometimes referred to as 'she'. 'She's not bearing well now,' they say. 'Not with that fancy dressing stuff.' Radnorshire is almost wholly agricultural. There are no industries to speak of, except for quarries. And apart from the places in the Wye Valley there are neither villages nor big country houses:

> *Alas, alas. Poor Radnorshire,*
> *Never a park nor even a deer,*
> *Never a squire of five hundred a year*
> *Save Richard Fowler of Abby-Cwmhir.*

'The Dyke?' said the old man on the tractor as if recalling a half-forgotten acquaintance. He switched off and remained silent for a moment. 'Now, down you go by Whitton. It's not far into a mile. Keep hard to the left like until you come to a proper old cottage with a pond in the garden. Behind the cottage you'll find the Dyke. I should know,' he said. 'I should know it well, for I was born in that old cottage seventy-nine years ago.'

Offa's Dyke-diggers dug wherever they could keep an eye on the Welsh. They didn't bother overmuch about whether they were digging into ancient burial mounds or Roman roads. Several of these lonely sites have the reputation of being haunted, as if unquiet spirits were still looking for somewhere to settle down.

In Flintshire, near the northern end of the Dyke, there is a cairn called *Bryn yr Ellyllon*, the Hill of the Little People. Long before the mound was excavated a woman claimed that at midnight she had seen the shadowy figure of a man in gold armour, on horseback. Many years later when archaeologists dug into the mound they unearthed, among other things, a gold peytrel - that is, the breast-plate of an armoured horse.

I located the Dyke behind the cottage as the old man foretold; it lay between banks of holly and yew, but it wandered off when I thought I had at last got to grips with it, and I never saw it again.

In the woods above Knighton that night the warm air throbbed with filibustering nightingales. 'Such sweet lowd musick they breathe', said Izaak Walton, that 'it might make mankind to think miracles are not ceased'. A pretty notion, but scarcely supportable. The birds are laying claim to territory. They not only shout at each other; sometimes they fight. One soloist I tracked down to a thorn-bush redoubled his chirruping when a rival flew in and started up nearby. In what was clearly far from harmony, they sang together for perhaps a minute and then joined battle. After a brief but furious scuffle one flew off, leaving behind a pinch of russet-coloured feathers.

At Knighton, to judge from the deserted streets, you might think there are more nightingales in the woods than people in the town, one of the biggest in the county. It looks deserted. In 1879 it had a population of 2,500, twenty-two licensed houses and two policemen. Today, according to Mr. William Cadwaller, Clerk to the Council, the population is about 1,850; the pubs have shrunk to eight and the constabulary increased by one. That man, a friendly fellow who played a very subtle game of dominoes, led me to a comfortable pub and put me on the right road the next day.

To get from thickly-wooded Radnor into the rolling downs of Housman country you take the road to Clun. On all sides are little Tuscan-like hills, bare on top and by the Forestry Commission scantily clothed below. This is Shropshire, renowned, they will tell you, for trout and Tories. It breathes a sort of airy, easy prosperity. East of Knighton the feeling is that the clash of the border is over and done with:

> *In the valleys of springs of rivers*
> *By Onny and Teme and Clun*

> *The county for easy livers*
> *The quietest under the sun.*

But Housman, of course, was a Worcestershire lad. And as for that sleepy old half-timbered town of Clun the noise was terrific. They were digging up the main street to lay a drain. By some mischance I walked into St. Catherine's Maternity Hospital instead of the not dissimilar Tile Tavern and had an embarrassed moment among the pregnant mums. They told me the pub was on the opposite side of the street. A pint or two there and I took to the hills again.

On the sun-bright and breezy top of Guilden Down you either stick to a little rose-hedged road or trespass into Forestry Commission forest. Those with an inclination to trespass I warn that this is not a good place to start, but with nothing but larks between myself and God I got carried away by Housman:

> *Laws for themselves and not for me,*
> *And if my ways are not as theirs*
> *Let them mind their own affairs.*

Forgive us our trespasses. In that coniferous labyrinth of larch and pine I went round and round in a maze of tracks that led nowhere. I even began to doubt the integrity of the map. Could it be that the cartographers were in league with the woodsmen in an effort to confound incursionists?

There is, I once discovered, a little-known trade called map-spoiling. An American told me it was his job to add small fictions to the sheets produced by his company. They were quite trivial: sometimes he put an extra wiggle into the course of a river or added a line of contour here and there; on occasion he rearranged the pattern of black dots that make up a village; all these contrivances were legally registered so that his company could detect and proceed against those who produced pirated versions of their sheets. It may be that something of the kind goes on in the Forest of Clun. The tracks and the shape of the green blobs of woodland on the map bore no apparent relationship to what the place looked like from the top of Sunnyhill. It took me about an hour to get out.

Beyond the forest you stride down to the great park of Walcot with its formal lake and lawns and cypresses, once the home of Clive of India. This is switch-back country. You feel you could roll down the hills and be carried halfway up the next one. Away in the far distance, the hump of that huge hill, the Long Mynd, looms up, bigger by far than anything else. It looks like a whale improbably stranded on the shores of Shropshire. At Plowden the head lies towards you, the back is foreshortened and the tail curls round until it gets lost in the miles-away haze. The impression is that the monster might roll over on its back.

There is some evidence that far back in geological time this actually happened to those very old Pre-Cambrian rocks. They were prised up by earth forces until they stood on end and then, after a long period of time, another shove from below pushed them completely over until they stood upside down. The Mynd today is renowned chiefly as a pleasure dome for those interested in walking or gliding.

I went up by Plowden, climbing rapidly, until vast tracts of Shropshire and Wales became visible from the top. Here the impression of an isolated leviathan vanishes, for there are scores of long rounded hills on either side, all surging north-east, towards the Midlands. On a very clear day, they say, you can see Snowdon.

On top the turf is elastic; the wind blew lightly and horses that had been left out to graze galloped away madly from the bat-like shadows of the gliders. I took off my shirt and still felt hot. I took off everything except my shoes and felt fine.

Try walking naked on a hill sometime for a kind of ecstasy unlike anything else I can think of, but a word of warning: keep a pair of britches at the ready for an unexpected encounter. I recall walking on the South Downs on a warm, wet day when, to keep my clothes dry, I stripped off stark and walked on. Nobody, you would have thought, would be about on that morning. But I still recall the embarrassment at seeing a young woman on horseback and seeing her, fortunately, before she saw me. As I peered out at her from behind a bush, dripping from all extremities, I wondered uncomfortably whether the circumstances would have sounded convincing in a police court.

You can walk on the very top of the Mynd for six or seven miles before reaching a deep canyon where I dressed and went down into the respectability of Church Stretton for supper. This done, the usual problem of where to put my tent down in the vicinity of a town became acute, for it began to rain.

Church Stretton is a very respectable-looking place. There are no vacant lots. Long tree-lined streets of aloof, detached properties, each with their own high-hedged gardens, stretch out into the country for a greater distance than I cared to walk. On impulse I settled for a little hut built in the fork of a tree for someone's child.

It partly overhung a dark and deserted street. I climbed up, put the fly-sheet over an awkward hole in the roof and settled down among a doll's tea service and a plastic machine gun. Late at night, before I slipped off to sleep, the door of the house opposite opened and, to my consternation, two women came out with a yapping poodle.

They were joined by someone else's dog. The women gossiped. I caught snatches of trivial conversation. The dogs scratched, sniffed, and cocked their legs up on what supported me. Here, I thought, is another situation that I shall have some difficulty in talking my way out of, the more since I daren't dress for fear of making a noise.

But nobody looked up. Not even the silly dogs. Only the blackbirds called *chick chick* angrily, incessantly, at the person who had invaded their home ground. The women went home. Doors slammed. Lights went out and Church Stretton slept.

I awoke under what seemed to be a gigantic udder. Above me, only a few inches from my nose, the fly-sheet sagged, heavy with rain. I dressed, hastily, before sending an impressive waterfall whooshing down into the daffodils below. At that dead-quiet hour it sounded tremendous.

With a bit of encouragement from the sun, the view from the top of Wenlock Edge might have matched some fine lines from Housman about the glittering pastures and the empty uplands, but Clunton and Clunbury and, for all I know, Clungunford and

Clun were blanketed in mist. From somewhere far below in the murk birds twittered and kine lowed. Trucks rolled out of the clanking limestone quarries; in the boot of his car a farmer showed me two dead foxes which he had gassed that morning. They were grinning, horribly. Feeling that things weren't quite what they should have been, I walked down into the prim, self-possessed little country town of Much Wenlock for a meal.

The half-timbered houses and inns are impressive. They are striped like old-fashioned mint humbugs. What's left of the Cluniac Priory is indescribably beautiful. As to local hospitality, I quote the standard guide-book, which describes it as 'unchanging, almost medieval'. Make what you will of this. Asked about the prospects of lunch and a bath, two hotel-keepers clearly wished me elsewhere. A lunch yes, a bath no. 'Inconvenient,' said one. 'Haven't really got a·bath to spare,' said another. The local butcher, a rather pompous fellow in a straw hat, seemed shocked by the suggestion that he might know somebody who could wash my underwear. 'Not in Wenlock,' he said, turning to a chauffeur buying fifteen prime steaks. I might have been enquiring about a bawdy house.

Thank God for small pubs. The manager of an unpretentious place offered me the use of his own bathroom. 'If there's nobody in it, it's yours,' he said. His wife hung my washing out and in half an hour it was dry. The lunch for the few shillings they asked couldn't have been better. 'Thee'st goin' through Coalbrookdale?' the landlord asked as I strapped on my rucksack. He spoke like Lady Chatterley's lover, direct, the accent unmusically Midland, but warm and friendly. In a two days' walk through Shropshire you can hear voices as diverse as any in one English county.

The Welsh lilt persists as far as the Long Mynd, where for centuries they retained the Welsh form of names, such as Richard ap Morgan. In Housman country the vowels broaden; they turn *a* into an *o*; a bank becomes a bonk and, for strangers, the negative forms of verbs sound rather curious. 'Ar hanna bin in Salop this ten years an' wunna go agean,' a farmer told me, expressing his dislike of the traffic in Shrewsbury. In Wenlock, especially to the north and east of the town, you begin to catch the loose, undisciplined vowels of the Black Country.

Coalbrookdale is a strange place to find in Shropshire, a county renowned for its sheep-sales, its rich dairying lands and its agricultural shows. But the name means what its says. In a steep gorge of the River Severn that lies some miles to the north of the town the great iron-masters of the eighteenth century began to use coal for smelting processes, a discovery that led to the Industrial Revolution.

To get there you walk down the northern end of Wenlock Edge, through Farley, following a musical little stream, the Farley Brook that drops into the Severn at the side of Buildwas Abbey. For the most part the going is pleasant and rural. There are still great vistas to the north and the west, but from a glimpse of distant chimneys and a pall of smoke the feeling is of the advent of dark, satanic mills.

I walked down into Coalbrookdale late that afternoon. The geological explanation for the great gorge there is that instead of wandering south to the Bristol Channel, the Severn used to flow north-west, towards Liverpool and the Dee, but during the Ice Ages the outflow became blocked by cliffs of ice. The river turned into an enormous lake. Eventually, the rising water broke through the narrow neck of the Wenlock Ridge and gushed down towards Bristol, much as it does today.

In the eighteenth century, when it became known that iron could be smelted with coal instead of charcoal that was destroying the forests, the great ironmasters found all the materials they wanted in this rift in the limestone. The river had laid bare seemingly illimitable supplies of coal and iron. Abraham Darby spanned the gorge with the first bridge in the world to be made of iron. It still stands there today, a symbol of the Industrial Revolution. But after a tremendous prosperity, it became clear that supplies of raw material were not illimitable. They began to run out. All that remains of the Darbys' enterprise are the grimy, derelict buildings, poised one above the other, like a blighted Tuscan village. And the bridge.

The ruined Norman arches of Buildwas Abbey are reckoned

to be the finest in England, but they were ruined by that infamous little toad, Thomas Cromwell, ecclesiastical wealth-provider to Henry VIII. It is a matter of no particular regret that he was eventually crushed under his own engine of tyranny, a bill of attainder, a trick for making things look legal. He was beheaded, messily, on Tower Hill.

Once over the river you climb up Beggar's Hill and beyond to what at that weary hour seemed like the slopes of the Himalayas, a little mountain called the Wrekin. There are two spurs, Heaven's Gate and Hell's Gate. I took the easiest path round both, encouraged only by the local folk who are friendly. They waved, they offered cups of tea and pointed out the most comfortable way down to Wellington.

Farquhar the poet said the kingdom 'cannot show better bodies of men . . . more generosity, more good understanding, nor more politeness than is to be found at the foot of the Wrekin', and on this I'm with Farquhar. A quarryman told me that the strange-shaped hill is the stump of an old volcano. But the smoke that drifts round it today comes from the new industrial centre of Dawley.

Easier going now. You pass through the great woods of Ercall with scores of picnic parties all sitting that late Saturday afternoon within sight of their cars. Below is a length of that most famous of Roman roads, Watling Street, which ran from Kent to a place near Shrewsbury. I branched off into Wellington, but not for long. A dreary place that used to be called Watlingtown. A meal and off again once more, slower now, the long day nearly done.

At ten o'clock I asked a gamekeeper if I could put my tent up in a wooded estate near the Shropshire Union Canal, a mile or two west of Wappenshall. 'It's all right by me,' he said, 'but don't upset those bloody pheasants or I'll lose my job.'

The Potteries

POTTERIES AND PEAK

Three incidents stand out from that night among the pheasants. First, the animal that tried to get in. Dog, I thought, from the snuffling noise and reached instinctively for the fudge. And a big dog, too, I reckoned. The animal seemed to be burrowing away under the canvas. Was it, I wondered, the gamekeeper's retriever or a sheepdog on the prowl? I poked my head out and snapped on the torch. A hedgehog scuttled away into the night. From the noise it made it might have been a wolf. I crawled back into my sleeping-bag and slept until the second incident, the birds, woke me up.

Now the dawn chorus, as I have said on several occasions, is a splendid thing, an example of natural ecstasy at its very best, but ideally it should be heard at a distance of not less than two hundred yards from the nearest choristers. At close quarters the principal singers can be a confounded nuisance. And of all birds that silly, strutting creature, the ring-necked pheasant, is a positive menace to the sanity of anyone fool enough to sleep within earshot of a well-stocked covert.

Karark they shouted at each other. *Karark, karark.* But this is a feeble imitation of the metallic, brain-stabbing quality of those feathered klaxon horns. Wearily I got up and paddled about, bare-footed, only to find a discomforting number of bumble

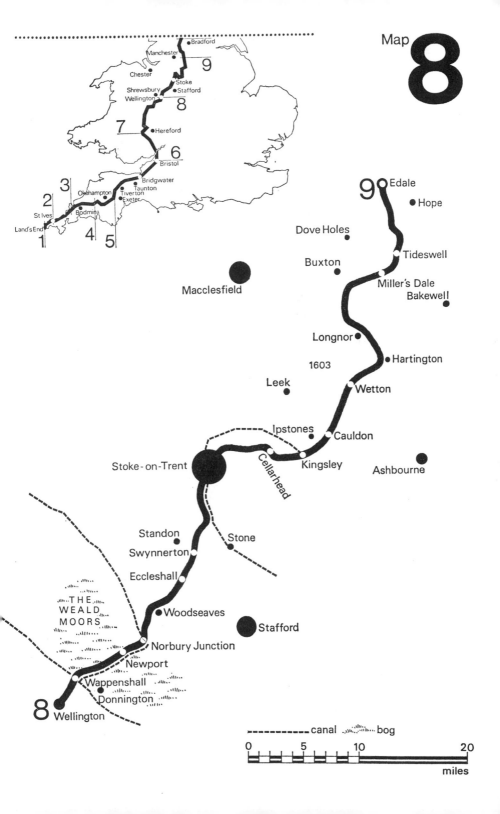

Map

8

Bradford
Manchester
Chester
9
Stoke
Shrewsbury • Stafford
Wellington
8

7
• Hereford

6
Bristol

3
Bridgwater
2
Okehampton
Taunton
Tiverton
Exeter
St Ives
Bodmin
Land's End
1
4 **5**

9 O Edale
• Hope

Dove Holes
Tideswell

Buxton
Miller's Dale
Bakewell
Macclesfield

Longnor
1603 • Hartington

Leek
O Wetton

Ipstones
Cauldon
Stoke-on-Trent
Cellarhead
Kingsley
Ashbourne

Standon
Stone
Swynnerton
Eccleshall

THE
WEALD
MOORS
Woodseaves
Stafford

Norbury Junction
Newport
Wappenshall
Donnington
8 Wellington

--------- canal .... bog

0 .... 5 .... 10 20
miles

bees in the grass. The bees were immobilized, wet with dew. This apparently happens if they spend the night out at certain times of the year. Several lay upside-down, buzzing feebly around my bare toes as they tried to warm up and take off.

A mile beyond that bee-loud glade is a dilapidated canal basin, a place where the barges used to pull in and unload. The canal is almost dry; the cranes are lying with their heads in the reeds, the pulleys rusted and the woodwork rotten. Yet almost hidden among those reeds is an old tow-path which led me through miles of marshland, in places strangely beautiful.

Here are the Weald Moors of Shropshire, a relic of a long time ago when ice-sheets changed the course of the Trent, and the Severn and the Midlands were deep under lake water. Here for centuries men poled about in flat-bottomed boats, decoying wildfowl and spearing fish. And here still are the soggy pastures, the pools of sour water and the almost endless avenues of reeds. Against the silvery-grey mist the wire-thin stalks stood out like the brush-strokes of a Japanese print. And at dawn when the sun caught the top of the giant grasses the plumes glowed with cold, incandescent fire. Out of this wilderness of vertical lines came the yelp of moorhen and the almost ceaseless jig-jag, jangly notes of reed- and sedge-warblers.

Two fishermen jumped to their feet as if to run off and then, seeing my rucksack, explained with disarming candour that they shouldn't have been there at all. They were fishing during the close season. 'They could do us for it,' said a man who introduced himself as Ted, hinting that they had been done several times before. 'You're not supposed to catch anything except eels until June,' he said, producing two pike each about a yard long.

His pal, Fred, who had caught about a dozen slimy bream, nodded towards a barrel-chested bull terrier. 'That's Herbert,' he said. Fred gave me a swig of biting hot tea, Herbert licked my bare ankles enthusiastically and Ted talked of the subject most close to their hearts: poaching other people's fish.

Both men came from Stoke; both were bricklayers 'in between times', as one of them put it. From January to December, come sun or rain, they cycled out to the most troutful, the most private lengths of the Dove and the Manifold. They poached forty miles of club water on the Trent and they apparently knew every landowner for miles around. 'When you've been pinched once or twice you get to know 'em,' said Ted reflectively.

As an article of diet he said he didn't much care for fish himself, although his missus was partial to a bit of grilled perch. Before we parted he asked me to keep an eye open for their pal further up the canal. 'Chap in a blue bonnet,' said Ted. 'He got put away last time he was copped and now he's a bit nervous like. If you see him, give him a proper toot like this and he'll know you've seen us.' He put two fingers in the corner of his mouth and vented a blast that made me wince.

I went on and on. And always through reeds. And always within sound of the jangling warblers. Past long dry stretches where only decayed lock gates showed that the Shropshire Union had once been a busy canal; past deep pools, bubbling with fish and weeds. Past low-roofed farmsteads, protected by windbreaks of Lombardy poplars. A few cows, but nobody about. A deserted fen known only to the likes of Ted and Fred. With a bit of tidying up, the wildly overgrown towpaths could at least be made into good walking country, and as for the reed beds they are ready-made bird reserves.

Near the sad grey little town of Newport the countryside looks a bit more cared for. Water from the dykes flows into the canal and apparently stays there. A good place for eel-fishing, too. On both banks anglers slipped eels shaped like roach, like bream and curiously like perch into their keep-nets. 'Eels?' I said. 'Eels,' they said. Some didn't even bother to turn round.

Feeling ravenously hungry, I turned into the emptiness of Newport on a Sunday morning. Only the shops that sold newspapers and bars of chocolate were open. Old men in cloth caps and shirt-sleeves shuffled in for the *News of the World* and shuffled out again, back into their still-curtained houses. The bells of St. Nicholas donged dolefully, but nobody seemed to be going in.

'Food?' said a lonely policeman, looking surprised, almost

shocked. 'Not here. Not in Newport. Good Lord, not on Sundays.'

Some way out of town I knocked on the back door of what seemed to be the smallest pub in the world. 'We're not supposed to be open,' said a young woman who looked precociously old. 'Oh well, come in, love. I suppose we can fix something.'

She started to talk as she cut the cheese and cress sandwiches. She talked as I ate them wolfishly, and asked for some more. She talked as I leant back, content, sipping coffee in the still-shuttered bar.

A man with his mouth slightly ajar came in, selected a glass and helped himself to about three inches of Scotch. 'I said wash the bloody things,' she screamed at him. 'And the bar wants polishing.' He went out with a trayful of glasses. He never looked up.

'He's a bit, well, you know,' she said, tapping her forehead. 'He's not a bad sort, really. You've just got to watch him, that's all.'

She kept on talking. For a turn-over of about a hundred and twenty pounds a week, the brewery paid her husband just over eleven pounds as manager. She got an extra three pounds as barmaid and virtually ran the place. Hard for a woman to get a licence, she said. Even when they had their troubles. And he'd got worse as time went on.

'Like to see my baby?' she asked.

Upstairs she went and down again, popping her head into the kitchen to say he could have another one, but only if he hurried up. She handed me a small, tattered photograph of a tortoiseshell cat.

'He went sudden,' she said.

I daren't ask how or when or whether he'd been replaced, for I thought she was going to cry.

I thanked her and paid and left. She waved from the door. She kept waving. I kept turning round and waving back until I could scarcely see the fluttering hand in the pub doorway.

Some miles beyond Newport the canal runs into Staffordshire and suddenly becomes busy with boats. That morning proud owners were busy fitting them out: launches and long narrow barges, beautifully done up like merry-go-rounds in sky-blue and scarlet. The bottoms of women in jeans bulged from the open cockpits as they bent down to wash up; their menfolk tinkered with engines and hauled up triangular flags on bits of string. Whole families, kids and all, helped to sandpaper and slap on the paint. They ought to have been ready to sail a fortnight ago, they said. But that weather, it had been *real* cruel. And with self-conscious modesty I said I knew just what they meant.

In the jolly waterside pub at Norbury they call each other skipper and drink not too much. 'Not much chance with the missus around,' said the man who invited me to have a look at *Mercy Jane*. I thought he meant his wife. It was a trim converted lifeboat. He invited me aboard to look at the little fridge and the place where, as he put it, he kept a bottle of the old stuff, for emergencies. He declared an immediate state of emergency.

He told me how to get to the next canal, the Trent and Mersey, the one that led to Stoke-on-Trent. But not, alas, on the towpath. Nor even across country. I had to make the best of twelve miles of busy roads.

Nobody, I realize now, should have tried to walk down the A519 between Norbury and Eccleshall on a sunny Sunday afternoon, not when people were out in cars, enjoying themselves. I developed a temporary persecution mania. They were intent, I thought, to terrify me. I literally ran the gauntlet. They whizzed past so close that I felt the onrush of air. On a road where there are neither footpaths nor grass verges there is no escape. On they came, one after another. *Wheee-ow*. I swallowed hard and trudged on. Why on earth couldn't they have given me another couple of feet. Already in the gutter, I vowed that next time I'd . . . *wheee-ow*. Too late. The car streaked on, driven no doubt by someone who cursed me as hard as I him. But there was a difference.

I took his number and promptly brought an action in the privacy of the skull cinema. I may say that in this sort of litigation I'm pretty terrific. Lawyers often ask my advice. The case of Hillaby *versus* the Motorized Hoodlums lasted for weeks. It began with a tart letter to the Pedestrians' Defence League. By some curious quirk, I found myself in High Court, not only as plaintiff and chief witness; I became the national champion of down-trodden road-users. The Press reported it at length, especially when I subpoenaed the Chief Constable and Lord Lieutenant of Staffordshire. I gave them hell. I recall putting the judge right on one or two points of *princeps ambulare*, especially *extra vallum* and *dubious spatiis tribusive factis*. Nobody could answer me. I put it to them again, the judge was astonished. 'Why,' he asked, 'hasn't this been asked before? It establishes an entirely new point in law.' 'Why?' I asked passionately. 'Why?' *Whee-ow!* Those car-drivers simply didn't know who they were pushing into the ditch.

The road climbed steadily and flattened out among ribbon-developed villages of no particular charm, curious places where they seemed to sell nothing except petrol, ice-cream and bars of chocolate. The traffic thickened. The holiday-makers were driving home. They hooted; they waved; they drove past like racing cars.

Tired and somewhat peevish, I tried to get a cup of tea in the little town of Eccleshall, where the guide-book says seven Bishops of Lichfield are sleeping. But not, I should imagine, on Sundays. And there's no tea. The publican explained that his missus was still asleep and he wasn't allowed in the kitchen himself. But he thought I ought to get a slap-up meal that night in what he described as 'that posh boozer' on Lord Stafford's estate at Swynnerton. But that was six miles away. Nothing nearer? Nothing, he said, and he said it with quiet satisfaction. I plodded on.

In an indeterminate trickle of water called the River Sow I washed out a pair of underpants and a vest and went to sleep for an hour in the sun. As the washing was warm but still wet when I awoke, I hung it on the back straps of my rucksack, not caring what dangling laundry looked like from the rear. In fact, scarcely anyone drove down that dreary little side road to Swynnerton. The *Wheee-ows* were over the hills and far away, belting along to Stoke-on-Trent. I could hear them.

What remains of the rustic scene hereabouts is effectively screened by a fearful-looking, heavily-guarded War Department chemical unit on one side of the road and the Drake Prison for Debtors on the other. The debtors played tennis and pottered about in the extensive gardens. There was no sign of the chemists behind the barbed wire.

I went into the skull cinema and got a clear and disturbing picture of the Stafford estate. Weren't they the Sutherland family, the Dukes of? The people responsible for the worst of the Highland evictions? I saw, inaccurately, his tavern-keeper, a tweedy gent, busy serving double gins to the owners of super-charged *Wheee-ows*.

'Beer, sir? Not here. In the back room, *if* you please. Some food? Well, there's chips, of course. A bed, sir? Good lord! *Not* on Sundays.'

I hastily switched off to the comfort I usually got from the running serial *Pilgrim's Progress*.

How far had I walked that day? About twenty-two miles. Total to date: about four hundred and sixty. Still to go? Maybe nine hundred. How far had I got? At this point I turned in my imagination the sort of map they show for the daily weather forecast. I saw myself, a lone figure in the middle of England, somewhere along a line between Nottingham and north Wales. A few days and I should be in north Derbyshire, at the foot of the Pennine Way.

A man with a startling resemblance to Anthony Eden turned up in the dusk: tall, dignified-looking, small moustache, black homberg. Who was he, I wondered. A debtor on parole? The boss of the chemical unit? Or maybe Lord Stafford himself. Curious to see a well-dressed man walking in that deserted place. We nodded. He smiled. I'm not sure that I altogether liked that smile. It seemed to have something of a smirk about it. It occurred to me, later on, that my dangling laundry may have amused him and I pushed it into the rucksack.

In the small annexe to the bar of that pub at Swynnerton, a place where the locals still sit on a bench, respectfully, madam said, coldly, that they didn't serve anything on Sundays. The argument would be tedious to recall. The door wouldn't slam; it was on a spring and I had to go elsewhere in search of a plate of food. I slept where, throughout the night, the traffic on the four lanes of the great motorway in the Trent Valley sounded like a prolonged growl.

At eight o'clock, when you might have expected at least a glimmer of sunshine, Darlaston, Barlaston, Trentham and Hanford, all the towns that lead up to Stoke-on-Trent, were hidden in a gassy-smelling haze. Out of it loomed the gigantic, the strangely beautiful shapes of cooling towers. Behind them, like a ski-lift, chains of little buckets on wires trundle over mountains of coke. Here, you feel, is the basic architecture of industry: the power stations are verticals, marked by pencil-thin chimneys; the factories are flat blocks. There is nothing pretentious about the Potteries. They make things and what they can't sell they throw away. Behind the Doulton Works are mounds of shattered lavatory bowls, bed-pans, bidets and basins. You can walk into Stoke by way of the Trent and Mersey Canal. The water that morning steamed and looked slightly iridescent. Two sad-looking swans, their under-plumage stained bright purple, cruised among bales of sodden hay and long streamers of toilet-paper.

The banks of the canal are capped by large blocks of ferro-concrete. Some of them are remarkable for their wildly erotic engravings, executed, I suppose, before the concrete dried. On either side of the water the factories rumble and snort steam with predictable regularity. Squeezed in between them are allotments where contented-looking old men in shirt-sleeves grow sweet peas and brussels sprouts and lean on their spades and gossip.

In the mid-morning shopping bustle of Stoke I looked round for a laundry, a barber's shop and a place to get a good meal. The noise you remember here is the click of stiletto heels on broad flagstones which sounds like a herd of startled deer.

In the help-yourself launderette a young girl took my little bundle of washing and pushed it into the whirler with her own. I noticed that from a large plastic bag she pulled out a man's shirt and a man's underwear with a deft hand ungraced as yet by a ring.

116

The barber seemed puzzled by the lemon-yellow powder on his comb. 'Never seen dandruff like *that*,' he said. He was probably right. It was pollen from the sallows on the Shropshire Canal.

'Like another egg, love?' said the bulgy, bouncy, jolly-faced girl in the little cafeteria. She looked anxious. I still looked hungry and I had already eaten four, not counting the bacon and tomatoes. There are no food problems in Stoke. I nodded. She looked pleased. I felt pleased. I like eggs. Come to think of it, I liked her, too. Really bouncy, top and bottom. She slid another one on to my rind-littered plate.

'Out walking, mate?' enquired the man at the next table conversationally. They are friendly people in Stoke. Old women are addressed as 'Mother', old men as 'Dad'. Male contemporaries are 'Mate' and up to the age of middle age the women say 'Love'. After that you become 'Mister'. Men as they remember them are mostly on their allotments, out of the way.

'Derbyshire,' I said. 'I'm heading for Dovedale.'

I told him how I proposed to follow the canal through Stoke until I got into the Churnet Valley.

'Could be difficult,' he said. 'Could be *quite* difficult.'

This, I discovered, was the understatement of the week. It wasn't difficult. It was downright impossible. Flood water from the previous month's rain had raised the level of the Trent and Mersey by two or three feet. In places where the canal narrowed at the humpy bridges the towpaths were deep under water. In an effort to avoid these bits I went up and down flights of stone steps, through the backyards of warehouses and in and out of a maze of water-side passageways.

'Not so fast, mate.'

A special policeman in the white tin-hat of the Gasworks Squad hove up and prodded my rucksack with his forefinger.

'We've orders to stop everyone we don't know,' he said, apologetically. 'They've just pinched a thousand quids' worth of copper piping from the new gasometer.'

Duty done and suspicions allayed, he guided me through short-cuts, introducing me to crane-drivers and checkweighmen, chatting all the time about what he called local villainy.

'Pinch anything round here,' he said. 'My mate's been in the Force for twenty years, and he woke up one morning to find they'd nicked all his outside pipes. Good old-fashioned lead, they was. Now his Dad lost the lining of a tank on the ruddy roof. On the roof, I tell you. There he was snoring away underneath while they're wrenching it out from the top of a perishing ladder.'

'Durbyshire?' he said. 'You going to Durbyshire this way? Oh, dear. Why didn't nobody tell you? I reckon all you need from here is a ruddy gondola or a diving-suit.' I had been cut off by the floods.

He told me to forget the Churnet Valley and strike due west. 'Make for Bucknall,' he said. 'The old chap who runs the pub at the crossroads is an old pal of mine. Tell him Charlie sent you. Then climb up the Cellarhead. Eight or nine miles, I suppose. It'll just about kill you. But you ought to be in Kingsley or Froghall for opening time.'

Dear Stoke-on-Trent. By far the dirtiest place I walked through and by far the friendliest. When I tried to pay for the pint I ordered at Bucknall, Charlie's pal, the landlord, genially offered to give me a dam' good hiding. A problem, here, since I wanted another pint. I offered to spin the landlord for drinks all round. I lost and he insisted on paying. Somewhat invigorated by strong bitter, I challenged a trio of bus conductors to a game of darts and missed the board with my first shot.

At closing time that afternoon we went upstairs and talked about canaries and pigeons, fishing and prize dahlias. And dogs, especially Staffordshire bull terriers. I mentioned the animal owned by Ted and Fred.

'Herbert,' said two men promptly. I might have been searching for the name of Princess Margaret's first-born. They knew the animal's sire, Pride of Longton. They knew its grandsire, too. But Herbert, now. There was a real dog. He might have been Champion of England, in Bucknall a distinction more revered than a pools winner or a Garter lord.

Staffordshire is an odd, rustic-industrial mixture, bursting with life, a place where they freely boast they breed the best dogs, brew the best beer and offer scope for the best potters and best poachers in the world. They are proud of what they are, unadorned. And given a chance they sing their heads off:

> *If the cause be right, we are the game to fight;*
> *We have never been known to yield.*
> *For this is the song of the Staffordshire men,*
> *In forge and kiln and mine.*
> *Our fires shall burn and our mill-wheels turn,*
> *And the Knot shall be our sign.*

We sang it two or three times, bashing our pint mugs on the parlour table until the landlord said if we weren't outside in three minutes he'd call the bloody police. I went out, bemused by the ale, by the good company and began to walk up that interminable road up the Cellarhead and down the other side, west towards Derbyshire and the Pennines.

For three days I walked fast and far, heading due north from the Manifold Valley into Dovedale and thence by Tideswell and Castleton into the Peak District of north Derbyshire. Anyone even slightly familiar with that splendid up-hill-and-down-dale country will realize the inadequacy of these fleeting impressions. They were written down, rapidly, whenever I sensed a change in topographical mood, a new industry, different plants, a different kind of stone. I talked to more people here than almost anywhere else, for the country is intimate and neighbourly. It gives the impression of having been used. Even the fissures in the deceptively soft-looking limestone crags are hung about with hawthorn and ash. They have grandeur, but they are not overpowering. You can spend the night among them, comfortably, as among friends. As for those rivers fished in and made famous by Charles Cotton and Izaak Walton, the old linen-draper of saintly disposition has said about all that can be said:

> I tell you, Scholar, when I last sat on this primrose bank and looked down on the meadows, I thought of them as Charles the Emperor did of the City of Florence, that they were too pleasant to be looked upon, but only on holy days.

Until your shoe leather begins to rasp on the gritty out-liers of the southernmost Pennines the keynote of the countryside is limestone. It is evident in the towering white cliffs, the quarries, the trees, especially the shivering grey-green ash and in the flowers, the wild roses, mountain pansy, and lady's mantle. But all this is far from being the privilege only of Derbyshire.

Staffordshire deserves more credit than it usually gets. People think of it as an endless industrial sprawl. They travel through it or away from it rather than to see what's there. They forget Cannock Chase and they forget, too, that in the north-east, some of the best dales scenery lies within the county border.

The gateway to these dales lies by Waterhouses, a stream-side village that comes as a relief from the enormous, smoke-vomiting limestone quarries around Cauldon Low, said to be the biggest in the world. The grass on the cracked face of the hillside is powdered like an old whore.

Behind Waterhouses a well-found track follows a little river, the Hamps, into a narrow cleft, three miles in length and remarkable for its almost silent out-of-this-worldliness. You walk into a mossy, grotto-like dampness of cliffs and faintly tinkling stream. In places the river disappears into underground fissures called swallow-holes and bubbles out again, lower down, leaving behind a pebbly bed used only in times of flood. The accent of the inhabitants is more rounded, more slow and controlled than the loose, friendly jangle of the Trent Valley.

In Derbyshire they introduce a slurring syllable into some words. A cow becomes a 'ky-ow', a cart a 'ky-art'. 'Far' rhymes with 'war'. In some places a spider is still an 'arrin', from a Norman-French word. And the second person singular is almost invariably used, except when they are talking to their betters.

'Ast come for?' asked a man repairing a dry-built wall with the dexterity of someone putting together a jigsaw puzzle he has done many times before.

'Pretty far,' I said.

He muttered something I couldn't catch. Seeing my puzzled look, he turned round and straightened his back. 'Ain't got many folk to talk to hereabouts,' he said. 'Reckon that's why we talk to ourselves now and then.'

It came out that he had lost over eighty lambs the previous week. In the cold, wet wind they had died as soon as they were born. 'Gave them old crows a proper breakfast it did,' he said. To add to his troubles, about a hundred yards of wall had collapsed and, as he put it, there wasn't a man in the parish 'fit to handsel a through'.

The old art of dry-walling is dying out. The skill lies in locking together a double row of grit or limestone blocks with long slabs called 'throughs', laid transversely. The marvel is that such permanence can be achieved so precariously. They are knocked down at lambing time by the pregnant ewes, who, when their time comes, try to get away from the rest of the flock. They jump on to the walls, kicking backwards as they jump down on the other side. The capstones are knocked off and the gaps widened by the rest of the sheep, who, being sheep, try to follow them.

At Wetton the Hamps joins the Manifold and the two streams flow away together, emptying, eventually, into the Trent. High up on the cliffs are caves, the homes, once, of Neanderthal man, whilst deep in the limestone are deposits of copper and lead. In the eighteenth century the profits were such that in one year they provided the Fifth Duke of Devonshire with enough money to build the famous Crescent at Buxton.

From the Manifold I moved across to that much-written-about stream, the Dove, following it dutifully, until it wandered off west, towards its source on Axe Edge. 'A contemptible fountain,' said Charles Cotton, 'which I can cover with my hat.' Christopher Hobhouse imagined the silvery stream flowing through the heart of the defile it has made for itself like a young princess between two ranks of grey-haired ministers, bowing as she passes.

The sad thing is that in its upper reaches today, especially between Hartington and Crowdicote, the waterside barns and farmsteads are hideously scarred by large tin-plate notices advertising soft drinks and ice-cream. The country between the pub at Earl Sterndale called 'The Quiet Woman' (the pub-sign shows a decapitated female) and Miller's Dale some five miles away is blighted with smoke. 'And without the smoke,' said a practical rustic, 'I'd be without summat to do.'

The dales are somewhat confusing. Ashwood Dale, Chee Dale, Miller's Dale and Monsal Dale all lie within a nine-mile loop of the River Wye, the southern boundary of the High Peak. The Peak, originally known as the Honour, was granted to William Peveril, the bastard son of William the Conqueror, but the Peverils lost the Honour when they made a bad job of poisoning the Earl of Chester.

Despite its spectacular beauty, the visitor soon realizes that Derbyshire is far from being an agricultural county. Lime quarries disfigure famous valleys; collieries are evident in the south and the east; and iron used to be mined wherever there was charcoal at hand to smelt it. All this, together with the ancient deposits of lead, the silver, the well-clothed sheep in the hills and the water-power in the valleys, depend ultimately on that useful rock called carboniferous limestone. It contributed to the investments of the great houses for which the county is famous: Chatsworth, Haddon Hall, Hardwick, Bolsover, Kedleston and many more. And it brings modern tourists into the dales.

Limestone is the floor of an ancient sea. The metals in the rocks are the products of volcanic fires that still smoulder deep underground, warming the mineralized springs in the spa towns of Buxton and Matlock. North of the Wye, towards the High Peak, the limestone is replaced by gaunt grit. The impression is of a progressively sombre landscape. The grass is darker and the flowers more scarce than in the dove-grey gorges to the south.

In Tideswell, where the great church is called the Cathedral of the Peak, you walk between lines of long, low, grey-black houses, like moored destroyers. At Castleton the horizon is heavy with gritstone tors, and at Hollins Cross you look down on Edale, the beginning of the Pennine Way and all that is usually meant by the North of England.

Dawn in Staffordshire

THE KINDER CAPER

The best view of Edale is from the south, on the crest of Hollins Cross, where an uncharitable notice on a gate says plainly that trespassers are liable to be shot. This is grouse-shooting country. Looking down, the impression is of a little Alpine valley seen through a glass darkly. But to get the feel of the village, you ought to meet the first train in on a Saturday morning, the seven-fifty from Sheffield. Walkers spill out in droves. By the time seven trains arrived that morning Edale began to look like a country fair. It swarmed with hikers, bikers, nudists, naturalists, motorists, coach and train parties, day-trippers, week-enders, the purposive and the indolent.

The purposive promptly scuttled up the narrow track towards Kinder Scout like a pack of beagles. They wore enormous boots. They sang. They carried ropes and rucksacks. They were not seen again until nightfall. The indolents mooched about or wandered off quietly in search of a picnic-place. Or somewhere to make love. And may God bless their union. A young clergyman confided that he walked in regularly from Glossop sustained only by orange-juice and rye bread. Good for a rather delicate stomach, he said. He waved to a noisy coach party from a Stockport pub. Obviously pleased by clerical approval, they cheered and waved their beer-bottles.

Edale, south gate to the Pennine Way

123

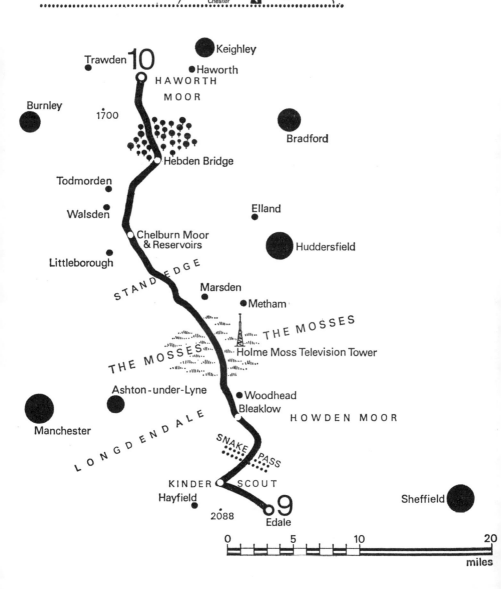

Map

9

Edinburgh
Lanark •
12
Newcastle •
Carlisle •
Appleby •
Kendal •
Ripon •
11
10
• Bradford
Manchester •
9
Chester •

● Keighley

Trawden 10
● Haworth

HAWORTH

MOOR

Burnley
·1700

Bradford

● Hebden Bridge

Todmorden

Elland

Walsden

Chelburn Moor
& Reservoirs

Huddersfield

Littleborough

STANDEDGE

Marsden

Metham

THE MOSSES

THE MOSSES

Holme Moss Television Tower

Ashton-under-Lyne

● Woodhead
Bleaklow

HOWDEN MOOR

Manchester

LONGDENDALE

SNAKE PASS

KINDER SCOUT

Hayfield

9

2088

Edale

Sheffield

0   5   10   20

miles

For those with a stake in the open-air business, Edale is a multiple store. The little village caters for everybody, especially walkers and climbers, and in the winter, skiers too. It lies between Manchester and Sheffield, the Potteries and the West Riding. Everyone seems to have been there at some time or other. But despite waves of visitors, the heavy traffic, the enormous sales of film, postcards, teas and refreshments, the Peak Park Planning Board has managed to keep the place in one piece. It looks a bit worn, but not battered. There are no garish advertisements. The trim church, the old mill over the tinkling stream and the cottages still retain the close-knit appearance of an old village.

Wardens marshal the traffic, pedestrian and mechanized. There are car-parks, camping-sites and a Youth Hostel. The constable said he had no trouble from them walking lads although he had reservations about certain parties that drove in from Derby and Sheffield on Saturday nights 'with their ruddy birds'.

Edale marks the beginning of that long upland track called the Pennine Way. In theory, at least, the walker can scramble up the gritstone staircase at the top of the valley and get up on the Kinder Scout plateau, the navel of the High Peak. From there on a surveyed track extends as far as the Cheviot Hills on the Scottish border. In all about two hundred and fifty miles.

Credit for opening up the track is due largely to a modest little man called Tom Stephenson, the Secretary of the Ramblers' Association. He and his friends struggled for years to gain lawful access through a tangle of private and municipal holdings. Most of the great moors of the Peak are private property. They are owned by grouse-shooters, who use them only for a few weeks in each year. The remainder are largely controlled by the water-works departments of cities, such as Manchester and Sheffield, who kept walkers out on the grounds that drinking water might be polluted. In the mid-thirties the walkers retaliated by mass-trespass; they invaded the High Peak in numbers too great to be resisted by a handful of keepers. This led to violence and, in some cases, to terms of imprisonment for the importunate pioneers. It also led, gradually, to the notion that city folk ought to be allowed to use land that is, at best, only marginally productive.

By dogged bargaining, barter and compromise, Tom Stephenson opened up a track from Edale to Bleaklow. He linked it up with the Brontë moors and carried it through the headwaters of the Aire and Ribble into Teesdale. It now winds along the crests of the South Tyne to the Roman Wall and beyond to the Border hills. In all it runs across ten sheets of the Ordnance Survey maps.

The bare bones of the route are laid out in a sixpenny pamphlet published by the Ramblers' Association, which I followed and found in places to be curiously indefinite, if not downright misleading. It may be that bits of the route are still in dispute. The pamphlet needs to be re-written with bearings and grid references to open country, difficult to get through in bad weather.

Kinder that week-end looked pretty good, but walkers came back daubed with greasy-brown dirt. 'What's it like up there?' I asked them. 'A push-over,' said the warden. 'Nothing to it.'

'Dreadful,' said a scraggy little schoolteacher from Leeds. 'All right on the way down,' added his friend, enigmatically. 'Don't try it,' advised somebody else. 'Squishy,' they told me. 'Don't get bogged down on the official caper. Head for the Snake Road on a compass bearing. Kinder's just a load of crap.' Aside from the warden's enthusiasm, opinions ranged from the stoical to downright depressing.

But what *was* it like? Thinking about those opinions now, I recall something that Jack Dempsey, the prize-fighter, said years ago.

During his bouts with Gene Tunney for the heavyweight championship of the world, the Press built up the image of Tunney as the athletic intellectual. They wrote about his reading, his prodigious memory and so on. By contrast, Dempsey seemed to be a dim-wit. But one reporter recalled seeing some books in his dressing-room. One of them was Jeffery Farnol's *Gentleman Jim*, the story of the prize-ring. He asked the prize-fighter what he thought of the book.

Dempsey, the inarticulate, shook his head, slowly, fumbling for words. 'It wasn't like that,' he said. 'It wasn't like that at all.'

Kinder and Bleaklow are only little hills. You can get over both of them in half a day. But they weren't like what I had been told. They weren't like that at all.

To get up onto the crest you follow a stream that gushes down the narrow V-shaped valley. It is, in fact, more of a corrie than a valley. It gets progressively steeper and then tails off into a cleft that ends in a natural staircase.

The weather that morning looked uncomfortable: misty, with rather nasty-looking clouds. 'It'll hold,' said the warden. And hold it did, just. The path beside the stream had been churned up like a football field by the pedestrian traffic of the previous two days, but there wasn't a bit of rubbish, not so much as an empty cigarette packet, to be seen. They are tidy folk, those northern walkers.

But where had they got to, those people who had swarmed into Edale? They had apparently all gone home. They were out for the day. In the eleven days it took me to get from Edale to the Border I saw in all only about seven or eight walkers.

Up the staircase I went, climbing rapidly, the supercharger undampened by the mist that got worse the higher I got. There is nothing particularly arduous about that spectacular cleft. The feet fall naturally on the dull grit-stone boulders rolled down by the floods. They lie one above the other. The surprise is at the top.

Up there you blink. A silent and utterly sodden world. This, surely, is not the summit of the High Peak. Mounds of bare peat rise in all directions, like waves, or rather a field furrowed by a gigantic plough. On the top there are no signposts, no markers. Only the choice of channels between the chocolate-coloured peat.

I took a compass fix on the highest point I could recognize, Crowden Head, drew a little cross on the map and hurried along the almost dry bed of a stream. There are several of these drainage channels. Too many. The one I followed swung off in the wrong direction. I tried another with the same result. *And* another until, fed-up with the sight of peat, I took off my shoes and socks and climbed on to a crest of the soggy stuff. I didn't sink in far, but the prospect from the top was appalling. The peat extended for miles. It rose, gradually, in the direction of a mound of rocks. And it steamed, like manure. Manure is the analogy that comes most readily to mind. The top of Kinder Scout looks as if it's entirely covered in the droppings of dinosaurs.

To get to the top of the waterfall that leaps off the ledge below Kinder I walked bare-footed, steering by compass which is a laborious business. The trick is to sound the depth of the peat. The light, the almost biscuit-coloured patches are infinitely more bearable than the chocolate-coloured stuff, which is usually wet and deep. It depends on how wet it is. The directions given in the pamphlet are unhelpful. They relate to the names of streams which all look much alike.

From the summit of Kinder, the official route takes you through at least two impressive bogs between Mill Hill and Featherbed Moss, just above the road called the Snake that dissects the moors. I cannot understand this Spartan predilection for what seems to be the longest and most arduous distance between fixed points. Perhaps the terrain has changed since the route was last surveyed, officially. There are people, I know, who speak highly of these south Pennine moors. They like the atmosphere of wilderness. I am not among them. I found them extraordinarily depressing.

From the botanical point of view, they are examples of land at the end of its tether. All the life has been drained off or burnt out, leaving behind only the acid peat. You can find nothing like them anywhere else in Europe. Here is the end-product of what botanists call a succession. The ancient woodlands that flourished after the ice melted degenerated into boggy patches of land, wet certainly, but rich in flowers. But as a result of burning, tree felling and overgrazing the land became progressively more sour. It lost its capacity to sustain more than a handful of plants, such as the bilberry, the mosses and the liverworts. On the summit of Kinder even the bilberry has gone. The heavily-dissected peat is bare. The faint cheep of pipits sounds like the last ticks of a clock that has almost run down.

Looking down on the Snake road I saw what from that height appeared to be a beetle lying on its back, surrounded by ant-like figures. A car had crashed and turned over. A model for which it is claimed that all the parts are replaceable had skidded, hit a rock and disintegrated. The driver, fortunately, had been thrown clear before it overturned, but the car had come to pieces.

You cross the road and climb up to another pike of shapeless rocks called Bleaklow Head, where the scenery is very much like Kinder. Perhaps a bit more depressing, for here and there are sheep and the sheep are filthy.

Towards mid-afternoon the mist thickened. With uneasy memories of Dartmoor, I hastened on, guided for the most part by the pencil-thin mast of Holme Moss television station. It lies due north. The pamphlet says: head due north. This is an error or, at best, a loose statement, since it leads you into a difficult defile called Wildboar Clough. I got in and, with difficulty, I got out. I didn't really mind, for the Kinder caper was nearly over and I don't suppose I shall ever go there again.

That night the couple in charge of the Youth Hostel at Crowden treated me with such warmth that I couldn't say anything about my dislike of the moors around them, and in the morning, of course, I felt much better.

Crowden lies in Longdendale. It lies beside a wide, wind-swept reservoir, one of about fifty that wink like watery eyes from the deep valleys between Edale and the Brontë country, some thirty miles to the north. Today, the Pennines are no more than catchment grounds. The uplands support no agriculture; the pasturage is scanty, the moors acid and ecologically dead. But because the moss and the peat are already sodden, the floods of soft water that flow from them can be skilfully canalized into the textile towns of east Lancashire and Yorkshire. The city corporations collect this inestimably valuable commodity in the great stores of Wadsworth, Rishworth, Saddleworth, Woodhead and Ladybower and what they can't use they sell. Looked down on from above, these water-stores remind you of moulds into which molten metal has been poured. If Longdendale were turned upside down it would leave, you would imagine, a mountain of solid silver. The reservoirs are bleak. Traffic through the Pennine gaps flow round them, but there are no houses.

In a day's walk hereabouts you can touch four counties: Derbyshire, Cheshire, Lancashire and Yorkshire. Here the Pennine Way runs between some of the most densely populated country in Britain, with Bradford, Halifax, Huddersfield, Barnsley and Sheffield on one side of the range and Blackburn, Accrington, Rochdale and Stockport on the other. Here, in several places, the gap between the advancing industrial sprawl has shrunk to a little corridor of high ground on top of the gritstone edges. The marvel is that the walker can still get through.

At Crowden you either take a chance of a brush with authority and cut through Little Brook, which looks very pleasant, or do what the directions say and march manfully through some upland bogs. I went up and came down resolved to walk only where it looked good. In fact, you can't win, for both tracks lead up to Black Hill, a monstrous chocolate cake of peat ringed by the candle-like heads of cotton-grass, a sedge with a fluffy top, like a blob of candyfloss.

Cotton-grass in abundance is a botanical danger signal, an indication that fertility has almost reached the point of no return. There are about 500 square miles of this rank sedge on the southern Pennines. What little humus remains below is now being washed away by ditching. The water carries it down Crowden Brook into Woodhead Reservoir. Silting is a major problem for the waterworks authorities. And I wish them luck, for the silt is all that remains of life on those southern Pennine moors. The rest is bare peat.

Listen, and you will hear at most only two or three birds: the cheep of the pipits, perhaps the harsh rattle of grouse and, occasionally, borne lightly on the wind, the reed-thin pipe of the golden plover. Look around and you will see at most a dozen plants and perhaps three or four insects, the daddy-longlegs, clouds of midges and maybe a beetle or two. This is biological penury. In the Derbyshire dales you could find fifty species in half an hour. With nothing better to do in a pause for breath I wrote:

Got bogged down several times in what I took to be Black Hill, the identifying cairn unapproachable in crappy ooze. Confirmed position in light mist by comforting back-fix on Holme Moss TV mast. Steep, easy descent down to what pamphlet describes as twentieth milestone on Saddleworth road. Twentieth milestone from what? Milestone unnumbered. Actual crossing-point apparently near Hollins Brown Knoll, where a nasty old woman offered to show me the site of the child's grave in that dreadful Moors Murder case. People often asked her to point it out, she said.

This is switch-back country with grey-brown gritstone cliffs on the heights. They call them Edges: Standedge, Stone Edge, Blackstone Edge. At the foot of the Edges are Black Moss, White Moss and Wessenden Moss. Place-names in this narrow, poverty-stricken part of the Pennines are lacking in imagination, but not candour.

At the Aiggin Stone on Rishworth Moor, where I looked, unsuccessfully, for the Roman road between York and Chester, a waterworks warden gave me ten minutes to get out of sight. The wind soughed through the dead sedge and the sheep looked dirtier than ever. From time to time it rained.

At eight o'clock that night, tired out and hungry, I reached a classy-looking pub near Chelburn Reservoir on the edge of my own, my native land. Madam, of course, said she couldn't provide anything, but with firm support from sympathetic customers I managed to raise a small and rather stale pork-pie which I ate out in the emptiness of Chelburn Moor. I put the tent down among rusting car-frames and bedsteads in a disused quarry, not far from the pub. This, I thought, is the rock-bottom, the ground floor, the very worst you can encounter. Survive this and you can survive anything. But somehow it all changed. It wasn't a bad night. It even stopped raining.

Chelburn lies on a ridge. Behind were the huge ferro-concrete walls of the reservoirs. To the west, far down, a host of little industrial townships: Todmorden, Littleborough, Bacup and

Rawtenstall. The centre, you might think, of the dark, Satanic mills. But when the light drained out of the sky the great industrial valley became freckled with points of light. The impression was of the sky turned upside down, a planetarium. I looked down on a galaxy of stars. Against this tremendous background, a couple walked past, slowly, hand-in-hand. They stopped and embraced. In silhouette they looked beautiful. It all looked beautiful.

But about four o'clock that morning the wind backed from south to east. I awoke to find the tent slapped by spray from the reservoir. In the half-light I packed uncomfortably, went behind some gorse bushes perilously and ambled off sleepily towards Hebden Bridge. Peewits whirled overhead like paper blown about in the wind. What with the spray and the wind it might have been somewhere in the middle of Finland, miles from anywhere. I rather enjoyed the occasion. Down I went by Stoodley Pike, the great monument to Wellington's victory.

On Erringden Edge I nipped over a fence, quietly, and put my foot down among an enormous flock of free-ranging but, at that moment, quietly dozing white Leghorns. Instant consternation. Off they went, like unguided missiles – all that is, except one rooster who seemed disposed to stand and fight it out. Terrified, I climbed back over the wall.

The skull cinema operator promptly snapped on a bit of comedy relief that happened to me, it seemed, centuries ago when the last British forces in France were trying to get out. We were dead tired. The gunners crouched under the eaves of a Normandy farmhouse whilst line after line of Stukas howled overhead. But the farm work went on and the sight of cows coming in to be milked was no less strange to those newly-arrived soldiers from the slums of Sheffield than the enemy aircraft.

The men speculated on the sex and edibility of the poultry and started to offer odds on the outcome of a chase between a rooster and fat hen. When the rooster was just about to mount the cornered bird, it saw a worm. The foolish animal stopped and ate it, enabling the hen to escape. 'By gum!' said a Yorkshire bombardier. 'Ah've niver bin as 'ungry as that.'

The Kinder caper

I heard the old familiar roar of the looms as soon as I crossed the river, but for some curious reason the smell had disappeared. As a native of West Riding, I had always associated the textile trade with a particularly pungent smell which comes, I think, from the processing oils. It reminds you of wet socks. Hebden Bridge is certainly a textile centre. The factories stand on each other's shoulders. They cling to the hillside. They are tucked away in yards and alleys; some are perched on the most improbable promontories. But what had happened to the smell?

I put the question, delicately, to the man in the doorway of an engine-house. No need to have bothered about the delicacy. No Yorkshireman worth the name betrays such an inadequate thing as surprise.

'Tha'll not get a whiff o' wool in 'Ebden,' he said. 'We go in for cords an' blewits.'

Corduroys and bluettes, the stuff they use for boiler-suits. I had forgotten that Hebden is a clothing, not a cloth town. It lies near the Lancashire border. But the accent is solid West Riding and a pleasure to listen to.

The standard response to the greeting 'Ow do' is 'Not so bad' or, if you feel particularly conversational, 'Could be worse'. The important thing is to keep to essentials.

'Going far?'
'Gargrave.'
'Over Wadsworth?'
'Seems best.'
'It'll be mucky.'
'Could be. Know a good cobbler?'
'Try Jim Cunliffe.'
'What about some grub?'
'Alan's place. Up t'hill.'

They don't suggest where you might go. That would cast doubt on their critical abilities. They *tell* you what to do. West Riding speech tends to be loud and declamatory. I did as I was told and got an enormous breakfast in a transport café.

Four locals, including a bus-conductor and a coalman, were

133

discussing the obituaries in the *Hebden Bridge Times*, a staple topic of conversation on Fridays.

Someone said Harry had gone out like a light. And wasn't that old neither he wasn't. Hardly seventy-four. Looked full o' fettle, too. And he'd leave a packet, they reckoned. 'Bow-legged wi' brass he was,' one of them added.

'And won't be wanting me this winter,' said the coalman, thoughtfully.

Nobody laughed, but if you looked hard you could see an almost imperceptible relaxation of jaw muscles which passes for amusement in the industrial Riding. Death had been cauterized by a pungent platitude. The macabre humour stems from a long history of poverty when talk usually ranged round unemployment, the dole queue, sickness and death. This survives still in an enormous repertoire of jokes calculated to horrify the stranger by the superficial denial of feeling.

'Where's t'wife?'
'Upstairs.'
'Takin' it easy?'
'Aye. She's dead.'

On this theme there are innumerable variations. One is of the neighbour who has come to pay his last respects. He stares long and earnestly at the deceased and says: 'Well, I must say she looks pretty good.' He pauses and then adds: 'Considering.' To this the husband says tartly, 'And she ruddy well ought to. She's just had a week at Blackpool.'

Apocryphal these stories may be, but on the formalities of the laying-out, the interment and the post mortem tea at the Co-operative café I can speak with some authority, for I wrote about them as an apprentice on the nearby *Dewsbury District News*. This meant interviewing the relatives and following the mourners to the cemetery for the names on the wreaths. The paper abounded in names. Each one, the editor said, meant three readers. During one lean week in the funeral business, I recall writing a slightly facetious biography of the cemetery-keeper, an elderly man who, I calculated, had put away about forty thousand of his fellow townsmen. The week after this piece of necrology appeared in print I approached the man with some circumspection, wondering if he had been offended by the article. Not a bit. He was delighted. 'Ah've bin thinking about that there article o' thine,' he said, 'and ah'm gonna tell *thee* summat that might do thee a bit o' good.'

He took me up to the highest point of the cemetery, where, with the air of a skilful gardener, he looked round carefully. Eventually he dug his heel into the ground and picked up a handful of earth, which he held under my nose. 'Look, lad,' he said. 'That's *real* dry stuff. When your turn comes you get right down there. You'll last for *years*.'

In addition to the obituary notices, we published little fragments of memorial verse which was not only paid for, but sometimes actually composed by the relatives. I recall one which ran:

> *Gabriel's trumpet sounded,*
> *And God said, 'Come!'*
> *The Heavenly Gates opened*
> *And in walked Mum.*

Yorkshire folk have the reputation of being offensively blunt; they give the impression of being as hard as nails. They make sure, they say, that 'a copper or two goes into the right pocket'. 'Each man relies on himself', says Mrs. Gaskell in her *Life of Charlotte Brontë*. He 'seeks no help at the hands of his neighbours. From rarely requiring the assistance of others, he comes to doubt the power of bestowing it: from the general success of his efforts, he grows to depend on them, and to over-esteem his own energy and power.'

Blunt they most certainly are, and offensive, perhaps, to those unable to sense their deep disdain for 'all that lardy-dardy talk that means nowt'. In fact, they are a deeply sentimental people and at heart generous. Hebden has the reputation of being an aloof, isolated sort of place, even by West Riding standards, a town that refuses to get mixed up in the rivalries between Lancashire and Yorkshire. I remember the place with warmth.

To get my shoes stitched the bus-conductor took me round to

Jim Cunliffe's little shop, where the cobbler spoke through a mouthful of brads, those little flattish nails not much bigger than a caraway seed. Picking them from between his teeth, one by one, he smacked them into a boot, rhythmically. Listening to his gossip, it occurred to me that the dialect of the West Riding often sounds as if it comes through clenched teeth. The trick is to relax the throat and keep the upper lip stiff, like a ventriloquist. The rest comes easy.

Jim fixed me up in no time at all, and when I tried to pay he told me to get stuffed.

Above Hebden Bridge you can afford to ignore the Pennine Way for six or seven miles. Keep to the well-defined track that leads through the woods of Hardcastle Crags, which are by far the finest to be found on the gritstone. On either side of the gorge are glades of oak and ash interlaced with honeysuckle. Below, a stream falls down from the Brontë moors, swirling round the mossy wheels of the old textile mills.

Here by the water's deep edge I watched the dippers, those curious portly birds with a white bib and cocked-up tail that makes them look like an enormous wren. They haunt streams, flittering up and down, making a metallic chinking noise, sometimes diving in and walking under water. They can do this by hunching their wings together and keeping their head down, so that the back of the bird acts like an aerofoil in reverse. The current presses them down on to the stream-bed, where they grub about for snails.

Here, too, is that blackbird with the white clergyman's collar, the ring ouzel, a bird that betokens the northern moors as surely as that little geranium, the cranesbill and the sticky sundews.

Between dippers and ouzels I frittered away the morning with my pack down under a tree. Why, I wondered, are these two unrelated birds dressed up in the same kind of bib? It is, I suppose, a courtship device, a means of giving a drab creature a touch of distinction, like a carnation in the lapel of a black suit. It is significant, surely, that they wear their bibs low, under their throats, so that the tell-tale flash of white can't be seen from above by a questing hawk.

On the map the gritstone moors beyond Hardcastle Crags are called Wadsworth, a cheerless place, chiefly remarkable for their association with the Brontë family at nearby Haworth. Here the sisters walked, with each other, or alone, creating their private worlds.

As I walked out into that great wilderness, it began to rain, at first gently and then with such extravagance that I reached a pile of rocks in the centre of the moor wet through. Rain is depressing stuff, and for the first three or four weeks of the walk it usually rained, hard, at least once a day. Showers I could tolerate, cheerfully. I did my best to ignore the sudden squalls, even to the extent of not looking over my left shoulder when I knew that massive, anvil-shaped clouds were billowing up from the southwest as if intent on washing me away. But there are limits to self-deception. Sustained downpours cannot be walked through for long, even in reliably waterproof clothing. Little trickles of water percolated through the lacing of my anorak hood until underclothing became unpleasantly sodden. Tiring of the meagre shelter and fearing that I should become both wet and cold, I squelched on through knee-high heather. In Ponden that night they told me that I had sought brief refuge under the Withins Stones, the setting for *Wuthering Heights*.

THE STRIDING DALES

Fortunately for poets and those who like to walk about in the open air, the beauty of landscape is not something that can be reduced easily to basic geology or a few ready-wrapped phrases about what places are used for. Preference and prejudice creep in. Mine are apparent in a love of limestone and a dislike of grit, two geological bed-fellows as unlike as chalk and cheese. You get the feel of both from the Wolf Stones on the edge of the Brontë moors.

Stand on that gritstone and look north and you are looking into limestone country. It looks far brighter than the moors to the south. The acid squelch is replaced by wholesome springy turf, the cotton-grass by fescues that sheep enjoy. Flowers abound in the hedgerows : water-avens, wild garlic, Solomon's seal and lilies-of-the-valley; the bird song is clamorous and the local inhabitants talk about something more interesting than the probability of rain.

As if to impress you with the sparkle and variety of their native stone, the dalesmen patch their pale walls with black splintery chert, full of the remains of ancient sponges; those shepherds push in bits of quartz-like grit and grey-brown slabs of Uredale sandstone a-glitter with mica and you feel there is something more than utility in those bright mosaics.

Malham Tarn on the moors and
overleaf *Tan Hill, the track to Teesdale*

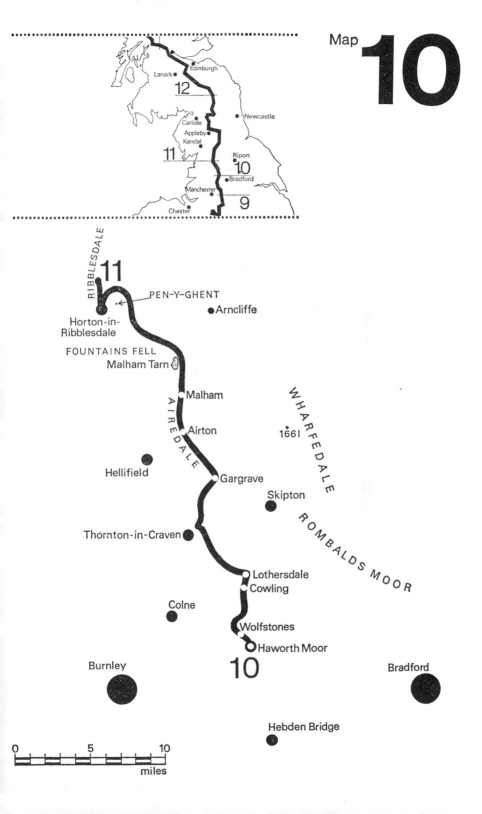

10

RIBBLESDALE

11

PEN-Y-GHENT

●Arncliffe

Horton-in-
Ribblesdale

FOUNTAINS FELL

Malham Tarn

Malham

AIREDALE

Airton

·1661

WHARFEDALE

Hellifield

Gargrave

Skipton

Thornton-in-Craven

ROMBALDS MOOR

Lothersdale

Cowling

Colne

Wolfstones

Haworth Moor

10

Burnley

Bradford

Hebden Bridge

0   5   10
miles

To get up on to the great arch of the Pennines I crossed the Vale of Craven by Cowling and Gargrave, following the River Aire to its source at Malham. From there on the track strides across Fountains Fell and Penyghent, Langstroth and Widdale. I run over these names with affection, since much of the way had for me the quality of a homecoming. Here, as a boy, I had fished and collected insects. I had learnt the names of plants and birds, taken home rocks full of petrified life and asked questions about how things got that way.

The boundary between the grit and the limestone is not marked by spectacular cliffs or fissures; both formations outcrop in each other's territory until the dull symmetry of the southern Pennines gives way entirely to the precipitous landscapes of Malham. The grit still clings to the top of the northern fells, such as Ingleborough and Whernside, but it's thin stuff, a mere vestige of the great beds of compressed sand that underlie Bleaklow and Kinder Scout.

On the hill that sits snugly around Lothersdale you find unmistakable tokens of limy soil in carpets of eyebrights, endearing little flowers like Lilliputian lilies. The village itself is remarkable for its early sweet peas, its comfortable pub and a water-wheel, nearly fifty feet in diameter, tucked away inside Wilson's textile mill. The contraption lies motionless these days, left dry by newfangled ways of pushing things round. Tuce Wilkinson, the engineer, claims that it's the biggest in Europe and rattles off its vital statistics with pride. He got the name Tuce, he says, from his old Dad, who came from Staffordshire.

'Y'know the way they speak there: one, tuce, free, four. Somehow I got stuck with Tuce.'

The accent of the limestone country is less broad, the speech more flowing than the tight-lipped ventriloquial commonplaces of the industrial West Riding. For about eighteen years - that is, between consciousness and young manhood - I assumed that all accents were aberrations of what I heard daily in the city of Leeds. It then began to dawn on me, gradually, that although half a million people spoke in that familiar and curiously aggressive manner, the accent was distinctly local, even for Yorkshire and as for people with the misfortune to be born in some other county they regarded it as quaint if not down-right vulgar. The aggressive quality, I think, comes from unusual, part-rhythmical stresses on certain words. They are not meant to be emphases, but they give quite ordinary expressions the air of a command. A Salvation Army captain from Leeds can make the twenty-third psalm sound like a speech for a Labour Day rally.

A few things that a little money can buy bring pleasure out of all proportion to the price-tag. High among them I rank a pair of good field-glasses; the smaller and the more powerful they are the better. You could put my Zeiss Telita in your breast pocket and not notice the weight, but they are there always for path-finding and the sort of unexpected pleasure I got out of them that morning.

In a rough pasture on the high tops above Lothersdale I walked by accident into a kindergarten of lapwings. The indignant parents whirled round, diving down, turning and twisting close enough to feel the waft of their curiously square wings. *Peee-wit*, they called. And also *peeerweet-weet-weet*, which I take to be extraordinarily rude in lapwing language. I looked down.

At foot level three nestlings crouched, quivering. A third made off like a mouse on stilts and then stopped dead, pretending not to be there.

In the air I counted about a hundred birds, maybe more. Say fifty pairs. In a three-acre patch of grassland about two hundred lapwinglets were being taught the hard facts of avian life: the difference, for instance, between a juicy wireworm and an acrid ladybird. Some spiders shalt thou touch, but not all. Keep out of sight of any bird that hovers and, above all, beware of that hairless biped called Man. I went off warily, still pursued until, out of the way behind some gorse bushes, I knelt down and focused the little Telita on a corner of lapwingdom.

Many birds possess what we loosely call grace. The need to keep primaries immaculate is vital to their survival; they respect their outmost extensions as a violinist his fingers. But watch the gulls and related hosts of birds called plovers for something unique in callisthenics. In the air they play with the wind, toying with it, rolling over, apparently not caring how the gusts strike them. But, the flight over, they glide down, landing delicately, scarcely seeming to touch the ground until with a little run they come to rest. For an instant the wings are lifted up and then swept back in the manner of a gallant bow. They settle down on their nests with a little shiver of ecstasy. Whoever invented the word grace, said Aldo Leopold, must have seen the wing-folding of the plover.

The Pennines are usually regarded as the spinal column of England, forming a natural barrier between Viking and Dane, red rose and white, cotton and wool. In fact, the mountains are split by gaps that run from east to west.

The first and most famous lies between Newcastle and Carlisle, where the Romans built the outermost boundary of their empire. To the south is a gap called Stainmore and a third, the Vale of Craven, immediately beyond Lothersdale. It was here that I had wandered, as a youth, looking for things like arrowheads and water-beetles which in those days ranked as treasure.

I recall a party of naturalists on one of their weekly outings. We stood on the top of the moors, looking down that morning on the Aire, one of the rivers that drains the east slope of the Pennines. The professor of geology talked about drifts and drumlins, moraines and impounded water. It seemed no concern of mine that glaciers had crunched down that valley, gouging out the dales. For a boy of eleven it happened so long ago it was past comprehension, near the boundary of eternity. But somewhere a phrase about an advancing wall of ice a thousand feet thick fired my imagination and I became interested. The tops of the glaciers, he said, had left scratch marks on the rocks. He showed us examples of these natural engravings and I never forgot what I saw.

Long before those glaciers crawled down the Pennine slopes earth movements wrenched the rocks apart in what is now known as the Craven Fault. The gap has been smoothed out by millions of years of erosion, but the rocks below haven't yet settled down. Sometimes they slip, only slightly, but enough to shake the cities of the West Riding. They are the last stirs of an old disturbance.

A tremor, I recall, shook Leeds in the late nineteen-thirties. It was more perhaps a hiccup than an earthquake; it rattled the china in thousands of kitchens, stopped a lot of delicately-balanced grandfather clocks and did some damage in Hunslet, the poorest part of the town.

The Yorkshire Post asked me to find out what had happened and the police directed me to the house of an elderly woman, who, they said, had an impressive crack in the wall of her bedroom. Slum property tends to crack without any assistance from the Craven Fault. The woman sat there, composed, sipping tea, rather enjoying the notoriety. With notebook and pencil poised, I asked her to tell me exactly what happened.

'Well, lad,' she said. 'It's quite simple. I was just bobbin' into bed when me teeth fair leaped off the dresser.' This struck me as a piece of straightforward observation and I duly reported it, but they sub-edited it out from what I wrote on the grounds of vulgarity.

On the way to Gargrave, the gateway to the Dales, the Pennine Way thrashed about in an incomprehensible manner; I couldn't make out what Tom Stephenson was up to. I climbed up on to a hill where, on a clear day, the country below looks like a map and the walker can decide for himself what looks most attractive and comfortable. The Gap itself is no longer a geological feature you could point to if you didn't know where it was. But on the way down those slopes, in and out of private land, I met with nothing but courtesy and that is how I remember Craven.

I must have been about nine or ten before I developed an extraordinary passion for dredging things out of ponds. In those days wealth consisted of a jar of newts, a frog, a hedgehog or a few caterpillars in a grass-lined box. For a town-bred boy hunting prowess meant being able to catch sticklebacks, butter-flies and, in the summer months, those vivid green tiger beetles which were treasure above emeralds. I went out on forays with the high priests of the local Natural History Society, collecting, trying to identify what I found.

Old Wilkinson, one of the best botanists in Yorkshire, was

blind, a strange, knowledgeable man who could name any plant put into his hands by running his fingers over the stem and leaves. Sometimes he smelt them. He also possessed the unique ability of being able to identify trees by the noise they made. In a field on a breezy day he used to crane forward, listening intently and then point unerringly to where he said he could hear a clump of oak or an ash, perhaps a hawthorn or a yew. He said anyone ought to be able to identify a Scots pine with their eyes closed and he knew the difference between other species, distinguishing them solely by the rustle of the wind in their leaves.

At school a little gnome of enthusiasm christened James Digby Firth, but known to everyone under the age of twelve as Bug Willie, taught us that beetles were the finest creations of God and threatened to thrash anyone who couldn't tell the difference between a weevil and a ferocious creature called the Devil's coach-horse. Out in the field, on the weekly expeditions, there were specialists who had their minds mostly on mosses, on birds, on the upfolding of grit and limestone and one, I remember well, with an unquenchable passion for midges found in oak galls.

Most of the specimens collected were exhibited and discussed at meetings in the local University buildings, where the amateurs could count on the authority of the academic staff. Among them were professors, such as Pearsall, who preached the new science of ecology, the philosophy that nothing in the world of plants and animals lives alone. These men were concerned about putting things together rather than in the usual scientific preoccupation of showing how easily they can be pulled apart. I took this to be little short of divine revelation.

It seems to me, now, that to have some sense of kinship with the land, to feel at home in the country, it's not necessary to know the name of all the willow-herbs, the warblers or the solitary bees. You may not be able to distinguish between yellow pimpernel and creeping jenny, chert and flint or boulder clay and the stuff laid down in the days of dinosaurs. To be able to make these distinctions immediately is helpful, but it doesn't necessarily make a naturalist, a person who I suspect gets more out of life than most people. Anyone who can use about half a dozen books competently can identify whatever he sees. More important by far, I think, is to know something about how things got to be the way they are. What has perished now that the hedgerows have become thin? Why are ponds important? Where is bracken likely to be found? When did butterflies become noticeably scarce? And why? If more people knew more about these sort of problems there might be more hope for that neglected, ill-treated child of ecology called conservation.

The Vale of Craven looked much as I remembered it. I expected to find the place spoiled by ill-development, but somehow it had survived. The market town of Gargrave looks as if the inhabitants are dependent on something more substantial than ice-cream and tea-shops. To get into the broad main street you cross the youthful Aire, a river still unpolluted by the dreadful stuff poured in from the sluices of the rag mills lower down. To leave the town you take the bridge over the Leeds and Liverpool Canal: for me a cataract of memories here, since in that canal I learned how to fish. No more than a few roach ever came my way, but they triggered off a passion incomprehensible to those who have never experienced it. Years later, when I learned how to use a fly-rod, I returned to the river at Gargrave, intent on trout. As I walked from the river to the canal that afternoon, I seemed to be closing the bracket of a long extended parenthesis. Why had that passion for fishing died? Without being sententious I cannot say except that, after mastering a sport, it's more exciting to find out how animals live than profiting, sensually, in the manner of their death.

By far the most spectactular section of the Pennine Way starts at Gargrave. From here to Northumberland, a distance of nearly two hundred miles, there are almost uninterrupted vistas, sky-wide and lonely. The route lies due north, an artificial highway in the sense that it cuts across the grain of the hills. Ancient man might have used sections of the track, but only to get from one settlement to another.

Through Craven lies a trail called Rombald's Way, which

has been used for many thousands of years. It linked the swampy hunting-grounds of the east coast of England to the communities that lived in the valleys on the western flank of the Pennines. The oldest sections are marked by the discarded flint tools of a race of Mesolithic hunters who populated the high ground soon after the glaciers melted, leaving behind great lakes. Rombald's Way came to be used by men in the ages of bronze and iron. When the native Brigantes, a race of war-like Celts, began to harass the advancing Roman legions, Agricola ordered a fortified road to be built through the gap.

I mention this cross-section of local history for the compelling reason that as a youth on a fishing expedition, alone, I found one of the little flint tools and wondered what it was. At the Leeds Museum they told me that the disk of flint with a sharp serrated edge was a Mesolithic scraper, used to dress the pelt of a animal, probably a wild ox.

High above Gargrave the River Aire gushes from its source beneath the foot of an immense wall of limestone called Malham Cove. The crag is riddled with underground streams which, after heavy rain, burst out of the ground like fountains. Originally, those streams poured down from the top of the cliff, but the rock is soluble in water containing a little carbon dioxide and the great scarps are now riddled with passage-ways and caverns. In the fields the boulders are longer than they are broad and rounded, like the paws of an animal. Among them you will find in-numerable flowers tolerant of lime, especially the eyebrights, small geraniums, rock roses and mountain pansies, pure yellow or yellow and purple.

To get to Malham, the gateway to the great Pennine moors, you follow that ambitious little river, the Aire, switching from one bank to another as it babbles through what appear to be out-crops of pumice-stone. Although the going is easy and official directions specific, many local farmers are hostile to walkers, saying they have never given their assent to the trail. Like Edale, the village of Malham manages to withstand periodic invasions of tourists without obvious deterioration. Two bus-loads of schoolchildren rolled in that morning and the effect when they poured out on to the little village green was almost explosive.

From Malham you climb up two thousand feet into curlew country, on to the very roof of the Pennines. The little road shrinks to a path, the path to a track and as the last visible farmhouse disappears far behind, the sense of space is tremendous and the view for ever. I went up Fountains Fell, to where Great Whernside, Littondale and Langstroth appeared as dark clefts in the undulations of the hills. The men who put names to the peculiarities of those places knew what they were about. There is Green Hackeber and Gauber, Gatekirk, Ellerbeck, Blackshiver, Quaking Pot and some deep holes called Boggarts Roaring. They look gigantic.

No less striking than the landscapes are the sky vistas. Like so much of nature the air in high places is an inexhaustible source of beauty. A cloud pattern seen once can be reckoned unique; it may not be repeated again for thousands of years. Instead of the lowering blankets of stratus that hung over the Hebden and Haworth moors, here above was cirrus so feathery it might have been chalked on the backcloth of the sky. Among the cirrus, wind, water vapour and sunlight combine to form splinters of rainbow known as glints, which usually betoken rain. That afternoon those glints hung suspended like bits of opal until the celestial scenery-shifters shifted them somewhere else.

Dalesmen are rare weather prophets. One strange man I remember from youthful days in those hills was not averse to giving the meteorological machinery a bit of a shove on his own. They called him Johnny Rainmaker. In times of drought he used to stand on the fell tops above Grassington and shout at the sky. For a few shillings he could be persuaded to holler his head off in the neighbouring valleys, too. There were those who said he was plain daft and it was a waste of good brass to start him ranting. But Johnny had a keen nose for a drop of rain that nobody else even suspected, and most of the locals agreed that when the becks ran dry it was at least comforting to see him shouting and waving his arms about. He had a hard life. No pension. He walked eleven miles to Skipton to get a skinful of free beer on his eighty-fifth birthday, and he walked back again.

Some may think he might have been better off, cosseted by the postal orders of the Welfare State, but somehow Johnny always managed to eat partridge, pheasant or grouse at the week-ends, in or out of season. For this is rich shooting country.

Over-plump grouse scutter ahead like mechanical toys, alarmed, clucking until they bounce into the air, turn in the wind and glide down the fell slopes on improbably small, bow-shaped wings. At your approach sheep panic, barging into each other until at a safe distance, with foreleg raised, they slew round and stare at you with mad, watery-blue eyes.

On I went that day, over the neck of Penyghent, the mountain with the lion-like head that hangs over Ribblesdale. Here are the western slopes of the Pennines. I had crossed the divide. The vistas are no less spectacular, but above Horton spoilt by smoke and a vile-green, bile-green lake in the middle of a limeworks. What gives the lake that colour I cannot say. Even fifty years ago a local guide-book described the place as unspeakable.

A meal in Horton and on I went again, up into the Ribble Valley. I felt good for another twenty miles. But it grew dark and I put the tent down where I could hear the river shrilling over the gravels.

I recall a boy in a red jersey. He pranced down the hillside, riding one of those invisible horses that little boys ride so well. And as he ran he called out names, insistently. They were the names of newly-weaned lambs. One by one they ran to him until young flock and young boy, still shouting at the laggards, pranced back to the farmstead to be locked up for the night.

I recall an immense night with an owl-like moon and Orion with the Dog at his heels. Now I know very well that the moon is a cold, airless sphere about a quarter of a million miles away. And I know, too, that Orion is a constellation of burning gases doomed to explode or go out, I forget which. But long before fellows like Fred Hoyle took all the friendliness out of the stars men gave thanks for that girdle of light. And so that night did I.

VIKINGS, ROMANS AND PICTS

I woke up feeling as brisk as a bird. A veil of mist, the horizons hazy, but no matter. It looked good: it felt good; it smelt good: a peaty, mossy, earth-born breath of the cleanest air anywhere. I decided to give myself a dew shower.

To do this you lower the outer-fly of the tent, dragging it away carefully, so that not a single ice-cold pearl is lost. Remove all clothing. Grasp both corners of the sheet, close your eyes, and clench your teeth. One shake is enough to produce a shower of needle-like spray.

Two pied wagtails turned up for breakfast. I tossed them bits of bacon sandwich, packed my gear, folded the tent, strapped it down on top of the rucksack and set off for Keld.

This is the country of Norse names: *scar* and *helm*, *garth*, *berk*, *keld* and *ghyl*. *Scar* means a cliff or a line of rocks, *helm* a cattle shelter, *garth* an enclosure, *berk* a birch-wood and *keld* a spring - not to be confused with *ghyl*, a narrow ravine that conducts the *keld* into a *beck* which is Norse for an immature river.

The Vikings came in here from the west. The shift in strategy is a little curious, since the attacks began on the east coast, where, in the eighth century, they sacked the Abbey of Lindisfarne. 'Never have such terrors as these appeared in Britain', wrote Alcuin, the scholar of York.

149

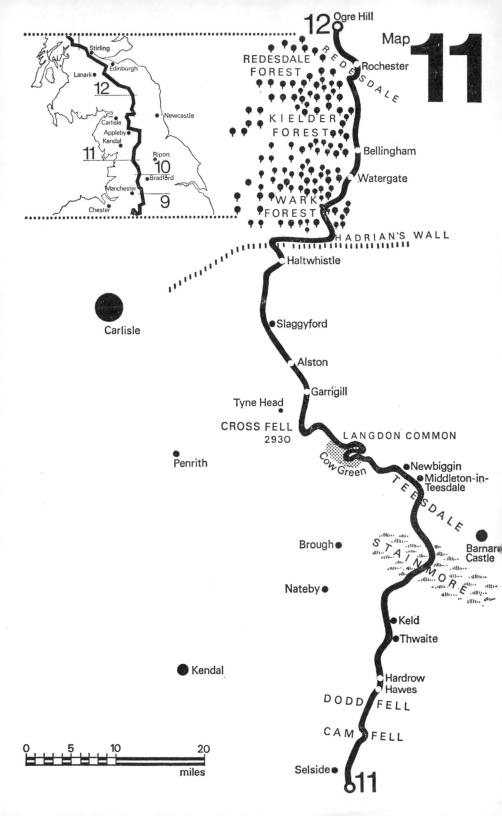

But the Vikings were far from invincible. When they attacked Jarrow at the mouth of the Tyne the following year, their leader was slain and his followers routed by spirited local resistance. For many years afterwards they sailed round the north of Scotland, into the Irish Sea, establishing a colony and eventually a kingdom in Dublin.

It is from the west – that is from landing-places in Lancashire – that the Norse advanced into the Dales. They cultivated what they conquered and ceased to exist as raiders when they found somewhere to settle down. Ships and weapons were a means, not an end:

> *In the evening can the day be praised*
> *And when she's dead a wife*
> *A sword when you have made a trial of it*
> *A maid when she's married*
> *Praise ice when you've got over it*
> *And beer when its drunk.*

In six hours I saw but one soul, a farmer who whistled commands to his sheep-dog from the driving seat of a tractor. He waved, I waved; I went on. In Ribblesdale they are friendly folk, but not given to gossip during working hours. And when you talk there are formalities to be observed. A man with his own land is always addressed as 'mister'. Among themselves they use the intimate 'thou' and 'thee', but with French formality. An importunate lad who addressed an elderly dalesman in a pub with the familiar 'thou' was told: 'Sithee, lad: thee thou them as thou's thee and not afore. Think on!'

I went up by Cam Fell, a soggy divide, where a drop of rain might flow west into the Irish Sea or be carried east through the Plain of York and out into the North Sea. One little dribble of water, the source of two rivers, the Ribble and the Ure, seemed to flow east or west in accordance with the direction of the wind.

With some surprise I found that the weathered woodwork of the notice-board that pointed down towards Wensleydale dripped with still-moist, bright red blood. It looked pretty ominous until I noticed that among the heather at the foot of the post were the entrails of mice and birds. Kestrel hawks had been using the post as a chopping-block for their slain prey.

Years ago, when the first high-voltage power lines were draped across the Pennines, the maintenance men were puzzled by blow-outs they couldn't account for. The clue came from the completely carbonized body of a kestrel found at the foot of a pylon. Naturalists soon realized that the hawks had mistaken the high-pitched squeak of faulty insulation for the noise of another bird and had attacked it. The result was a flash-over that blew the circuit, sometimes putting a whole region in darkness.

This is a place for the lonely. The kestrel hangs head down in the wind, tail outstretched like a fan, a solitary hunter calculated to turn on intruders, immediately. The helicopter becomes a fighting plane. The grouse have a communal life of their own, secretive, you know them only by the noise of their going, and as for the curlew and the plover their cry has all the sorrow in the world.

Beyond Cam Rakes there are valleys like Dodd Fell so steep that the sun rises hours after they have seen it in Cam Pastures and it sets again in mid-afternoon, dropping down behind Whernside and Widdale, leaving only short shadows in summer and winter.

'A bit doomy,' they say on Durley Bottoms, using the word in its old sense, of something laid down for ever. Doomsday is the book of reckoning; the boundaries of the old courts of judgment were marked by doomstones. They couldn't be moved.

Below Dodd Fell lies Hawes, a village once renowned for the famous cheeses of Wensleydale. They were brought to Yorkshire by the monks of Jervaulx Abbey and made, originally, from ewes' milk, but the bit I bought with keen anticipation tasted of nothing in particular. It came from a factory miles away, together with the butter and the bread they used to make in the village. Most of their food is delivered by van. 'It's difficult, you know, here in the winter,' said the woman in the shop, an understatement, since the snow has been known to cover the local station so deep that the station-master couldn't find the train he was supposed to flag out.

Even on that bright May morning a few patches of unmelted snow hung about in the hollows of Shunner Fell. They looked innocent enough, but at least one proved deep and I turned round to retrace footsteps which stood out clear, like the tracks of the Abominable Snowman. I looked at the impressions with more than casual interest since, in nearby Grassington at the beginning of the war, a strange woman had likened the walk of some of the Dales farmers to the great stride of the creatures who, from newspaper accounts, were thought to haunt the Himalayas. Asked to tell me more, she said she had either met or maybe corresponded with - I forget which - a certain Madame Alexandra David-Neel, a woman who had spent fourteen consecutive years travelling through Tibet.

Before she left Europe, Madame Alexandra had studied philosophy, specializing in the elegant scepticism of Descartes, but in mystic Asia she underwent the complex psychic exercises of esoteric Buddhism and, eventually, her adopted son became an ordained lama. Both sought the strange contentment of the *void* which, in Lamaist terminology, means the inexpressible reality.

Among learned lamas and mystics there are, it seems, several sects that practise rigorous austerities. One consists of breathing exercises and conditioning processes that enable the void-seekers to endure acute cold and to walk high up in the snows for a day or two without stopping on their way to neighbouring monasteries. They are called *Lung-gom-pa* and it is they who, my informant thought, gave rise to stories about the Abominable Snowmen.

The usual explanation for the imprints seen in the Himalayan snows by western mountaineers is that they have been made by an animal, either a bear or a langur which is a sort of gibbon-like creature remarkable for the long journeys it makes in high places.

I became interested in the *Lung-gom-pa* and discovered that Madame Alexandra had written several books about her travels in one of which* she describes how, through field-glasses one day, she had seen one of the Snowmen moving like a black speck but, clearly, with enormous strides. She said the man did not run. He

With mystics and magicians in Tibet (Penguin Books, 1936)

seemed to lift himself from the ground, proceeding by leaps. It looked as if he had been endowed with the elasticity of a ball and rebounded each time his feet touched the ground. His steps had the regularity of a pendulum. She said her servants dismounted and bowed their heads to the ground as the Snowman passed, but he went on his way, apparently unaware of their presence. He seemed to be in a trance, and although she would have dearly liked to question him, she could not guess what psychic disturbances might have arisen from such a course.

Back in the place where I had started from I dropped all pretence of being a Snowman and slogged up the length of the Buttertubs Pass by way of Hardraw Force. The Force is an almost perfect column of bright water which drops a hundred feet from a ledge of rock at the back of a pub, the 'Green Dragon', where they charge you the not excessive fee of threepence to look at the biggest waterfall for miles around. The Buttertubs get their name from natural holes in the limestone at the top of the pass. At the Green Dragon they will tell you that the holes are bottomless and, as one old man put it, 'some are deeper than that'. That night I reached Keld.

High-perched Keld clings to the western slope of an ash-lined scar. There is a Norse clang about the name and a Norse look about the country. It reminds you of a fjord. The Vikings who got there must have felt at home. But climb over the brow of the hill and look north and the change in scenery is dramatic. Instead of deep ravines and hanging cliffs, the eye ranges over the immense valley of Stainmore with its bogs, becks and isolated farmsteads.

Here is another of those gaps through the north march of the Pennines. The Vikings came from the west; the Danes from the east. Whether they engaged or avoided each other, as dogs do, history bears no account. The places they subjugated are implicit in what they are still called and the names seem to be about equally divided.

Beyond Stainmore lies Teesdale, and it took us about a day of hard walking to get there. I say 'us' and dwell on that plural pleasurably, for I had pleasant company, a young student who had decided to wander about for a few weeks with a rucksack before he went off to Cambridge. I'm pretty sure he had no intention of walking twenty-fives miles that day. And nor, for that matter, had I, for it seemed scarce half that distance on the map. But I persuaded him to make Middleton that night. This became something of an embarrassment, for, with a quite spurious air of familiarity with what we were about, I led him into some exceptionally unpleasant bogs. But he never complained and after a month on my own it was a privilege to have a companion.

Nowadays there is scarcely a tree to be seen on the heathery uplands of Stainmore Forest, but there, they will tell you, stock-raiders called moss-troopers sought refuge in between their forays. There are reports that in earlier times the swamps were so deep they engulfed wild oxen, and from what we walked through I wasn't in the least surprised. Rivulets as palatable as soda-water pour down from the fells. Here too they are called 'becks' - the Greta, the Syke, the Rennygill, Hargill, Arngill, Deepdale, Hunder, Balder and Black.

You cross the Greta on a flat slab of limestone the size of a barn floor, called God's Bridge, and there in the valleys, especially by the edge of the water, I began to look for the pink primrose.

Until I walked down into Teesdale I had never seen one. I knew the ordinary primrose, a flower more picked than any other except, perhaps, the bluebell; I knew its relations, the oxslip, the cowslip, and its cousins, the loosestrifes and the pimpernels. But search, as I once did years ago, the pink species had eluded me, and yet botanists of the competence of Geoffrey Grigson have said that if one made a selection of the dozen most exquisite natives of the British flora, the pink primrose would be among them. Among other places, the plant grows in Upper Teesdale which had become that month the most talked-about botanical site in Britain. The story is sordid but needs to be told.

Imperial Chemical Industries had applied for permission to build a huge reservoir where some exceptionally rare plants grow. The pink primrose was perhaps the least rare of those frail relics of what the flora of Britain used to be like when tundra winds blew across north Britain, but, like the dotterel and the ptarmigan, the plant carries the rights of old inhabitants to be looked after in isolated retirement. This is unrecognized by those who run big industry.

The whole dismal affair arose from a series of administrative muddles involving not so much I.C.I. as the local Water Board and the Nature Conservancy, the Government agency responsible for keeping an eye on sites of scientific importance. I.C.I. wanted more water to exploit a new method of making fertilizer at their chemical plant near the mouth of the Tees. They couldn't draw supplies locally, for the river there was heavily polluted.

They decided to build a reservoir about thirty miles upstream. For geological reasons, they chose the one site that botanists value more than almost any other in the north of England. This is Cow Green, a little basin up in the hills upheld by a hard rim of black rock called dolerite.

The struggle for the possession of Cow Green became a national issue. Government enquiries led to a full-scale debate in Parliament. To meet the legal costs of fighting the case, the botanists launched an appeal and raised £20,000. It emerged from the evidence that the local Water Board had completely miscalculated their future requirements. And, worse, the Nature Conservancy, with a research station nearby, hadn't realized until far too late that a unique place, a bit of land unmatched anywhere else in Britain was threatened by what is, ironically, described as development. If the site went a link with the past would be cut for ever.

Cow Green which, until the arguments arose was no more than a map reference, lies above Middleton-in-Teesdale, a handsome, decaying sort of place from where most of the young folk have wandered off to take up jobs elsewhere. The night we arrived there, late, the reservoir issue still hung in the balance and the oldsters gave the impression they didn't give a hoot, one way or the other. What they wanted, they said, was more people and more trade. A warden from the Nature Conservancy offered to show me round the botanical battleground the next day and I went to bed distinctly sore, for in the scramble to get down into the village before dark fell I, in turn, fell off a wall, on to a post, and bruised some ribs.

The pink or, as botanists call it, the bird's-eye primrose is an exquisite little plant, only a few inches in height, putting you in mind of those little Japanese confections that open out in a glass of water. I found several clumps in a crevice between boulders not far from the river, and felt that I had made a great discovery. The petal stars are delicately poised on a rosette of pale green leaves. In colour the flowers are between lilac and rose and more fragile by far than those of the ordinary primrose. It comes as no surprise to learn that the plant is found throughout central Asia. My host offered to meet me at a point some miles up stream and drove there in his Land-Rover. I set off early and walked up the river, doggedly determined to remain a whole-time pedestrian.

My ribs ached, but I moved fast, infected by the earthy vigour of that bright morning. Spring, you felt, had been held back that year. It flowed north far later than usual, and, wherever I got to, I always seemed to be slightly ahead of the tide. Looking back on the trip, I think that if I had holed up somewhere for a few days I might have walked in company with warm winds instead of almost always in front of them.

Upper Teesdale is remarkable for an outcrop of black rock called dolerite, curious stuff which hangs over the river like the ramparts of a medieval fortress. It is lava, squeezed out through cracks in the limestone by volcanic action. The river pours over the top of the rampart at Cauldron Snout and gushes down towards Middleton in a series of waterfalls. When the dolerite was originally squeezed out, hot, it baked the sedimentary rocks into coarse crystalline stuff aptly called sugar limestone, the home, now, of many rare plants.

No botanical name-dropping can give an adequate impression of the botanical jewels sprinkled on the ground above High Force. Here you find the little Teesdale violet, smaller and more downy than the bankside flower, also asphodel, sandworts, alpine meadow-rue, lady's mantle, and high slopes bright with spring gentians.

In this valley a tundra has been marvellously preserved; the glint of colour, the reds, deep purples and blue have the quality of Chartres glass. For me Teesdale was more beautiful than I could have imagined; certainly more strange and evocative than I could have foreseen.

There are marked differences in the posture of some of the plants found on those fell-sides. They lie close to the ground, as if still cowering from Arctic winds. Here are lineal descendants of flowers which, like the Celts, took to the hills when the islands were invaded by hosts of new plants. The invasion took place when the ice retreated and the valleys became clothed in forest and blankets of acid bog. This explains many of the similarities between plants of the high, treeless places and those found near the seashore. Both are places of refuge for the dispossessed.

The day ended drearily. At a place where the boundaries of Yorkshire, Westmorland and Durham converge on a stream-meet below Cronkley Fell I said goodbye to the warden and set off once more on my own. It began to rain and for hours it continued to rain, vindictively. Somewhere ahead it had been arranged that I should be met by another representative of the Conservancy, but somehow, for some reason, he didn't turn up and I set off across the moors again with the visibility down to fifty yards. This sounds of small account, but on those high moors mist and rain can be deeply depressing.

The Cow Green affair has now been settled. Although the Bill was opposed by every biologist of distinction in the country, the Government got cold feet and approved the plans for the construction of the reservoir. The valley is to be flooded. I knew nothing of this as I walked across Moor House that afternoon, but the decision could have been predicted. In Britain conservation is largely in the hands of organization men, smooth, cautious and committee-minded. They can be relied on, as an American once put it, to keep an agency or a bureau functioning with a minimum of friction. Regardless of any inward convictions of their own, they hesitate, like astute politicians, to take up a strong position on any issue unless they can detect ready-made support from their peers. They seldom stir up bitterness, even among their opponents. Likewise, they seldom enlist enthusiastic support from their friends. That is what society has come to expect. Controversy is unpleasant.

The propaganda of conservation is mostly pitched in support of the exotic and far-away. Children are asked to give a proportion of their pocket money to save the Javan rhinoceros at a time when the factory at the bottom of the street is turning the only stream they can paddle in into a stinking sewer. Under Rafferty's Rules for pollution, it is not illegal to poison your neighbour; it is only forbidden to poison him all at once. Cow Green might have been saved for the nation if the government agency responsible for its protection had been courageous enough to fight. But it slipped through the feeble fingers of officialdom.

It continued to rain, hard. After searching vainly for a glimpse of the Pennine Way, I turned north-east, hoping to encounter the source of the River Tyne. Most of the small streams had become impassable, filled with flood-water from the slopes of Cross Fell, which in pagan times, they say, used to be called Fiends' Fell, but, during one of his northern missions, the Blessed St. Augustine drove the evil spirits away and, on the summit of that stark crag, inplanted the cross that gave the fell its present name.

I trudged on, keeping to a stream that flowed away from the moor. 'Where am I heading for?' I asked an old man, expecting to be told the name of the next village. With what at that moment I took to be unseasonable humour, he said that if I kept going for sixty miles I should probably reach Newcastle-upon-Tyne. I thanked him and walked on to Garrigill, where I spent the night. It rained for seven hours. A local saying from which I derived no comfort is that if you can see Cross Fell it's going to rain and if you can't it is raining.

For those wise enough to ignore what you are advised to do beyond Garrigill, where the Pennine Way gets hopelessly complicated, the going is easy. There is only one way, and that way is due north: the way the legions went. The valleys are parallel-sided and the biggest flanks the north-bound Tyne. Follow it to dark, stone-built Alston, the highest market town in England, but otherwise unremarkable. Cling to the river until it winds round a village with the unpromising name of Slaggyford, and then climb up the western side of the valley, as high as you can. This means clambering over a cross-gartering of mossy walls. For those neither ashamed nor afraid to trespass there are ample opportunities here. It pays to shout 'Good morning', loudly, to authority, especially those in breeches and gum-boots, and the chances are they will shout and wave back, cheerfully. The important thing is to get up high above the knuckles of the valley, where, on the top of the slope, a dead-straight Roman supply road called Maiden's Way heads for Hadrian's Wall. To stride along it that May morning was well worth the climb.

The Durham uplands are made up of the same sort of limestone that shelters those lovely little purple and yellow pansies in the central portion of the Pennines, but the rock, called the Alston block, is far more stable. It hasn't been cracked and twisted by earth movements. When the ice-sheets crawled down from the high latitudes, they ran up against this barrier, squeezing through only in places where the Pennines were riven by such gaps as the Craven, the Stainmore and the Tyne. The immense horizons are horizontals, relieved only by the great breasts of the fells. Down in the valleys, the grey farm buildings are roofed by heavy slabs; the holdings look prosperous enough, but the upper limits of cultivation are severely bounded by walls that mark the open moorland.

Gone, now, are the broad vowels, the slow and aphoristic speech of the dalesmen. On the boundary between Cumberland and Durham the accent lifts from that relaxed, deep-throated *ahh* as you hear it in 'Ah wer' going' for a walk' to the higher-pitched 'eh' of Newcastle and Geordieland. Scotland, you feel, can't be too far away.

Through field-glasses from the top of Byers Fells isolated bits of the Wall become visible far ahead on the most distant horizon. The ramparts crop up irregularly from behind a line of electric pylons. By nine o'clock that night I had outflanked the dilapidated mining town of Haltwhistle and reached what, nearly two thousand years ago, was substantially the northernmost boundary of the Roman Empire.

Some of the great monuments of antiquity are hard to take in at a glance. You need a guide, a knowledgeable person to explain the significance of old stonework. The Wall is an exception. You can see exactly what the Romans were up to. The impression is of an enormous roller-coaster, soaring exuberantly up and down one hill after another. At a distance it looks too sinuous, too graceful for the brutalities of fortification. And yet there is not a curve, not a dip in its original length of forty-five miles without military or structural significance. Much of it has recently been restored, stone by stone, with, if anything, too much precision. But the reconstruction means that you can walk on the top of the ramparts for a long way, and that I did that night, staring out into the dusk towards the land of the Picts.

Towards the end of the first century A.D. the Romans tried to subdue the southern tribes of Scotland. They fought their way into the lowlands as far as Strathmore, beyond the Tay, but the refuges that the mountains afforded defeated them and they fell back on the Tyne. When the Emperor Hadrian came back to Britain in A.D. 122 his engineers had already surveyed a convenient ridge across the narrow neck of land between Carlisle and the mouth of the Tyne. The hills, they found, were studded with towering outcrops of black rock some hundreds of feet in height. This is dolerite, the same volcanic lava that scars Teesdale. Hadrian ordered the wall to be built, not merely between, but up to and over the very summit of these crags, linking one to another.

I climbed up to the highest point, Winshields, and slept in the lee of a turret, but instead of dreaming romantically of the watch, of the sentries pacing ceaselessly between the signalling stations, I got up several times during the night to put bits of the wall on to the tent to hold it down, for it blew hard until the first flush of an ominously red dawn.

Four o'clock is a poor time for sight-seeing, but I walked on behind the wall, thankful for the protection it afforded. At first light two large lakes, Greenlee and Broomlee appeared unexpectedly, some hundreds of feet below the ramparts. The cliffs are vertical; nobody could scale them, but the wall on the top is as thick there as anywhere in the blockade. The Romans left nothing to chance.

I fingered the blocks of smooth gritstone. They are less than a foot in length so that they could be man-handled and they were carefully tapered from front to back to fit snugly, one against another. They were hewn from local quarries, where on the rock-face antiquarians have found the sort of scrawls that soldiers the world over leave behind, some obscene, some boastful. Up the First Cohort of Hadrian's Own Marines! The names of the units sounded strangely familiar. Originally the wall stood between twelve and fifteen feet in height, so that it could not be scaled by a man standing on another's shoulders. But for centuries the fortifications have been used as a source of free building material and the easily recognizable blocks are to be found in the walls of local farmhouses, churches and castles.

From the dispatches sent to Rome by the Governors of Britain, it is known that about twelve thousand men were required to patrol the ramparts and man the supporting garrisons.

Three legions dominated Britain throughout most of the occupation: the Sixth (*Victrix*) stationed at York, the Twentieth (*Valerian*) at Chester and the Second (*Augusta*) at Caerleon in Wales. In between local engagements, the legionaries took turns at wall duty, backing up the Auxiliaries, who, poor fellows, were permanently stationed there. Although they took the brunt of the fighting, the Auxiliaries were in every way an inferior grade of troops. They were raised from among the non-Roman tribes of frontier provinces: Gauls, Spaniards, Moors, Dacians from central Europe, Nervians and Tungrians from the borders of Germany and Hamians, who were renowned as bowmen. They all served on the Wall, speaking their own languages, worshiping their own gods.

At six o'clock that morning I reached the famous fort of

Housesteads, or *Vercovicium*, manned, originally, by about a thousand Tungrian infantrymen and some local mercenaries called *Numerus* Naudifridi or Nottfried's Irregulars. I saw Nottfried as a short-built, heavily-moustached Celt, the model for sergeant-majors everywhere. Square pits in the ground mark the site of the headquarters building (*Principia*), the commandant's house (*Praetorium*), the hospital (*Valetudinarium*) and a large communal lavatory with the seats arranged over two deep sewers. In front were the water channels for washing the sponges, the Roman equivalent of toilet paper.

The main gate-posts are still intact and from two deep ruts in the stone guard-blocks it is possible to determine the breadth of the chariots that ran over them. It is about fifty-six inches, which is still the gauge of British railway lines. This is not to suggest that George Stephenson got his measurements from Housesteads. He took the average breadth of about a hundred farm-carts, but they in turn reflect a tradition that probably began in Rome.

Excavations behind the wall at Housesteads have disclosed a village with shops and taverns. One of them, called the Murder House, owes its name to the skeleton with a knife-point in its ribs; the man who died there was surreptitiously buried beneath the floor of the back room.

When the northern tribesmen grew restive, the Romans used the wall as an almost impregnable base and also as a screen for an offensive. The Auxiliaries were mustered behind the ramparts, where they couldn't be seen and then, at a signal from their commanders, they poured out, enveloping the enemy, 'reducing them' as the dispatches put it. During part of the occupation it looks as if the wall served more as a Customs barrier and trading post than a fortification. On at least three occasions it was completely overrun.

On the few occasions when the natives got the better of their oppressors, the Commander, the *legatus* at York, sent in the local legion, drawing sometimes on mobile shock troops, *vexillatio* from Chester or Caerleon. The legions were by no means invincible. One, the ill-fated Ninth, left York, but never returned from a foray against a large and powerful tribe of Celts, the Brigantes. What happened nobody knows, but from surviving fragments of the legionary records in Rome it looks as if they put up a poor fight and scattered or, worse, they surrendered. They were not slaughtered, for the names of some former officers of the Ninth appeared in other theatres of war, significantly reduced in rank.

For Britain the Roman conquest was more of a flood than an upheaval. The soldiers had little contact with the natives. They employed Celtic craftsmen and labour forces; for women they went to the brothels. When the flood subsided and Magnus Maximus led the last of the legions back to Rome, the Celts reverted to a state of barbarism. They re-fortified the old Iron Age hill-forts; they built villages of mud huts outside the walls of towns where patricians once lolled in steam-heated luxury. They even forgot how to use stone, for they soon began to refer to the crumbling masonry as the work of giants.

For most of that morning I trotted up and down the slopes between the forts and the mile-posts, poking about under stones, hopeful that I might come across at least a coin or two. Although the great days of treasure finds are long since over, a few isolated specimens turn up now and again. Among those most sought after are the brass coins of the consulship of Pius which commemorate the pacification of North Britain after the great disturbances of the year A.D. 155. They depict Britannia sitting disconsolate upon a rock, her hair dishevelled, her head drooping and her shield cast aside.

Towards noon I returned to *Vercovicium* and slipped out through the chariot gate. Within a mile you enter a forest as dark as any that ever sheltered a painted Pict. The transition is sudden, dramatic. Behind are the towering cliffs. In front is a close-planted arboreal slum. This is a man-made forest, the biggest in Britain and by far the most unpleasant I encountered. It stretches from the Wall to the Border and beyond, an area of nearly three hundred square miles. Throughout this great tract of country the

Forestry Commission has planted young trees, mostly Canadian spruce planted so close that, apart from the forest rides, it is impossible to get between them. The eye craves for variety, for something less monotonous than the endless corduroy of conifers. Although the Pennine Way runs through only a very small section of the forest - in all perhaps no more than about four miles - in that distance the walker is likely to get lost, misguided by signposts that point in the wrong direction and pulled up short by rides blocked by brushwood. It rained, hard, as it so often did on those occasions and I went round and round like a rat in a laboratory maze. Wet through and annoyed that one could be so badly treated by a public authority, I managed to get out of the Christmas trees near an isolated farmhouse.

Instant hospitality. When had I last eaten? asked the young farmer. Would I care for a bath? Everett of Watergate had been at home for two days, entertaining the children whilst his wife was in hospital having a baby, their third or fourth. The place looked upside-down and everyone seemed extraordinarily happy. My host even phoned up a local schoolmaster so that we could have a bit of a party that night. We talked for hours. I slept, eventually, on the kitchen floor between the open fire and the table, marvelling again on the unpredictable oscillations of Fortune.

The contiguous forests of Wark, Kielder and Redesdale extend northwards for about twenty-five miles. Remembering only too well what had happened the previous day in Wark, I carefully avoided Kielder and nipped through only a corner of Redesdale because there was no way that I could see of avoiding the place. The North Tyne is crossed at the austere-looking village of Bellingham, pronounced 'Bellinj'n', where even the big houses seem curiously barn-like and inhospitable. They were built that way, they will tell you, to escape the attention of billeting officers and looting parties, which, up to the eighteenth century, probably amounted to much the same thing. This is Border country. You can sense something of the old strife from the fortress-like appearance of the isolated farmsteads. There are ruined castles in the hills and hair-raising stories about what went on there. But this is history preserved in aspic for tourists' consumption. The English seem completely indifferent to the boundary and all that it used to mean. Nobody in the bar of the 'Black Bull' at Bellinj'n seemed to care a damn that a Douglas or a Kerr, a Maxwell or a Scott from over the Border had slaughtered most of his ancestors. But on the other side of the Border, only a few miles further on, they are a bit more touchy; an injudicious reference to names like Percy, Neville or Clifford can start a row, even today.

Bellinj'n church is dedicated to St. Cuthbert, that most gentle of Celtic saints. Grey seals are said to have kept vigil with him as he prayed on the shores of Lindisfarne. Aside from the Danes, the Devil and his works, he fled only from the presence of women, a fear attributed to a false charge of seduction laid against him by the daughter of a Pictish king.

The high road to Scotland passes through the middle of the Redesdale Forest, where for mile after mile you walk through a cleft in the conifers. The Forestry Commission has tried to disguise the walls of dank spruce by planting a few chestnuts and flowering cherries alongside the road, but the screen, one-tree thick, tends to accentuate rather than detract from the dreariness within.

Here among the spruce and out on the moors above Redesdale are some of the biggest artillery ranges in the north of England. The noise at times is fearful. By a curious quirk of history, the present artillery headquarters lies within half a mile of High Rochester, known to the Romans as *Bremenium*, where, on the hillside, the legionaries built immense catapults, capable of hurling boulders down on the Picts who plagued them. The weapons were mounted on solid square towers and protected against counter-missile action by outlying earthworks. High Rochester served as an outpost from which cavalry could patrol the wide no-man's-land north of the Wall.

Up there today they are firing off rockets. Redesdale, like Salisbury Plain, is a good place for military manoeuvres. In mock battles on this historic defence line Northland fights

Southland and the Picts the Scots. They were at it that day. The roads were blocked with lines of armoured vehicles. Disinterested soldiers brewed tea or, with earphones at the ready, waited for a radio call to trundle off somewhere else, equally disinteresting. An elderly brigadier who had been coming up there for years as a divisional umpire had thoughtfully established his headquarters in the 'Redesdale Arms'. Hadn't heard about the catapults himself, he said, but thought they were extremely interesting and reckoned his chaps ought to know about them. Where had I picked up the information? I referred him to the guide to the National Parks published by Her Majesty's Stationery Office, price five shillings, and he said he was hanged if he wouldn't buy a copy. They knew a thing or two those Romans.

To get into Scotland from Redesdale you can either cling to the forest road or cut up through the trees into the Cheviot Hills, holding to an ancient Roman highway called Dere Street that curls round the back of Carter Bar and drops down into the valley of the Jed.

I went up into the Cheviots at first light and got lost on what I took to be Ogre Hill, near the limit of the trees. The Cheviots are the highest and wildest part of Northumberland, a dome nearly twenty miles across. I missed the catapults, but pressed on through what seemed to be a distinctly Roman landscape: straight tracks and rounded volcanic hills, grass-covered with scarcely a rock to be seen. Below you could imagine, as perhaps the legionaries did, the plain of Latium. There is something Roman in the appearance of those Cheviot sheep with their aquiline noses and supercilious expressions. They are a very superior breed of sheep. I hurried on, climbing rapidly, conscious that most of the landmarks, even the distant peaks, were rapidly disappearing in the mist.

Here it was in the seventeenth century that little congregations of Presbyterians known as the Covenanters held holy service in secret. The Reformers had bound themselves by oaths to resist attempts made by Roman Catholics to regain their lost hold on Scotland. The Covenanters knew they risked death if they were caught. The story is that during one of their congregations the famous preacher, the good man they called Savoury Mr. Peden, was offering up thanks to God when, to his consternation, he saw a company of dragoons advancing up the hillside. Not wishing to alarm his flock, he concluded prayer with the words: 'And lastly, O Lord, cast the lap o' thy coat ower puir auld Sandy and his friends.' And they say that before the troopers reached them a mist rolled down from the heights of Broad Law and Mr. Peden and his friends got safely away.

SOUTHERN CALEDONIA

By walking down into Jedburgh and Selkirk, two Border towns of credit and renown, I thought I might get an instant taste of whatever it is that makes Scotland different from anywhere else. But, as usual, it didn't work out that way. There are bits of both countries in the Cheviot Hills; the Border is no more typically Scottish than, say, cosmopolitan Glasgow or pawky, self-contained Edinburgh, which in character are as unlike as any two closely-situated cities can be.

To me, at that stage of the journey, rural Scotland was merely an elevated and largely unexplored part of Britain. As a small Boy Scout I had been goaded down a long, wet length of the Great Glen by a bustling master who said, rightly, that I would never forget the occasion. Years later I made short trips into the hills from Dundee and Glasgow, where, as the only Sassenach on a very popular newspaper I had worked, briefly, against appalling linguistic difficulties. About innermost Caledon I knew little more than could be seen from a train on Press trips to such un-Gaelic monuments as the atomic power station in Caithness. I had a lot to learn. But what of the Border?

The Border is bonnie. No other word I can think of catches so well the feeling of sprightliness. The villages look trim; the hills are lightly clothed in ash and beech. They are furrowed by burns

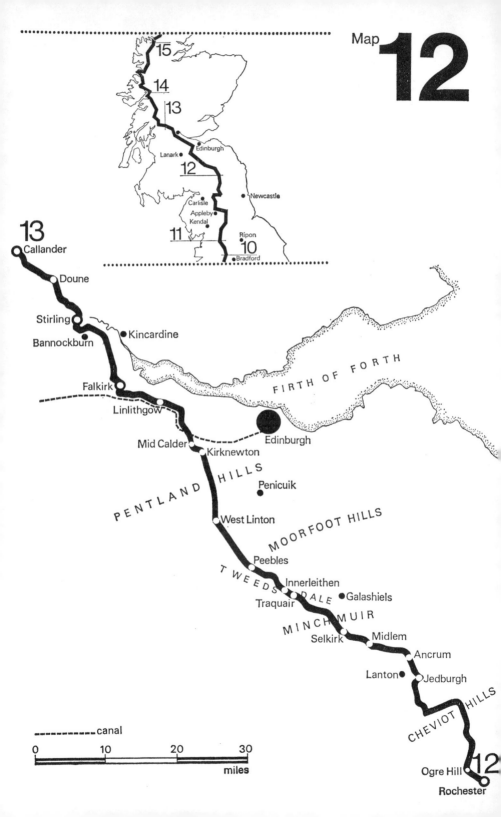

Map **12**

15
14
13
Lanark • Edinburgh
12
Carlisle •
Appleby •
Kendal •
11
Ripon •
10
Bradford •

Newcastle •

13
○ Callander
○ Doune
Stirling ○
Bannockburn
● Kincardine

Falkirk ○
Linlithgow ○
Mid Calder ○
Kirknewton ○

FIRTH OF FORTH

● Edinburgh

PENTLAND HILLS

● Penicuik

○ West Linton

MOORFOOT HILLS

Peebles ○
Innerleithen ○
Traquair ○   ● Galashiels

TWEEDSDALE

MINCHMUIR

Selkirk ○   ○ Midlem
                              Ancrum ○
Lanton ●   Jedburgh ○

CHEVIOT HILLS

Ogre Hill ○
Rochester ○ **12**

------------ canal
0   10   20   30
                              miles

that bubble down into the whisky-coloured water of the River Jed, a tributary of the Tweed. The girls look bonnie too. Standing under a tree, miles from anywhere, on the Great North Road were two youngsters carrying small suitcases. They were improbably dressed in tight sweaters and mini-skirts. A local said they were 'just a couple o' wee whores', waiting for the long-distance truck-drivers. But they looked bonnie for all that. I wrote down the word as if I'd thought of it myself and added a lyrical if somewhat unoriginal note about the incidence of the bluebells of Scotland. In this mood I reached Jedburgh.

The townsfolk call it something that sounds like Jeddut or Jethart. At first I attributed the elision to a temporary relaxation of throat muscles induced by liquor, the more since several natives said, dispassionately, that they'd been on the hard stuff for days. Jethart was hell-bent on celebrating a great occasion, and there's nothing I know of, anywhere, to rival the Jethart capacity for putting it away.

Accordions played in the back rooms; men sang mournfully, loudly, apparently undeterred by the fact that their more boisterous companions were being chucked out one after another. This is a recognized Scottish custom. The ejected party has the choice of cooling his head in the street for ten minutes and coming back, meekly, through another door or staggering off in search of another pub.

Fascinated, I watched a bouncer throw out two rowdies with the muscular economy of a coal-heaver. The first picked himself off the pavement and might have got back in if he hadn't encountered his companion on the outward part of the night's routine. The chucker-out, a slim young fellow, watched them, critically, as they zigzagged down the street, arm in arm, singing *Farewell to Sorrento*. He seemed to be looking at me, too, I thought, as if I were somehow responsible for their behaviour.

After a walk through the town I slipped through the back door of a pub, hired a room and settled down in the bar with a pint of the local stuff, which is pale and potent. To my consternation, I found I had strayed, unwittingly, into the house patrolled by the agile young bouncer. He walked over with his hands raised, poised, in the Hollywood tradition of a gun-fighter. This, I thought, is it.

'Ye're not taking this amiss, I hope,' he said. 'Will ye shake?'

Shake hands? From somewhere underneath vast waves of relief, I tried to give the impression that I had walked from Cornwall to Jethart for no other purpose. We solemnly clasped hands, not once but several times; he insisted that we were all friends and that, as far as he was concerned, the past didnae matter a hoot. As he saw it there were good chaps to be found on both sides and for his part he was prepared to forget and forgive. Before I got the hang of what it was all about, two of his pals came up and went through the ritual again. They all forgave me. By the time we had exchanged several drinks and photographs of sweethearts, wives and children, they seemed a bit disappointed to find I wasn't a Border man at all.

At ten minutes to seven several of the company rushed out to escort their lawful spouses to the local bingo hall. At ten past seven they returned thirstier than ever, explaining that no respectable woman could be seen leaving the house by herself on a Saturday night. The neighbours would talk. And anyhow it wasn't nice to leave the puir lassies on their own.

Erchie, the bouncer, told me confidentially he had been inside twice for a bit of trouble (assault), which, as he put it, might have happened to anybody. He was a ju-jitsu expert and prison had put an end to his ambition to enter a karate school. He said the police kept a record of all trained men and the karate instructors wouldn't have anything to do with anybody who had tangled with the law. He had been thinking about taking a correspondence course in the subject, but felt it wasn't quite like the real thing.

Local festivities in Jethart that night were associated with that most venerable of Border customs: the Common Ride. I say 'associated' since the relationship seemed neither obvious nor direct.

In the merry month of May Jedburgh, in company with Hawick, Selkirk and other border towns, elects a popular citizen to lead them in a rollicking ride around the statutory boundaries of the burgh. The man is the Cornet or Standard-bearer. The Ride commemorates bygone times when common property rights were reinforced by an annual show of strength called a 'wapynshawe'. They rode hard and they stopped only to drink confusion to encroachers. They still ride and they still drink prodigiously, but as I discovered from the affair in the bar, they were prepared to forgive their former enemies. Jedburgh had already celebrated the election of their champion. All that remained was the excuse to toast the success of the Ride the following week.

When the pub closed we went down to an underground vault near the town bridge where amid a great deal of bottled beer his friends forgave me yet again. They asked me repeatedly what I thought about Lintalee and Todlaw, naming places I had walked through on my way in. Easy questions to answer, since these little villages that stand above the Jed were among the most beautiful I had seen. But, they said, have you seen anything *anywhere* to match Jethart? And I said truthfully that by God I hadn't.

For the rest of that night and until far into the morning my friends told stories and sang boisterous songs about the Lads o' Wamphray, Dick o' the Cow, the Battle of Otterburn and Leslie's March.

Border history is terrible stuff. One can understand the long fight for independence, the efforts to repel the constant incursions of the hated English. What the mind boggles at is the amount of treachery, feuding, cattle-lifting and slaughter that went on between Borderers at least nominally united against common enemies. On the English side the Charltons, Fenwicks, Herons and Melbournes were chronically at each other's throats, whilst on the other the Scotts raided the Kerrs and the Grahams, Elliots, Turnbulls and Armstrongs joined in whenever it looked profitable. Throughout it all the law of retaliation prevailed. 'All is dishonarabell', wrote Alexander Napier, 'quhair there is not eie for eie and tuith for a tuith.'

Scott o' Buccleugh slew Kerr's kinsfolk at Dornick; they in turn murdered auld Buccleugh in Edinburgh High Street. The aged Lady of Buccleugh, born a Kerr, was burned to death in her castle when her husband's men were out raiding with the English. Elliot of Stobs, a follower of Buccleugh at the time of the Dornick affair, ravaged the Scott country, killing scores of his fellow countrymen, including women and children. Lord Maxwell, dying on the field of battle, begged aid from Lady Johnstone, the wife of his adversary, who had come to the field to see how the day had fared. She charitably dashed out his brains with the heavy keys of the castle. Fifteen years later Maxwell's son sought a 'friendly interview' with Sir James Johnstone with the avowed intent of patching up the quarrel. During a carefully-arranged diversion he shot him in the back. The assassin fled to France, where he remained for four years. On his return he was betrayed by his kinsman, Sinclair, Earl of Caithness, and beheaded at Edinburgh.

Meg Lawson, an elderly woman, was refused a glass of water before they burned her at the stake on a trumped-up charge of witchcraft, for, as her captor said, 'the drier ye are ye'll burn the better'. After a raid by the Regent Moray, twenty-two prisoners were thrown, bound, into the Teviot 'for lack of trees and halters' and the rest were hanged. Hundreds died on the banks of the Jed, the Tweed, the Ettrick and in the dowie dens o' Yarrow. In ballad metre their names sound romantic enough: Kinmont Will, Ill-drowned Geordie, Jock Half-lugs, Red-neb Hob, and Tommy Fire-the-Braes. But what they did and how they died is dreadful even in ballad and song.

Through it all, belatedly, comes a note of regret, sometimes even of repentance. 'Though I have slain the Lord Johnstone,' said Maxwell, 'what care I for their feud?' King James deplored the 'auld and detestabel monster' of clan strife, but fanned the flames by giving the wardenship of the western marches first to a Protestant (Johnstone) and then to a Roman Catholic (Maxwell). For some hundreds of years the country between Solway and Tweed must have been the most-used tournament ground in Britain.

Elements of the old strife linger on in a love of litigation. Only a Lowlander could confess to his minister that he knew of 'no greater pleasure on airth than a weel-gowin' law plea'. It lingers on, too, in prickly regard for the honour of the family and the community, even where fighting is disguised under the name of football.

Somebody that night made a disparaging reference to one of the players in a forthcoming match. It brought the man next to me to his feet with a 'Wullie's a cousin o' mine and there's nobody here who'll gainsay *that*!' He banged his pot down and glared round aggressively. If Erchie hadn't shaken his head slowly and decisively the incident might have ended in a brawl. Erchie neither upheld nor gainsaid the proposition. He merely acted as a reference-point in a place where skill at arms is deeply respected.

About two o'clock in the morning and for no reason that I can recall, a sad-faced youth began to sing the *Ave Maria*. He sang it, moreover, in Latin, which seemed rather surprising in a country dedicated to ridding the Kirk of altar, candles and crucifix. The light tenor voice climbed up to the pinnacle of the *ad uxorem mundi*. It broke very slightly on the *exultimus* and rolled down on the *coelis advenit*. A splendid effort. Some of us began to think there were things in life more noble than bottled beer. Tears rolled unashamedly down my neighbour's cheeks. 'That kid can certainly sing,' I said to Erchie. 'Aye,' he said. 'He's had a lot of practice. He's just done three years in the Catholic reformatory at Gattonside.'

The Jed winds round the back of the rose-red Abbey of Jethart; it scampers under an immense cliff and then ambles off north, slowly, losing its identity, first in the Teviot and then in the Tweed. Looking back on the maze of streets the following morning, it occurred to me that in joining in the local celebrations I had done less than justice to the sights of this attractive town. The 'Spread Eagle' is reputedly the oldest pub in Scotland. There at different times stayed a local advocate called Sir Walter Scott and, before she moved to a little place of her own in an adjacent street, Mary Queen of Scots. There she lived with the dissolute Bothwell. 'Would that I had died in Jedworth', wrote the Queen in exile.

To get to Selkirk that night I crossed about sixteen miles of flat rain-soaked farmland distinguished only by villages with curly names, such as Ancrum, Lilliesleaf and Milrighal, most of them the sites of dreadful conflict. At Ancrum, for instance, the Regent Arran and the Earl of Angus by a smart feint routed an army of English at least three times bigger than their own. At sundown, when it was difficult to see what they were up to, they hid their troops in woods and thickets on a steep hillside. And then by displaying their cavalry in a mock retreat they lured the English away from prepared positions to a place where they literally fell on them. So great was the slaughter that the victorious Arran was moved to pity and called his men off. As usual, a sprinkling of Border men were of uncertain allegiance. The Kerrs, several Armstrongs and some Turnbulls fought on the side of the English invaders. When they saw how the day was going they tore the red cross of St. George from their arms and joined in pursuit and plunder. The battle is renowned for the somewhat improbable exploits of a young girl called Lilliard. The story is that she followed her lover to the edge of the fray. Seeing him fall, she rushed in, seized his sword and polished off a few of the Southrons before she too fell. On the hill which bears her name, to this day an inscription says:

> *Fair Maiden Lilliard lies under this stane.*
> *Little was her stature, but muckle is her fame;*
> *Upon the English loons she laid mony, mony thumps*
> *And when her legs were cuttit aff*
> *She fought upon her stumps.*

Outside the tourist's routes the Scots are still strict Sabbatarians and on that Sunday I couldn't buy so much as a bun or a cup of tea. 'Ye've no *occasion* to be trampin' aboot this day,' said an indignant storekeeper, a woman who had been looking at the telly in her back parlour. I sighed and tramped on, hungry. It continued to rain, hard. Heavenly disfavour, I thought, and sought shelter under one of the Lord's newly-opened umbrellas, a massive oak tree. It leaked badly. In the spring, when the foliage is thin, a chestnut provides by far the best cover, with new sprung beech and a thick old conifer a good second and third.

Late in the afternoon I stood, Cortez-wise, on the heights of Selkirk golf-course and looked down on what I reckon to be the very heart of the Border. This statement, I know, is calculated to provoke armed reprisals from Hawick (pronounced *Hoik*), which regards itself as by far the most important town in Scotland, a sentiment shared by Galashiels and Melrose. But Selkirk, I consider, has the edge on them all for surrounding splendour. It lies on the banks of the Ettrick, which is yet another tributary of the Tweed.

The town is renowned for the tweeds, plaids and shawls it manufactures; it looks ancient, but the English fired it at intervals, and today there is scarcely a building more than two hundred years old. For some reason which I have forgotten, it used to be called Scheleschyrche. From where I stood on the eighth tee the great hills on the opposite side of the valley - Foulshiels, the Three Brethren and Peat Law - stood out like homely Himalayas, impressive but by no means overpowering. Much the same can be said for the citizenry, who, for their association with an early period of shoe-making, are called Souters. Nowadays they weave cloth and compound a delicious bun of which I shall have more to say later.

I walked down into Scheleschyrche in the company of three chatty golfers. They wore traditional costume - that is, baggy waterproof pants, a zipped-up jacket and a cloth cap of florid check or sett, representative of nothing more than aesthetic whim. Golf in Scotland is a democratic game, and I may have been in the company of almost anybody from the Provost to his Sheriff's most junior clerk. The talk was good Border talk of the unpredictability of football results and Italian competition in the rag trade.

Souters exude a feeling of self-confident superiority. It would not have occurred to anybody to forgive me. Or ask to be forgiven. Yet in their talk, especially in their questions, there is much of the latent passion of the Borderer. The town's monuments proclaim their history. Of the Flowers of the Forest who marched out to fight at the disastrous Battle of Flodden only one returned. High up on the wall of Muthag Street there is a metal plate as big as a barn door. In large letters it says the street was:

> Named in grateful memory of John Muthag, first Provost of
> Selkirk who, with Bailie James Kein, was slain upon 25 July 1541
> by James Ker of Brighteuch, Ralph Ker and William Reston when
> riding to defend the Burgh lands before the courts of Edinburgh.

The crime took place over four hundred years ago. It has not
been forgotten. Souters are prepared to bury the hatchet, but,
like Yorkshiremen, they mark the spot.

In addition to the usual Common Ride around the boundaries
of the town, Selkirk ensures that the ancient hill-paths are kept
open to all by the regular excursions of a local walking club called
the Plodders. They conduct their club business in the open-air
and have challenged their own Council on the issue of a closed
right of way. A few groups of this kind in England might ginger
up the fossilized institutions nominally dedicated to pedestrians'
rights.

Two bakeries in the town offer for sale a rich delicacy known
simply as 'the bun'. This is an elaborate confection of heavily
spiced pastry and fruit somewhat of the consistency of Christmas
pudding. For some curious reason, it rarely appears in the local
hotels, which, instead of dinner in the evening, serve the traditional Scottish high tea at about half-past five. For this meal the
visitor is offered a curious combination of steak or chops and
commercially-manufactured iced cakes and scones. But no bun.

I stayed in a small hotel where a long, unfurnished bar still bore
signs of the previous night's celebrations. At least seven regular
customers, the landlord informed me, confidentially, would not
appear there again for at least a week. Among the chastened
survivors I countered delicate questions about Border loyalties
with a noncommital nod and the suggestion that much could
be said for both sides. In Scotland this can be done by emitting a
long-drawn out 'Aye' at appropriate moments, adding, 'That's
so, it is. That's so.' I learnt, too, to substitute 'mind' for remember,
salt for sugar (in porridge) and to say 'butter and bread' instead of
the reverse. In Selkirk the word 'bun' saves a number of words.
I bought one before I tackled the hills on the way to Peebles the

next day and found that half the confection would have sufficed for twice the distance strode.

Beyond the town bridge you encounter the site of yet another battle symbolically marked on the map by a minute drawing of crossed cutlasses. The battle is Philiphaugh, for Southerners an unusually complicated affair, for the defeated hero, Montrose, Earl Marischal of Scotland, was both a staunch Presbyterian and a royalist. On that famous occasion in Edinburgh in 1638 he had signed the Covenant against the display of popish relics, but he could be governed 'by no other sway than purest monarchy'. And his King was King Charles of England, Scotland, Ireland and Wales. At Philiphaugh his former ally, General Leslie, the leader of the Covenanters, caught up with him.

Montrose was trapped between cross-fire on the banks of the Ettrick and whilst the people of Selkirk watched, as if from the gallery of a playhouse, his slender forces were shot to pieces. A few prisoners, including some women and children, were butchered on the spot and their leaders hanged or beheaded, later, at Edinburgh. On hearing this joyful news, David Dickson, Moderator of the General Assembly, expressed his pleasure that the 'work gaes bonnily on'. Montrose escaped by galloping off towards where he thought, wrongfully, that friends could be rallied to his support, but he was eventually captured and hanged.

A man driving a tractor around Philiphaugh Farm looked puzzled when I asked about the battle. He said he couldn't rightly recall the matter himself, as he hadn't been employed there very long. He came from Galashiels. A cheerful little boy of about eight walked up and gave me an exciting account of the affray from what he had learnt at school. Even better, he conducted me through the thick skirt of trees around the farm. From there I went high up into the hills, confident about the route which had been carefully plotted for me by Donald Moir of the Scottish Geographical Society. It had been arranged that we should meet in Peebles for a day's walk together over the Pentland Hills to the west of Edinburgh.

The twelve-mile climb over the Minchmuir from Selkirk to

Traquair by the side of the Tweed is by way of an ancient
cattle-track or drove-road that runs between the peaks of the
Brethren and the Broomy Law. The track is high and spectacular,
but easy to follow, and I made the stage in five hours, hampered
only by a wind of unusual violence.

It came at me head-on and hard. I managed to make some
progress by leaning forward and lifting my feet up high, but it
was like walking in a dream or in some space-fiction world of
excessive gravity; the unexpected gusts threw me sideways.
Tiring of the buffeting, I sought refuge in a little wood where a
thread of a stream, a daughter of the Ettrick, appeared to have
lost her way. There I stayed, lunching on squashed bun and burn
water, listening to the shriek in the tree-tops and staring fascinated
at the carpet of pine needles that rose and fell uneasily as if something beneath had been buried alive.

It still blew fitfully as I ventured out, but I could see the thin
ribbon of track running ahead for miles. It had been pounded flat
by thousands of Highland cattle that were driven south annually
until the great treks ceased in the latter part of the nineteenth
century. The cattle were accompanied by hardy drovers, who
made the long journey to the marts of England, sleeping beside
their beasts at night. In the early days there were no bridges and
the animals had to be pricked through the rivers, although many,
they say, took to the water like spaniels. Those that came from
the Western Isles were pushed into the sea and towed behind
boats, linked nose to tail. On the upland tracks they usually made
about twelve miles a day, since forced marches were reckoned to
be 'fair ruin on the bestial'.

Dr. A. R. B. Haldane of Edinburgh, to whom I am indebted
for most of my information,* says that in the far north a herd of
perhaps two or three hundred were reinforced at recognized
trysts until in time a river of animals flowed south, mostly towards Crieff and Falkirk and thence over the border into England.
In the eighteenth century the trade satisfied the British Navy's
prodigious appetite for salt beef, but it is doubtful whether at four
or five shillings a head for the whole journey the drovers made

The Drove Roads of Scotland (Nelson, 1964)

much out of it. They were agents and the majority of them seem to have been honourable, hard-tried men.

Over and above the hardships, the months away from their own villages, they had to meet heavy dues; their cattle were often inflicted with pestilence and on the Border they were constantly beset by thieves, who have been given the romantic name of reivers. In the long wars against England the Borderers had grown out of the way of raising crops for others to reap: cattle were the only form of transportable wealth. They stole from each other and they stole from those who were driving food into the stomachs of the hated English. The drovers paid for elaborate systems of protection, but once outside a recognized way-leave they were likely to be pounced on by clansmen who had no cause to love those who had given them local indemnity.

Here again are the names of Bothwell, Kerr, Home, Turnbull, Maxwell, Armstrong, and, of course, the Scotts. Old Scott of Harden, the most notorious riever of them all, was married to an outspoken woman who, in hard times, served her lord and master with a pair of silver spurs for dinner as a plain hint that the time had come for another moonlit ride. Scott lifted everything he found. Returning one night with a herd of cattle and horses, the 'spoil of two houses and gowlde mony and insight worth £100', he saw a haystack and remarked that had it but four legs, by his soul, it wouldn't stand there long. Willie, his son, was caught red-handed lifting Lord Elibank's cattle and condemned to be hanged on the gallows tree, a piece of domestic furniture which no family of repute was ever without. With a mind on a profitable alliance, Lady Elibank persuaded her husband to give Willie the choice between the rope or of marrying their daughter, Margaret, who, from the width of her mouth, was known throughout the Border as Muckle-mou'ed Meg. Willie took one look at his chance of survival and opted for the gallows. But, as he said, life is sweet, and when they actually put the rope round his neck he changed his mind. They married. Documents attest the match. Sir Walter Scott, a descendant, used to point to his well-developed mouth as proof of his ancestry.

The drovers faced direct assault by night and by day. Stuart of Ardvorlich stampeded the herds by sending 'twa bagpypis blawand' ahead of his gang and snatched up what he could. Cattle were constantly coming down from the north and, on the few occasions when they were recovered, it was often very difficult to trace the legitimate owners of stolen beasts. Affairs got so bad in the early part of the seventeenth century that the Privy Council ordained that driven cattle could be slaughtered only in the presence of someone who knew the brand-marks. In a more forthright approach to the problem, the Earl of Dunbar, His Gracious Majesty's Commissioner, summarily hanged over a hundred of those described as 'the most nimble and most powerful' in the business. But all in vain. As a chronicler puts it: the survivors went on with the dance.

I reached Traquair, the great house on the banks of the Tweed, about midday. To Traquair Montrose galloped after his defeat at Philiphaugh. He found the gates locked. They were locked when I got there. It wasn't visiting day, they said. A retainer told Montrose that the master and his son were not at home, 'although there be gentlemen of credit that testify they were both within'.

To avoid the miles of busy road between Traquair and Peebles, I walked across much private property beside the river. This led to a brush with two bailiffs and the gradual evaporation of the enthusiasm worked up on Minchmuir. However, a little Scotch and Tweed served to keep me going until I slipped into the kilt-swishing streets of Peebles. There you are likely to see more Highland dress than anywhere else in Scotland.

Borderers, as I understand it, may not wear Gaelic garb, and you next to never see it among native Highlanders, but ex-patriated Scots, especially those from overseas, delight in tartanry. In the bar of the 'Cross Keys' a Mackay from Nova Scotia wore dark green, blue and black. He chatted to an Australian Campbell in a not dissimilar kilt, but with the addition of a yellow and white line. They explained the difference to me, carefully, whilst a red Hamilton from Ontario looked on. That night, at the great Hydro outside the town, a building far bigger than Buckingham Palace, the members of the Grocers' Federation were gloriously got up for their Annual Conference dinner. The Highland game is far from played out in the Lowlands.

Describing Highland dress to Henry VIII, Father John Elder of Caithness said the 'tender delicatt gentilmen of Scotland call us Reddshankes'. Their brogues or pampooties, he said, were made of hide picked with holes to let the water flow both in and out. Thus it was that they were sometimes styled 'roghe-footide Scottis'.

My own problem was footwear. The soles of the shoes that had carried me up from Cornwall had been smoothed out flat, and before tackling the Highlands they had to be repaired. This took time. I telephoned for advice. The upshot was that a new pair of soles were eventually stuck on indifferently well and Donald Moir, my Scottish route-master, came in from Edinburgh to guide me through about thirty miles of country between Peebles and Midlothian, territory which he knew intimately. It was good to have his company that day.

We went by Newlands, West Linton and the great drove road that straddles the rolling line of heather-clad hills, the Pentlands that lie to the west of Edinburgh. Pentland means the country of the Picts, the people who were among the principal adversaries of the Romans at the time when the legionaries raised the Wall. Almost nothing is known about them except that they may have painted themselves, hence the name *Picti*; they were almost certainly polygamous. Royal descent came through the female line for they reckoned you could be reasonably certain who a person's mother was, but not his father. The traditional form of execution was to chuck adversaries and felons into a deep river with their arms and feet tied. Some clues as to where the Picts dwelt come from the prefix *Pit* in Scottish place names, but not a single sentence of their language has survived on vellum. A few words have been found on their weird monuments on which are carved the outlines of warriors, oxen, stags and salmon. Most of what scholars know about the distribution of the Pictish tribes comes from Ptolemy's map of Great Britain which was drawn in the first century A.D.

Pictland is much of a mystery and the Pentlands today are still magnificently deserted. Apart from reservoir keepers and a few shepherds the most noticeable inhabitants are plovers or peewits, the birds they call whaups in the Lowlands. The accents you notice most in the village tea-shops are middle-class Edinburgh, the sibilant speech of Princes Street, which has been likened to a mouse scratching about in an empty deed-box.

At nightfall Donald and I parted company in a sad little place called Mid Calder where I thrashed about for longer than I care to remember, looking for something to eat and a decent place to put my tent down. I carried a few dry sandwiches and an apple, but I felt that a good day ought to end on a note slightly more heroic than a bed on a vacant lot near the town dump. Besides, I felt very hungry.

Those who haven't tried the vagrant life might think that with a pack on your back and money to spend the world is a picnic basket, ready to be opened and enjoyed at any time. In places like Mid Calder the shops (two) snap shut at six and the publicans (three) were politely unhelpful. They were too busy to serve food. The nearest hotel was six miles away. I telephoned. No room there, either. The proprietor asked why didn't I take a bus to Edinburgh or Linlithgow. They slid past, those buses: warm, well-lit affairs, filled with well-fed people obviously bound for where the action was. Why didn't I take one? Obstinacy, possibly.

The Good Samaritan of Mid Calder turned out to be a young engineer busily painting the front door of his wife's hairdressing business. He thought he 'might know of someone', but felt he ought to telephone first. It was, I might have guessed, his wife. They invited me to their little home on a nearby housing estate, where I ate an enormous amount of food. They looked surprised and pleased and brought out all that remained in the larder. The next morning when I tried to pay something the man shook his head and his wife, a very pretty woman, put her arms round my neck and kissed me, warmly. This is one of the two things I remember about Mid Calder.

The other is the school bus that pulled in to the courtyard of some old-fashioned tenement houses on the outskirts of the town.

The driver hooted. Kids rushed out, pulling on their jackets, shoving each other to get at the front seats. The bus seemed full. The driver knew better. Somebody was missing. He hooted again, insistently. High above the courtyard a window opened and a woman leaned out and bawled: 'Wullie canna come noo; he's on the potty just.'

The waist of Scotland is laced-up tight between Edinburgh and Glasgow. To get into the central highlands, Moir suggested that from Midlothian I should strike north-west, across the Campsie fells to Loch Katrine. Or else work my way round the industrial squalor of the Firth of Forth, towards Stirling and Callander. I took the east route, following the towpath of the canal to get to the old cattle tryst of Falkirk, now a very ordinary town. I recall little that I want to see again in that part of Scotland.

Beyond Mid Calder the villages are hidden among brick-red volcanoes, the spoil-heaps of the shale oil industry. Some are perfectly conical in outline; others are being carved up into improbable shapes for road material. A few have almost disappeared. A pity, since they give some distinction to a sad landscape. On the canal to the south of Falkirk you walk for a time among soft-green birchwoods, but not for long. To the north the smoke rolls in from Grangemouth and Bothkennar. It smells foul and makes your eyes burn.

Down I went into the pall, past the great ironworks of Carronside that gave its name to the guns of Nelson's fleet, the carronade; I kept on, past the oil refineries and out into a network of cinder roads through the marsh. In the pubs there were scenes reminiscent of Jethart. One was filled with seamen on strike. They had plenty of money and on that afternoon, an hour before closing time, they were raising hell.

'An' whurr ye from?' said one who had noticed my pack. He spoke thickly, but with no evident aggression.

I might have parried the question and said I was mooching around. Anything. But I had been chatting to the barman and he answered for me. 'He's from England,' he said. 'He's walked.'

The drunk looked incredulous. 'Ber-luddy liar!' he said.

No heroics were called for, since the barman merely said 'Outside!' and out he went. 'There'll be no ill-will in *this* house,' he said, apologetically.

To my dismay, the drunk reappeared within five minutes, cautiously, protesting that he'd 'just got òne simple lil' question to ask. What's yon chap trying to prove?' he asked the company at large. 'Stands tae reason, if he's walked *all* that way he *must* be trying to prove something.'

Sensing somehow that he had touched on a vulnerable point, he kept up the catechism until he was chucked out again. Why, he said, should anyone walk with money in their pocket? What were they walking for? They must be trying to prove *something*. It stood to reason. What was it? Why wouldn't I *say* what it was?

I couldn't think of an adequate answer and the more I thought of the fellow afterwards the more I disliked him.

At Bannockburn I slept for an hour under the post that pointed to the battlefield, but, too tired for off-route diversions, for I had covered about twenty-eight miles, I pushed on to Stirling, intending to eat there and decide whether to walk through the night.

With its slope of historic buildings and Castle perched high in the air, Stirling is no less dramatic than Edinburgh, but for some quite unfathomable reason the burgh councillors have pulled down or modernized what they should have been proud to preserve, especially in the lower town. Stirling is a mixed-up sort of place, neither ancient nor modern. For that matter, Stirlingshire is a unit only in the most arbitrary sense of the word. Between one end and the other there is practically no coming or going. I entered it during the afternoon and left it at night. Somebody has likened it to a huge brooch that clasps together the Highlands and the Lowlands. But this is scarcely accurate, since the Highland line, that subtle boundary between Saxon and Celt, the breeches and the kilt, runs diagonally across Scotland, from the south-west to the north-east.

At midnight, some five miles beyond Stirling, I had for company only ghostly swans on the River Teith. Tiring of the trucks that thundered down the road from the west, I took to the stream at the Hill of Drip in Kincardine where she joins the Forth. Callander lay only eight miles ahead - say, two hours' hard walking. Already the air seemed wholesome. With luck I should be among the hills at dawn. But somewhere near Doune Castle I felt unbearably tired and pitched down under a lemon-like slice of moon without even bothering to put up the tent. What on earth, I asked myself, *was* I trying to prove?

TARTAN FRINGE

If it hadn't been for the arrival of a massed pipe band, I might have stayed in Callander for hours, making up for lost sleep. As it was, at the first wild skirl I shouldered my pack and fled up into the Pass of Leny. Callander has this much to be said for it: you can clear out in a hurry. The road north makes a determined effort to climb up into the sky. On either side are birch woods and towering cliffs, with Ben Ledi in the background. At some point I suppose I must have crossed the Highland line. There is some dispute as to where it is, but, as far as I'm concerned, the boundary is where *Lament for Lochaber* can no longer be heard or is, at best, no more than the murmuring of bees. I like the pipes, but I felt there was some danger that afternoon that the sound would set fire to the heather.

I had arrived in Callander in time for breakfast. I ate one in a café and another at a hotel. Apart from the pubs and ice-cream parlours, the main street is almost entirely devoted to little shops that sell plaster models of Highland chieftains, Scottie dogs and tam o' shanters adorned with sprigs of plastic heather. Behind the trinket-marts a handsome river flows out of Loch Venachar; there is also a coach-park the size of a football field. On the grassy green where I tried to sleep beside the river, little girls came up and threw bread at me. They were, in fact, aiming

Map **13**

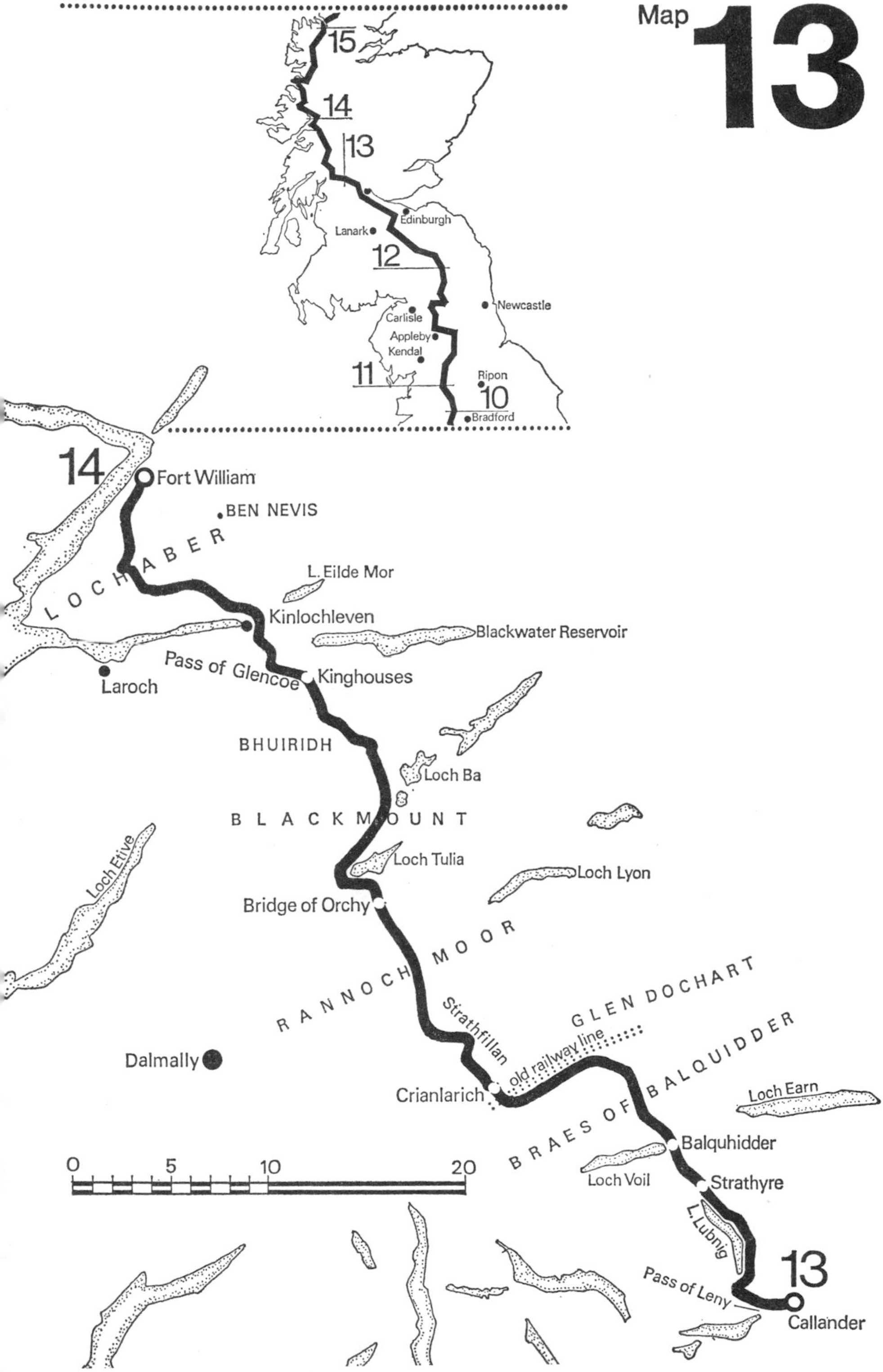

15

14

13

Edinburgh
Lanark ●
12
Newcastle ●
Carlisle ●
Appleby ●
Kendal ●
11
Ripon ●
10
Bradford ●

14 ○ Fort William
● BEN NEVIS
L O C H A B E R
L. Eilde Mor
Kinlochleven
Blackwater Reservoir
Pass of Glencoe
Laroch ●
Kinghouses
BHUIRIDH
Loch Ba
B L A C K M O U N T
Loch Etive
Loch Tulia
Loch Lyon
Bridge of Orchy
R A N N O C H   M O O R
Strathfillan
GLEN DOCHART
old railway line
Dalmally ●
BRAES OF BALQUIDDER
Loch Earn
Crianlarich
Balquhidder
Loch Voil
Strathyre
L. Lubnig
0   5   10   20
Pass of Leny
13
Callander

inaccurately at some much over-fed swans which in Callander, I'm sure, touch nothing less than shortcake smeared with Dundee jam. The sight of the bread reminded me that I was still hungry. I took another snack and tried to settle down again, morbidly conscious that the town was filling up like a bath. Coaches began to roll in, massive affairs from Glasgow and Dewsbury with built-in toilets and flags on the roof. The police shunted them into the coach-park and the population pressure built up on the green. Vendors shouted something that may have been Gaelic for Pepsi-Cola or ice-cream. It all sounded very strange. I was only half asleep when the City of Glasgow Police Pipe Band marched in with pipes skirling. I left them to it.

Up in the Pass of Leny I settled down again and slept, head on rucksack, birch overhead. No sound except the sustained roar of traffic intent on reaching Strathyre that afternoon. For the second time that day I awoke to a fearfully familiar wail. For a moment the thought occurred that the police pipers had marched up in the wake of the cars. But far from a hundred pipers, a little man by the roadside had released the pressure from the cloth bag under his left armpit and all the anguish of the Highlands drained out in one despairing drone. He saw me and came straight over.

'Can you oblige me with a cigarette and a match as well? I have nothing whatever to smoke.'

Before lighting it, he said he would like to play something in return for the courtesy for, as he put it: 'I am not a beggar, you understand. I play the pipes for those who like the sound.' He played. I doubt if I could have stopped him. He walked up and down, fingering Strathspeys and pibrochs with a dexterity a concert flautist would have admired. This done he shook my hand, lit the cigarette, sat down and introduced himself formally as Roderick Duncan Macgregor.

Roddy tramped the roads, playing for tourists, specializing in captive audiences, such as caravanners and roadside picnic parties. That afternoon he intended to walk up to Balquhidder, the home of his forebears.

'Including Robert Macgregor, commonly known as Rob Roy,' he said. 'Of whom you have, no doubt, *haird*?'

Tartan fringe

I said I had.

'But not, I hope, through that auld fool, Walter Scott,' he observed. 'We were the descendants of native hereditary kings who reigned doun at Dunstaffnage; we possessed the crown of Alba originally, and still have hereditary rights to it.' He intoned the words, adding something in Gaelic which I didn't understand.

I suggested we might travel to Balquhidder together.

'A most excellent suggestion and one that should be consummated forthwith,' he said, producing half a bottle of pale malt. Thus it was we went up towards Loch Lubnaig and Strathyre. I shall relate what I can remember of the day, for of all the people I met in the Highlands Roddy was perhaps the most remarkable, certainly the most entertaining.

Born somewhere on the west coast, he said his father had been taught to play by a MacArthur, a member of the hereditary pipe-playing family, who he reckoned were technically more competent than the famous MacCrimmons of Skye. Father taught the son to play and for forty years he had wandered about 'earning enough and a little more for a dram'. He reckoned that, like a man who could mend a watch, a pipe-player would never starve. He spent most of the summer months on the water-fronts of Mallaig and Rothesay and where the steamers pulled in on Loch Lomond. Once a year he made a pilgrimage to the grave of Rob Roy Macgregor in Balquhidder churchyard.

Like certain classes of drugs, there seems to be something about pipe music that amplifies the prevailing emotion, whether pleasurable or otherwise.

One family who were packing up their tea-things rushed to their car and drove off in a panic, leaving behind a plastic cup. 'No poetry in their dispositions,' observed Roddy, pocketing the cup.

Another car coming in the opposite direction skidded to a standstill as soon as the driver caught the first squeal. The delighted occupants clapped their hands in unison and made high-pitched, enemy-scaring *hooching* noises. Eventually they got out and danced to *Strip the Willow*. Two other cars pulled up behind and Roddy collected twelve shillings.

An American with his family said it was the finest playing he had ever heard anywhere. Fascinated, he asked for the performance to be repeated. This done he thanked Roddy and gave him twopence. My friend took both coins gravely, thanked his benefactor and trusted he had no trouble with the British currency.

'Some people,' he said as the huge car pulled away, 'are *curiously* mean.'

In the Pass of Leny the road climbs for three miles and then winds round Loch Lubnaig, a mountain-reflecting mirror of uncommon beauty. The great trees on the hillside are a credit to the Forestry Commission, who utilize most of the land. In between stops for refreshment and capital gain Roddy talked of his travels. Wherever he went there was usually someone with whom he said he was on 'the best of terms' and there was clearly someone to be seen that night in Strathyre.

'We have a duty,' he said, 'to comfort the afflicted, and widows, I take it, are among them for, God knows, they have a lonely life. No one in the Highlands counts it a sin to be on hand at a time of need. To the white crest of the green wave I liken my love. All who deviate from orthodoxy must arrange their lives as best they can.'

On the subject of marriage he held to one firm view. He was against it. A fine ceremony, in his opinion, but, as he saw it, 'a man should be off and away before he got into the habit of staying precisely where he was'.

His father had told him that among the MacArthurs there was a custom that when a marriage had been consummated on the wedding night the bridegroom rose and took up his pipes and played, just as among the Bedouin the husband fires off his rifle. These are among the pipe tunes called 'exultations'. He played one. It sounded terrific. It also sounds strange since the nine notes determined by the chanter are unlike any other diatonic scale. They are not even strictly in tune with each other. 'All a matter of having a guid ear and being able to handle the warbles,' said Roddy.

By 'warbles' he meant the grace notes which are liberally

sprinkled about to disguise the almost constant discord between the melody and the drone. If he spotted a likely patron, Roddy could throw the drones over his shoulder and pull out a tune in no time at all. But if he gave the instrument what he called its rightful dues he wetted his lips carefully and stroked and patted the bag before he began to blow. By the time we reached Strathyre he had made about three non-deductible pounds. We parted there, fraternally, on the understanding that we should meet again that night at ten o'clock which, as he put it, was an accommodating time for a friendly stroll.

Whenever the people of Strathyre open their mouths they take in great gulps of mountain air. This, I suspect, has a tonic effect on the vocal cords. Perhaps it induces song in the way that yodelling is peculiar to certain Swiss villages. There is certainly a lot of singing in Strathyre. They were at it in the forester's lodge when I passed by; the house shook. There was also guitar-playing and singing in the pub where I ordered a meal. This was a spontaneous *ceilidh*, something markedly distinct from the boozy ballads of Jethart. Most of the singers were young people with a fine repertory. I sat back and enjoyed the occasion, delighted that a musical afternoon should end that way. As it turned out, it had not ended. It had scarcely begun.

At one point during the evening I heard what I took to be the sound of pipes coming from somewhere behind the pub and wondered whether Roddy was keeping up the MacArthur tradition, but I may have been mistaken about the noise.

Shortly before ten I said goodbye to the company and slipped out to look for the piper. But he wasn't there. Wondering if I had mistaken one end of the village for the other, I went back for half a mile. Still no sign of Roddy. Disappointed, I walked on towards Balquhidder alone.

I discovered later that, stripped of all its romantic trappings, the story of the real Rob Roy is pretty sordid. A cattle-rustler with no particular regard for anything except immediate gain, he was called Roy from the flaming colour of his hair. But Robert Macgregor was obliged to change his name to Campbell by those who had suffered most from his band of armed thieves. An agile man with exceptionally long arms, he is reckoned to have been the best swordsman on the fringe of the Highlands. He married the daughter of the clan chief, the Gregor Macgregor, and, though he was not the nearest heir, he gained control of lands stretching from Balquhidder to the shores of Loch Lomond. By what seems to have been stark duplicity, he gained the favour of Montrose and Argyll, his noble neighbours, and plundered both. Siding, nominally, with the Pretender in the rebellion of 1715, he took no active part in the Battle of Sherriffmuir except in plundering the dead on both sides. For various exploits he was outlawed, eventually forgiven and died more peacefully than he deserved to.

A mile from Strathyre I heard the sound of pipes from the opposite side of the river. It sounded more like a lament than a salutation. What went wrong that night I never discovered. A small crowd had collected outside a row of cottages. Doors slammed. Roddy hurried up, saying there had been a few complications and it would be as well if we left then and there.

For two hours we walked and played and sat down and talked. It was a night, he said, for the *Ceol mor*, the big music, the laments and the salutations. In his father's day the young pipers underwent an apprenticeship lasting several years. They practised in the open air, where they might spend months repeating phrases of three or four notes so that in time they built up a memorized repertoire of the traditional lullabies, reels, the slow marches and lastly the pibrochs (*piobaireachd*), the tunes composed in memory of great happenings. In particular I recall the indescribably beautiful *Lament for the Children*, the story of how a way of life was destroyed. This is the hard stuff of Gaeldom, almost incommunicable to those who know little of her history.

Roddy stopped to play whenever he felt inspired, but not everyone, not even in pipe country, was equally devoted to his musical meditations at that hour. Chained dogs became hysterical and those on the loose had to be sternly met. At a sneezy sounding little place called Auchtoo, we were told loudly to go away.

About midnight we arrived at the low, railed-off tomb of Rob Roy and his family just inside the entrance to Balquhidder church. On top of the graves were bunches of wind-blown narcissi and yellow poppies. I felt tired and looked round for a place to put my tent down. Roddy threw the drones over his shoulder, but with a thought, perhaps, for the remonstrance at Auchtoo, he sighed and put the instrument back in the old sack he carried. A cold wind began to blow across from Loch Voil. We had a final drink, shook hands and parted: he, I suppose, back to the cottage in Strathyre. I slept for eight hours near the tomb of his ancestors.

In ordinary life, that is to say in an apartment in Hampstead, I spend a great deal of time in trying to persuade inanimate objects to go away and leave me alone. Books, papers, unanswered letters, broken spectacles, lens filters clutter my desk. I shove them away in drawers, pile them up precariously, and hide them away in the spare room, anywhere. The object is to get them out of sight. I like to imagine myself entirely unencumbered. On this walk I became obsessed with the counter-notion that my meagre store of possessions were trying constantly to escape.

In the tent in the early morning I conducted a roll-call, mentally ticking off in order of priority nylon rain-gear, spare clothing, maps, compasses (two), knife, purse, camera, notebooks, emergency food supply and important little things like the tool for prising apart sections of the aluminium tent-poles. Unsatisfied with what I counted, I usually assembled the company outside for final inspection before I packed up and set off. On wet mornings this became an arduous exercise, conducted in a bestial, crouching posture, for I could barely sit upright without touching the little pyramid of canvas.

In Balquhidder that morning it poured down. I ate breakfast of rye bread, cold bacon and apples in the church porch and looked at the map, not liking much what I saw.

On the Ordnance Survey of the Highlands the closely-packed loops and whorls of the uninhabited contours resemble enormously magnified colour photographs of finger-prints. On most of the high points are scratchy little lines in black ink that look as if they have been drawn with a corroded steel nib. These are faces or vertical cliffs: *creag* in Gaelic. Above me were far too many *creag* for comfort.

In trying to describe what it felt like to enter the Highlands that day I have the feeling of trying to recapture the beginning of a strange and lonely dream. From Cornwall to Callander I had grown used to my own company; I liked the feeling of being self-contained, but for most of the way I knew that villages were rarely far away. This is not so in the Highlands. I travelled not merely alone, but often without seeing a soul from one desolate glen to another.

Balquhidder lies in a deep valley that runs approximately east and west. To get into the next parallel valley, Glen Dochart, I had the choice of going due north, direct, climbing over the crest of a steep escarpment, or keeping to the road that winds through Glen Ogle, a detour of several miles. In the church porch that morning I vowed that if I could find a direct track anywhere I had done with roads. The rain had ceased; the heights above were misty, but a notice-board at the foot of Kirton Glen pointed boldly to where I wanted to go and, rashly, I took a Forestry Commission sign at its face value.

The outcome is predictable. The old right of way had been turned into a horseshoe-shaped logger's track that climbed up through the trees to a height of about two thousand feet, turned round and, I suppose, came down again. At the apex of this disappointment I tried to get through something that resembled a path and eventually followed a steep burn through a firebreak until I found myself, alone and palely loitering, above the trees, but on the edge of an impressive *creag*. I cursed the Commission, blackly, for this misdirection.

I sat up there for perhaps half an hour until the mist lifted, whereupon, on the very summit of the escarpment, I saw a little lochan, *Eireannaich*, steaming like a cup of tea. This gave me a map reference-point. I edged my way towards the water, worked round it and found a cleft down through the *creag*. Far below, looking vast and uninviting on that grey morning, Glen Dochart extended as far as the eye could see. It began to rain again as I descended, but with visible landmarks I endured the soaking philosophically until I reached a disused railway in the valley, where I sought about for somewhere dry to spend the rest of the day.

Glen Dochart lies across Breadalbane – called *Brid-albin* – a tract of mountainous Perthshire that covers in all about a thousand square miles. It gave noble title to ·the Campbells of Glenorchy and, in particular, to the first and infamous Sir John, author of the Glencoe Massacre, a man described as having neither honour nor religion but where they are mixed with interest. What you notice nowadays is that although the valleys seem fertile there is nobody about: the population has drifted away. Until I reached a hotel in Glencoe the following night I met very few people. 'What did you expect in Campbell country?' asked a West Highlander to whom I related my experience there.

Although it seemed months since I had trod the cinder tracks, the little bridges, the goblin-sized gradient signs and the rusty rails were oddly familiar. At the ghost station of Luib – I repeat that slowly in case you suspect I have invented it, *Luib* meaning the loop – you have the impression that the staff fled before the last train to Crianlarich pulled out. Clearly to be seen through the cracked windows of a Lilliputian left-luggage office are dusty trunks, labelled suitcases, a bundle of fishing-rods and a bicycle with flat tyres. What on earth happened that night when Stationmaster Campbell went home, never to return? Nobody has yet been able to enlighten me.

From Luib you walk on, past a signpost pointing to nothing identifiable called Corriechaorach on the one side of the track and a huge mountain called Stobinian on the other. Between the two, approximately, you will find a plate-layer's cabin with a burnt-out chimney. I confess freely that I burnt it myself, but commend the place still for a decent doss down in the rain.

I turned in there, wet and tired, and lit a fire with those chunky little blocks that keep the rails in place. They blazed briskly and a few minutes later, not to be outdone, the chimney caught fire. Disconcerted, I ran outside and, for lack of water, threw a couple of large wet sods on to the blaze, whereupon what had been no more than a roar in the flue became an enormous and unapproachable smoke generator. It looked as if a new volcano had erupted in Breadalbane. I waited, nervously, until most of the smoke appeared to be coming from the chimney rather than the door, and then went inside, poking about in the grate until the place became moderately habitable. I spent the night there, grilling bits of corned beef on an upturned shovel and reading five-year-old news items from a yellow page of the *Highland News*. I also tried to learn some Gaelic.

This is a useful accomplishment - not for speaking to mono-lingual Gaels. I didn't meet any. Everyone I met, even in the wildest parts of Wester Ross, spoke immaculate English. What the Highland walker needs is a working knowledge of the technical terms used on the Scottish maps. I have mentioned that ominous word *creag* meaning crag or cliff face. Equally dangerous is *coire* or *choire*, a blind valley or corrie that almost invariably leads nowhere except in most cases to a *creag* on the other side.

'Ben' or its Gaelic equivalent *beinn* is, of course, a hill which may be *mor* (big), *beg* (little), *dubh* (black), *rhuadh* (red) and very often *glas* (grey). If the peaks of the mountains (*monadh*) are pointed or spiky at the top, the word to look out for is *sgurr*; less formidable affairs are called *meall*. All this I learnt from an excellent little book called *Gaelic Without Groans*, by John MacKechnie, M.A. It is *gasda* which is good.

By the time I had mastered the little black loch (*chuala*) shaped like a shoe (*cuaran*) I got carried away by some rather esoteric words like ice-cream (*cè reoidhte*), boxing (*dornadh*), radio (*beart dith-dhealgach*) and wet (*fliuch*) pronounced 'floo-chh'. I have particular regard for *fliuch*, since I was so often wet. Unfortunately, until I met a deceptively reticent shepherd on Ben Douran (*Beinn Doireann*) I had no opportunity of exercising the little I had learnt.

I met him the next day. I followed the railway track to Crian-larich where, instead of getting mixed up in the traffic in the trough of Strath Fillan, it takes to the side of the hills, where you can get an eagle's-eye view of the mountains that converge on Glencoe some eighteen miles to the north.

I hailed the shepherd boldly. '*Ciamar a tha sibh?*' I said. How was he? To my consternation, he responded in voluble Gaelic. I took this to mean that on the whole he felt quite well and wanted to know how I was. '*Gasda*,' I said, guardedly, hoping it sounded like pretty good.

He looked puzzled. Obviously I shouldn't have lapsed into English platitudes. I wasn't very well. I looked like a drowned rat.

'*Tha mi fliuch*,' I said, apologetically, adding in about the last phrase in which I had any confidence that I had been walking for a long time. From the way he repeated the word *fliuch* I think he wanted to know why I remained out there in the rain when I might have been in the pub at Bridge of Orchy enjoying myself. Repressing a ridiculous desire to expend my last drop of Gaelic capital and say I had been boxing with an ice-cream, I shrugged my shoulders and looked at the sky. '*Fliuch*,' I said again.

In exquisitely phrased English he said he hadn't much of the Gaelic himself, although his father had encouraged them to speak it at home. Apart from the broadcasts put out by the B.B.C., it was rare, he said, to hear the language spoken. But he hoped I would continue to take an interest in it, as so few people did. 'Goodbye,' he said, politely. 'Goodbye,' I replied. I never tried to speak Gaelic again.

From Ben Douran I went round the western end of Loch Tulla and the great Moor of Rannoch, keeping to a bridle-track until I reached the mountain called the *Buachaille*, the Shepherd, at the entrance to Glencoe. Much of this became a forced march in the sense that I hoped to spend the night warm and dry in the hotel at Inveroran halfway there, but the place had been taken over by a party of fishermen. Madam referred me, apologetically, to the wife of the head keeper at Black Mount, who, she said, might be able to put me up. In a variation of a phrase I had heard before, that stern woman pointed to a little thread of a track that led over the moor and said, 'It's just ten miles,' adding, aggressively, 'Ye shouldnae be aboot the glens if ye've nae car.'

Rannoch Moor puts you in mind of the first act of *Macbeth*. On that wild evening I shouldn't have been in the least surprised to see the witches. Three or four monstrous-looking peaks loomed up from the north-west. They appeared to be constantly changing their relationships, so that I could never be sure how many there were or which was the *Bhuiridh*, on the map the biggest of them all. The moor seems to extend for ever, an expanse without apparent bounds. But it was far from hard going. The track could be relied on and I walked briskly, pausing only to refresh myself from the little streams that poured down into Loch Ba far below. Towards dusk a lemon-yellow shaft of light fell down on the entrance to Glencoe. 'A perfectly terrible place', said Charles Dickens, who thought the glen formed 'such haunts as you might imagine wandering in the very height and madness of a fever.'

Much of the awe is generated, I suppose, by the thoughts of the massacre of 1692, when the wicked Campbells upped and slaughtered their traditional enemies, the Macdonalds, whose hospitality they were enjoying that night. The legend is that for twelve hours the streams of Glencoe ran red with blood.

The facts are that the warring clans were offered a free pardon if by the end of the year they formally submitted in Edinburgh to the rule of William and Mary. Alasdair Macdonald turned up on the last day, but he came to the wrong place and several days elapsed before he could attest his loyalty. This provided the Campbells with a royal excuse to settle an old account with those who had been raiding them for years. Under pretence of friendship - they had been playing cards before they picked up their claymores - they fell on their hosts. As a modern historian, John Prebble, sees the affair, the slaughter, though wholly dishonourable, was grossly exaggerated by Jacobite pamphleteers anxious to put the Hanoverians in a murky light. For all that, about thirty-seven people were hacked to death and some that managed to get away probably died from exposure. William comes out of it pretty badly. It looks as though the Campbell faction induced him to sign a document that ended: 'If . . . that trybe can be well separated from the rest it will be a proper vindication of the public justice.' The massacre was planned at a building in Kinghouses which is now a three-star hotel, and there I spent the night.

The road through Glencoe, one of the wildest-looking glens

accessible to traffic in Scotland, is now, inevitably, a tourist high-way. All day long a procession of coaches and cars rolled along a ribbon of tarmac entirely hemmed in by blue-grey mountains. At the head of the pass is the most famous of all, the great *Buachaille*, the Shepherd, a peak that looked extraordinarily difficult to climb. But even before the morning mists had cleared young men draped in coils of rope hung about, massaging their calves, waiting for a turn on one of the almost vertical ascents. On both sides of the road the peaks are divided by corries that project from the pass like the exposed ribs of a Dover sole.

You can avoid the traffic by climbing up a spectacular zigzag called the Devil's Staircase. By climb I mean trudge, for although this old military road looks perilous, it winds backwards and forwards, ascending gradually to a height of about two thousand feet. There on a bare sandstone shoulder between Glencoe and Loch Leven you are obliged to stop and look around, for on a fine day the vista is full-circle.

It was more than fine that morning. The sun burned down. Lying there, dressed only in shorts and shoes, I looked down on wide splendour.

I am asked, sometimes, what parts of off-beat Scotland can be tackled confidently by those who want to storm mountains without relying too much on maps. I can think of no better walk than the trail north from Crianlarich, around the edge of the Black Mount and Rannoch Moor to Glencoe. Thereafter, the Staircase leads you up onto the roof of Lismore and Appin. There is no arguing with this onward-going track. It knows what it's about. Behind is the hard background to the Campbell affair, an extraordinarily dour landscape which, geologists will tell you, was sculptured by the splash of lava and the effect it had on the surrounding rocks. A mountain slipped onto the vent of an exceptionally big volcano.

Ahead are about a dozen peaks dominated by the snow-capped nipple of Ben Nevis. You can get from Glencoe to Fort William in a vigorous stage of about twenty-four miles, taking in the aluminium plant at Kinlochleven and trusting the well-signposted track to the north of the town. Like the Devil's

Staircase, it starts as a zigzag and then, getting into its stride, it goes on and on, through deserted glens and the overgrown stones of the two-roomed hovels until it meets a road of sorts high above Loch Linnhe. From there it runs down quickly to what the local people still call the Fort.

Fort William still retains something of the atmosphere of a frontier post. Everyone seemed about to be going on somewhere else. The town itself has developed new industries, especially pulp-making. It draws immense power from water that thunders through a conduit buried under Ben Nevis, but, like so much of the west of Scotland, it depends essentially for its livelihood on visitors that come in by car and coach party.

I sought advice about how to work my way round Loch Arkaig and reach the coast opposite the Isle of Skye. A bearded young man in a kilt at the information centre warned me about a number of stages, especially Glen Dessary and Assynt in Sutherland. Assynt I knew about. In my imagination, it had already become the ultimate obstacle, but I had not anticipated trouble in Dessary, which I hoped to reach the following night.

As it looked as if I should be on my own for about eighty miles, I stocked up with several pounds of oatmeal, excellent stuff which can be mixed with water and eaten raw. This is what they call brose, but to make it a bit more palatable I bought some dried fruit, cheese and a few onions. With this I reckoned I could keep going for five days.

Before I set off the following morning I spent an hour in the local museum, a little building, rather dilapidated, but stuffed with unexpected treasure. Here you can find armorial china, ancient weapons, jewellery, spinning wheels, models of the mountains and an illustrated history of the kilt. Perhaps the most strange, certainly the most ingenious, object is a piece of wood about a foot square, splashed with paint, mostly reds and blues, but in no apparent pattern. But when an upright cylinder of steel is placed on the board a portrait of Prince Charlie appears on the polished surface of the metal. This is the famous secret portrait, carried out by his friends after 1745, when it was an offence to possess even a likeness of the Pretender.

Larach, a place that was

THE DEAD VAST

Tremendous landslides have choked the floor of the glen with large, irregular shaped blocks of rock that glint with mica. No trees. No grass. Only rocks sculptured by fire and ice. In places they are piled high, one above the other in chaotic architectural form as though, during a violent spasm, a cathedral had collapsed. This is Glen Dessary, a rift in the edge of Lochaber. *Daysary* the sheep-gatherers say, lingering on that first syllable of desolation, as though it betokened the end of the world. I never saw a wilder glen. Dessary drops down to a fjord-like inlet from the sea called Loch Nevis, opposite the southernmost tip of the Isle of Skye.

To reach that wild glen from Fort William I walked up the Caledonian Canal for about eight miles and then struck west, along the shores of Loch Arkaig, where the air is lightly scented with birch. At dusk or, indeed, at any time this is a beautiful loch. Red pine and still water with a back-drop of hills. I rested there that night, watching the rings of rising trout until it grew too dark to see. The next morning, early, I entered Dessary.

Squeezing in and out of the rocks wondering, apprehensively, if I had strayed into an unmapped corrie, I came up against a coarse grey boulder that appeared to be spattered with drops of blood. Surprised, I fingered the surface to find that the rosettes,

203

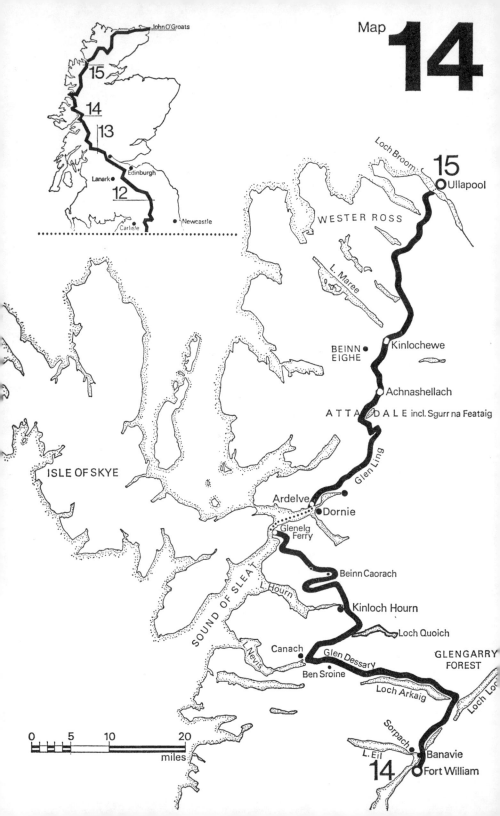

Map **14**

John O'Groats

15

14

13

12

Lanark • Edinburgh

Newcastle

Carlisle

Loch Broom

WESTER ROSS

15
○ Ullapool

L. Maree

BEINN
EIGHE • ○ Kinlochewe

○ Achnashellach

A T T A D A L E incl. Sgurr na Feataig

Glen Ling

ISLE OF SKYE

Ardelve •
○ Dornie

Glenelg
Ferry

Beinn Caorach •

SOUND OF SLEAT

L. Hourn

Kinloch Hourn

Loch Quoich

Canach •
Glen Dessary

GLENGARRY
FOREST

Nevis

Ben Sroine •

Loch Arkaig

Loch Lochy

Sorpach

0   5   10   20
miles

L. Eil

14
○ Fort William

Banavie

each about the size of a shilling, were composed of wine-coloured crystals. They were garnets and in the half light of dawn the impression was of a colossus. You could imagine an immense statue of a leopard carved out and inlaid by some ancient race. With some difficulty I knocked out a handful of small treasure. Looking at them, munching a mouthful of moistened oatmeal garnished with raw onion, I began to weep like a child. Even today my eyes tingle at the thought of onions and oatmeal, diluted as they were that day with a little Scotch and Dessary. But to return to the garnets.

In the glen miles away I talked to a morose old man busy gathering sheep into what in the west is called a *fangh*, a handling-pen. He had, as they say, the Gaelic, or at least enough to disconcert strangers. He said something incomprehensible. I shook my head. I could foresee the complications. In perfectly good English he then asked what I was doing in the glens and what I found of interest there. I shrugged my shoulders and for want of better excuse I showed him the garnets. 'Foul slewy,' he said, or something like it. So what, I thought. They're not worth much. I knew that. But what in fact he'd said, I discovered later, was *Fuil nan sluagh*, meaning the Blood of the Hosts.

In the Highlands there is an old legend that at death the souls of fighting men are gathered up into the air, where for years they are cast backwards and forwards, over the hills like migratory birds, unable to gain peace until they make expiation for their sins on earth. Sometimes on windy nights they can be heard fighting high up in the scudding clouds, and in the morning the rocks are spotted with blood.

Dessary is reckoned to be one of the most complicated geological formations in Britain. Earth movements over a period of many millions of years have folded the rocks back on themselves; those that were originally lying flat have been up-ended, bent into the shape of a horseshoe and turned over so that now only the stumps of their feet are exposed. The walker is obliged to make elaborate detours, and five hours elapsed before I reached the narrow arm of the sea at Loch Nevis. Should you venture into that dead vast I warn you, solemnly, to watch out for the deceptively simple outlines of a mountain called *Sroine*. It lies foursquare across the glen and beckons seductively towards Loch Morar, an easy primrose path into a *cul-de-sac*. The route is to the north-west of that peak. I mention these pedestrian pitfalls, hopeful that one day there will be a track through the length of the Highlands.

At Finiskaig on Loch Nevis the shallow water is tufted with salty samphires and glassworts and there an eagle rose, startled at my approach, clutching something alive and dangling from extended talons. A rabbit, it seemed, or maybe a young hare. With easy wing-beats it gained height rapidly, making for a cliff face. At this two ravens pitched off a pinnacle and attacked it in mid-air. One robber kept to short-range tactics, pecking, fluttering, seeking to distract the laden bird while the other repeatedly swooped down from on high. The grunts and barks sounded dog-like. The result, I thought, was a foregone conclusion. Surely the hard-pressed bird would drop its prey, but with occasional side-slipping movements and an almost leisurely swerve of great wings the eagle seemed strangely unconcerned. All three birds passed out of sight behind the cliff, where for several minutes I could still hear the clamour. Eagles, they say, can lift ten pounds in weight: one was seen to carry a struggling wild cat to a height of fifteen hundred feet before dropping it to its death on the rocks below.

Keeping to the edge of the salt marsh for about a mile, I struck north, up yet another narrow cleft, this time the gulley of a cascade called the Carnach, hoping to reach Glen Barrisdale before the night fell. In this glen the walls are richly clothed in trees, especially rowan and birch. On drier ground, standing tall and aloof, are stands of old Scots pine, their trunks as red as Celtic gold. Among them I came at last to the track I sought, an old drove-road, cut into the face of the glen, hundreds of feet above the furious water. In places where the gorge narrows and winds round the feet of towering cliffs, the marvel is that herds of cattle could be driven without frequent casualties.

Some of the high platforms have been washed away. The walker finds that what look like short-cuts across rocky meanders progressively deteriorate, leading nowhere. Time and time again I turned back, clambering down into the stream bed, where, eventually, I became resigned to laborious progress among stern rocks in the torrent.

This is red deer country. Groups of hinds with scampers of fawns at foot grazed unconcernedly in meander pastures where, thanks to the down-wind and the thunder of the stream, I often saw them before they scented me. Usually the alarm came not from the herd, but from an old matriarch, isolated on sentinel duty high above the river. The short, explosive bark was repeated first by one hind and then another until a dozen animals with forelegs partly raised for a quick get-away swung round in my direction. And then off they ran with youngsters protectively encircled. Bits of shale tinkled down the slope long after they had gone.

Although the sexes congregate only for about six weeks in each year, red deer are intensely social animals. The stags have a club life of their own. On high crests at sundown I got a glimpse of heavily-antlered animals in dramatic postures. But never near at hand and I often wondered where they went during the day.

I had reason that night to wonder where I was going myself, for I missed the track to Barrisdale and felt tired. Instead of trying to climb out of the glen, I swung east and followed a tributary of the Carnach to the head of Loch Quoich. There I settled down to a nourishing if uninspiring meal of oatmeal and raisins. I lit a fire for company, but put it out before I went to sleep.

Throughout the night came the sound of gentle squeaks and blabbering noises. The deer were talking to each other. I had pitched down where the tent would be least conspicuous and this proved rewarding at dawn when, by peering through a gap in the fastening, I had an intimate view of their family life.

Half a dozen fawns scampered about like lambs, chasing each other, butting and frolicking, racing up and down hillocks, often falling flat on their noses. The games were broken off, temporarily, when they returned to the hinds for yet another suck. And then off they went again. Like lambs, too, they were disposed to bounce into the air as if on springs. Or else they sniffed at the dewy sedge grass or rolled over, kicking legs that seemed too spindly to support them.

I guessed that the majority of youngsters were no more than eight or ten days old. Deer are usually born at the beginning of June and remain hidden in the bracken for a day or two until they move on with the rest of the herd. In between gambolling and feeding they are licked vigorously by the hinds, usually about the eyes and ears, an action that appears to give both parties intense pleasure, the calves particularly, since they almost invariably lift up their muzzles for more. As the light increased and loud wails from either grebe or loon rang out from the misty surface of the loch, the deer moved off up the glen and I started another day.

Loch Quoich is a water-store, one of the many topped to the brim by the Scottish Board, and what appeared to be a maintenance road, a relic of the days when they built the dam, follows the shore-line. Along this well-found path I strode happily, singing, hoping it went on for miles. But before long the track swung round and plunged down into the depths of the loch where I could see it shimmering bright green beneath the water. The water-level had been raised; the old shore-line had gone and the road had gone with it. This left me stranded on the braeside, unable even to make my way along peaty banks heavily under-cut by chattering wavelets. Unwilling to go back, I struck inland, following a stream that took me up on to the roof of the brae. How I got down by wading through a bog on the other side is painful even to recall. The sphagnum wasn't deep. But the place was lonely. And there was nothing ahead I could recognize. I had the feeling that I had strayed into an entirely unmapped, un-known corner of Inverness-shire. Bird cries still rang from the invisible loch. Above them I heard other sounds: deep and throaty, like the lowing of cows. It was, in fact, a large herd of Highland cattle grazing behind the brae ahead and at the sight of a man in what I had taken to be an uninhabited corner of the Highlands they came lumbering up at the double. I couldn't shake them off. They followed me and by following their well beaten track through the moss I came at last to Kinloch Hourn, the loch of Hell.

Each chapter of what I have written brings together a portion of Britain as I experienced it. Looking back on the regions – Devon and Cornwall, the Welsh marches, the Midlands, the Pennines and the Border – each now becomes an entity remembered. The Highlands are much less of a piece entire, for in places the hazards were greater than I had experienced and I became largely preoccupied with route-seeking through what seemed to be a tremendous void.

In two days I made about sixty miles, that is from Dessary and Carnach to Quoich and then up and over the hills that lie between Loch Hourn and Glenelg to the narrow strip of water beneath the mountains of Skye. From Hourn you climb through a rich man's estate called I have forgotten what, although I remember clearly the azaleas and the eucalyptus trees, a testimony to the warm current that sweeps into the west coast of Scotland. For four or five hours the going was hard but uncomplicated, a rare pleasure in upland country with no especial grain, but at the foot of *Beinn nan Caorach*, the Mountain of the Sheep, I had to choose between narrow alternatives and I chose wrongly.

The light that pours down on those high tops has a super-transparent quality. It makes peaks look nearer than they are. Even to avoid gross error on open ground you have to watch both map and compass constantly. *Caorach*, like *Sroine*, beckons from afar. You walk up to it with confidence, only to discover that the mountain is one of several scattered about in less orderly fashion than would appear from the map. A deviation of only a few degrees here and you will find yourself, as I did, on the brink of a dizzy drop down into Glen Arnisdale about a thousand feet below. I pulled up hard and turned back, adding another four or five miles to that long day's stint. Keeping to the east of *Caorach*, I took a chance and scaled an immense corrie where, once over the top, I coasted downhill for seven miles. And, as it proved, in the right direction. Thereafter I relaxed and looked around, for even on bare open ground there is always more going on than one expects to find.

Flying rapidly over the dewy grass were specimens of that most adventurous of British butterflies, the Painted Lady. These long-distance travellers breed on the edge of the Sahara. They cross the Mediterranean, winging their way, purposively, through the passes of the Alps and the Pyrenees, stopping only to lay eggs, from whence come fresh broods. These fly on, across the Channel, advancing steadily towards Scotland and the most northern isles. Those on *Caorach* were still flying north, impelled by that urge called instinct for want of better explanation.

The plants of the high tops are modest, retiring but jewel-like in their solitary settings. Saxifrages, bedstraws and speedwells looked out from the most ungenerous soil, whilst on bare shale the butterworts opened greasy green leaves to the sun. The plants resemble starfish. The leaves are covered in mucilage; they curl inwards to trap and digest insects that alight on them. I unrolled several to disclose a host of Lilliputian wasps, fruit-flies and midges, all dead in the clasp of the carnivorous vegetable. The law that governs life here is simple but exacting: plants and animals must be able to withstand extremes of weather. In winter the ground is frozen; in summer it bakes and in between times, probably for most of the year, the hills are thrashed by gales. Plants can survive only by cultivating thick skins, cushion-like growth forms or furtive, strictly economical habits. If they are pollinated by insects and not by the wind they must stand out star-bright and offer reward to the moth or fly that gently strokes their anthers.

As with plants, so too with animals. For shelter and insulation, hares, foxes and ptarmigan are competent to dig holes in the snow. The deer move down into the glens. In days when the Celts buried their dead on islands to keep them from wolves, the deer were creatures of the forest. Now the forests that clothed the Highlands have disappeared. Men burnt them down. The dead vast is not so much the product of climate as of man's hand and of the insatiable appetite of his domesticated animals. Only the relics remain.

In lodgings behind an outcrop of Torridonian sandstone I came across three of the oldest inhabitants: three old pine trees had

lived there together since the Act of Union and it seemed that
when the wind passed through them they sighed.

Throughout the West Highlands human habitation has
vanished almost as if it had never been. The word for these imprints of wrecked homesteads is *larach*, literally the site, the place
where something was and is no longer. Time and again I struck
out for a locality named on the map, hoping to find at least a
cottage, only to discover a little pile of stones or, nearer the
Glenbeg River, where the soil is richer, a bed of nettles and no
stones. Everything else had been carted away. *Larach* stands
testimony to that most terrible of Highland events, the evictions.

After the inglorious and wholly unsuccessful Jacobite rebellion
of 1745, led by Charles Edward Stuart, the Bonnie Prince, the
clan system was torn to shreds, the Highlanders disarmed. They
were forbidden even to wear kilt or tartan. The chiefs, their
hereditary lords, the central figures of complex patriarchal
societies became business-men. Tradition and successful business
rarely go amicably hand in hand. The chiefs replaced their cattle
with sheep and turned out tenants, the majority of them small-
holders, to make room for animals that could look after themselves. 'Lochaber no more' sang the emigrants as they set sail for
Nova Scotia. 'I'll never, I'll never, I'll never return.' And return
they never did, for there was little or nothing to return to. Their
homes were burnt down and the stone used for sheep-pens. Only
the *larach* remains. And 'the world is strewn with shingle from
the dwellings of the past.'

On the map the west coast of Scotland has a distinctly dissi-
pated appearance. It is slashed by rivers and sea lochs and dotted
with islands. This natural violence has been wreaked by that great
ridge called the Drum Albyn, the spine of the highlands. Far
from being a central feature like the Pennines, it lies to the west and,
as I discovered in Dessary, it sometimes lies within only a few
miles of the sea. The rivers here are short and turbulent, but with
the strength of countless thousands of burns they have torn the
coast to shreds.

You sense the upsweep of Drum Albyn from the brow of
the corrie behind *Caorach*. The impression is of a wave that

mounts majestically, attains full stature and rolls on, less steep, but undiminished in vigour. It carries you into a cleft between *Sgurr Dearg* and *Creagan Dubh*, where a stream takes up the momentum, plunging on, over waterfalls, round the foot of Ben Chappail and down to the gentle meanders of the Glenbeg River.

There in the Forest of Ellanreach is larch and oak and the thin clamour of wrens. I walked on, marvelling at the splendid light. Ahead, appearing starkly black against the sinking sun, were the peaks of Skye. Within an hour I hoped to be in the coastal village of Glenelg and might have been there earlier but for the great brochs that loomed out of the dusk.

Brochs or, as they used to call them, Pictish towers, are fortified homesteads, the refuges of the Iron Age people that lived in the north and the west over two thousand years ago. Originally about fifty feet in height, these great towers are roughly cylindrical, but pinched in towards the top. The walls are hollow. They are nearly vertical inside, but incurved externally, the two faces being tied together by horizontal slabs used as an internal spiral staircase. Today, they are hung about with ivy and tenanted only by owls and redstarts.

From their resemblance to the Cornish forts built to protect the tin trade, brochs were thought to be the homes of chieftains who fled north when they were repeatedly attacked from the Continent. Recent excavations suggest that the towers are a very sophisticated form of local architecture, a development perhaps of the wheel-house and the hill-fort. Brochs could be built without scaffolding – that is, by masons standing inside the hollow, economical walls. In times of trouble the inhabitants and their flocks could resist almost any form of assault except fires lit against the walls or a burning brand tossed into the open top of the tower.

A forester offered me a bed in Glenelg, a luxury which I accepted gratefully, for my feet were bruised by the scramble down from *Caorach* and I had lost a couple of toe-nails. The next day I intended to walk round the headland and slip across Loch Duich to Ardelve on the ferry, but halfway there the local postman told me that in a brave gesture of solidarity the boatman at Totaig, alone, had joined in the national strike of seamen. Fed-up with it all, I turned back to see what I could charter in Glenelg.

It began to rain, first lightly and then with spite. There is something about Skye and the Sound of Sleat that attracts the most baleful clouds in the north Atlantic. In Glenelg it had been raining for days, although up in the hills I had experienced nothing but sunshine. It rained as I bargained with a rather furtive character outside the pub. I may be prejudiced about everything that happened that day, for the boatman swindled me and, still smarting from this hurt, I got bitten by a dog. In the Sound of Sleat it never rains; it pours.

'Not *varra* guid the morn,' he said as we chugged away from the pier. And even without knowing what I was in for I agreed.

In fact, I enjoyed the trip, since we cruised between the points where in the great days of the droves the cattle were induced to swim across the Sound of Sleat. Each year about six thousand beasts passed between Skye and the mainland. They were shipped to Skye from the Outer Hebrides and driven into the water at places opposite Glenelg and Bernera. Ferrymen tied a noose around the animal's lower jaw which, in turn, was tied to the tail of the animal in front. When they were linked up, one behind the other, a man in a rowing boat towed the great horned beasts across the narrow channel with its surging, river-like currents. What a sight it must have been to have seen them in the water.

There were complaints from dealers that some animals had to be sold with their tails missing. Others gored each other on the voyage over from the Outer Isles. But by far the majority reached the trysts of Crieff and Falkirk intact. Great drovers, men like Thomas Bell, Cameron of Corriechoillie and McTurk, were known throughout the Highlands for their integrity. They suffered tremendous setbacks from Border rievers and from pestilence, but on their own they were adept at getting their charges through the most difficult places. Even so, things some-times went wrong. In a letter to his partner after one disastrous trek south, Thomas Bell wrote: 'I am positive we have lost three thousand pounds already. I shall be home at Candlemass and people may do with me as they will. They shall get every groat we have and we can do no more.'

Towards sundown that night I sat on a ledge, filling in my diary for want of something better to do. The incident of the boatman, the dogs, even the long haul up Glen Ling became trivialities, something scarcely worthwhile putting down, even for the sake of continuity. What concerned me urgently was that, without either map or binoculars, I had got on to the crest of *Sgurr na Feataig*, from which there appeared to be no way down. And a cloud made it impossible to see for more than a few yards ahead. The old story and this is how it happened:

A mile off Eilean Donnan, once the stronghold of the Sea-forths and now the most photographed castle in Britain, that damned Glenelg boatman demanded double the agreed dues, the price, I suppose of hiring blackleg labour. Arguments led to threats to knock him overboard, an unheroic gesture on this party's part, since he was rather a small man. Unamicable settlement with shouting on the quayside. There must be better ways of entering Ross and Cromarty.

From Ardelve, the centre of a clover leaf of lochs - Alsh, Duich and Long - I slouched north-east to Nonach on the advice of a village constable who said his very, very old friend there, the keeper of the big estate, would put me right in no time at all. The keeper wasn't at home, but his dogs were, and what seemed at first to be a particularly friendly black-and-white sheepdog, one of several, ensured remembrance by battening on to my left calf. I beat him off with a Japanese camera and ran off until I remembered I ought to be limping. Exuberant bleeding, but no evidence of torn muscle. I plastered myself up and followed the River Ling for miles and miles until it got lost in a *dubh*, or black water - that is, a stream which winds through peat hags. That night I hoped to be in the little hamlet of Achnashellach, no great distance ahead, but detached from me by a range to the west that could only be scaled by mounting an impressive corrie.

June 11: Seems I'm stuck on this damned ledge for the night. Followed R. Ling into tree-lined gulley. Discovered too late that map and field-glasses had fallen from ripped jacket pocket. Went back. Unable to find them. Abandoned stream for 1,000-ft. contour and descended to eerie-looking Loch Laoigh. Mounted corrie, remembering what I could to track bearing. Reached crest to discover northern face drops sheer. Looks foul. Sought about for path down to the east. Found new-born deer shivering in hollow. Fur wet. Seems unable to stand. Cloud blew across like smoke. Visibility about 10 ft. Am staying until it lifts. . . .

It lifted suddenly. A puff of wind and I found myself in the rubescent light of the setting sun, apparently isolated on a long, narrow ridge. Far below on both sides a second layer of cloud hid the valley floor. I packed up and approached the edge. It seemed less steep higher up, but before I made more than a few hundred yards the cloud rolled over again.

After two or three rounds of nebulous hide-and-seek, it became apparent that the clouds were unlikely to cover me for long and that in between times I could look for somewhere to get down. To my dismay, the ridge narrowed and, in places, fell away, vertical. What I had taken to be a slope turned out to be a scree, too unstable to be scrambled down. A flock of ptarmigan pitched off a hair-thin ridge, making an odd belching noise. Hinds scampered ahead. I reasoned, unreasonably, that if they could get up there I should be able to get down.

In an ample *cirque*, about a mile from where I had climbed up, I found a zigzag that apparently went down for ever. No deer track this. Each zig matched the zag immediately below: a fine piece of hillside engineering carried out, I liked to imagine, by some mathematically-minded Pict or *broch*-builder. I went down singing what I could remember of the Eighteenth Psalm, especially that bit about 'my God, have I leaped over a wall'.

Towards dusk the rim of the cloud layer below became rose-pink. Out of that highly chromatic cotton-wool a bird - a hawk of some kind - appeared for an instant. It circled once or twice and then sank back again, like the fin of a fish seen through the ice of a pond. Soon after I edged into the layer myself to find it even danker and darker than I feared. A step off the track brought me to the edge of something that fell away into the gloom.

Imagining precipices on all sides, I put up my tent and settled down in more comfort than I deserved.

> *June 12:* Awoke to find I had slept on a track about a mile from Achnashellach Railway Station. Am undaunted by lack of valour, since ridge behind looks far steeper than it did from the top. Bitten calf looks a bit puffy, but apparently not symptom of sepsis, as other calf looks even puffier. Waded across river to Youth Hostel for breakfast, where agreeable young man in charge accompanied me to Beinn Eighe Nature Reserve, about twelve miles away. Treated myself to half-day holiday to brace up for what looks like arduous eagle-watching exercise tomorrow.

The day came and went without hazard, but not without sweat, for we travelled a long way, the warden and I. Richard Balharry, a tough young Scot who looks after the Reserve, guided me from Kinlochewe, his station headquarters, to the foot of the Dundonnell Forest, a transect through much of Wester Ross. He took short-cuts through the back-stairs of the hills, squeezing into gullies I might never have found on my own. When he left me at a place where a Land-Rover picked him up and took him home, I went on by myself less certainly to the shores of Loch Broom opposite Ullapool, covering in all that day about twenty-eight miles. Looking back on the occasion, it becomes for once direct, relatable narrative instead of a series of dramatic episodes. I had become tired of path-finding. All the pleasure of pioneering had drained away; I wanted nothing more than to conserve what energy and enthusiasm I had left for the one remaining obstacle ahead, the crossing of Assynt. Anyone can go twist or bust, irrationally, on the last hand of the evening, but, as I saw it, the cards were still being dealt out, slowly.

Dick Balharry led me through peaks that seemed to be topped by snow. This is gleaming white Cambrian quartzite, splendid to look at from a distance, but sadly lacking in the stuff that makes soil. Yet in Dundonnell there are glimpses of what Scotland looked like when the great Wood of Caledon, perhaps the biggest pine forest in Europe, stretched from coast to coast.

With the exception of Scots pine, the trees of the glens,

especially the birches, the alders and rowan, are a pliant, wind-tormented lot; they are built to bend before and not stand up to the gales. By contrast, the pines are rock-hard and anchored deep in the ground. They have a trunk like the foremast of a sailing ship, golden-red at the cross-trees, a colour perfectly offset by the bottle-green foliage. Altogether a noble tree. Nothing else in the streets of the mountains gives such a sense of pageantry. They have about them the quality of a bugle blast.

The Vikings started to fire this forest, and the custom was taken up by everyone else who roamed here in the days of the early Scottish kings. In the seventeenth and eighteenth centuries iron-smelters helped to create the wilderness by prodigious felling. The sad few trees that remained blazed furiously at a touch from the fire-sticks of the flock-masters at the coming of the sheep. The Nature Conservancy is now charitably warding pockets of these coniferous Old Contemptibles in the hope that by studying their decline and fall they may one day be made to grow again.

With the brash insistence of the visitor who wants to know everything at once, I asked Balharry about his local parishioners: the herds of unharassed deer, the pine martens that rustled about in the woods above Loch Maree, and especially about eagles. There are over twenty pairs in the neighbourhood, some in the Reserve itself.

He knew them intimately, for it was part of his job to protect the birds and learn something about their habits. On misty days he sometimes climbed up to within a few feet of the eyries to see what their youngsters were being fed on. He said they are largely eaters of carrion, although during the eaglet-feeding season they may take an occasional grouse, ptarmigan or other live animal. Unless they are obliged to range far for food, they spend much of their time sitting up on pinnacles like vultures, just watching what goes on below.

I thought it strange that he could approach their nurseries without getting scalped, but he said romantic stories about birds attacking intruders are - unfortunately - untrue. He had never heard of anyone being attacked and he had been brushed by their pinions as they swept down to land. As the birds are still being persecuted and their eggs stolen, they might be better off if they lived up to their reputation for ferocity.

In Wester Ross you are affected by the sense of sterilized grandeur. Postcard scenery attracts the coach parties and the climbers. It has enabled the Nature Conservancy to do what it likes with a large piece of land cheaply acquired. Parts of Inverness-shire and Sutherland are as wild as Ross, but they seem burnt out, dead. Short of a miracle, you can't imagine anything bringing them back to life. This is not the impression in Ross. Notwithstanding the centuries of devastation, the land, you feel, is ready to burst into life. The woods in the glens, the pastures moistened by the Atlantic, all seem potentially fertile. The sad thing is there is nobody there to get on with the job of restoration. Ross is deserted.

Walking on the high track that leads down to Loch Broom, you come across the wrecked shells of black-houses, the hovels in which the Highlanders lived until they were driven out to make room for sheep. They were built without a chimney: a hole in the roof served as vent for the peat smoke from the mid-floor hearth. They had minute window-niches or none; the walls were three feet thick and only a low partition separated the living-room from the byre. Without communal heat from man and beast, the cold would have been insupportable in such primitive dwellings. In almost every instance they were sited where they trapped the warmth from the midday winter sun, usually on some height or slope, free from the mists and in summer the mosquitoes. These were the homes of the people to whom the romantic tradition of the Highlands has been attached.

They were a people who were always faithful to their chieftains, fighting for them, honouring them in death. In 1830, when Lady Mackenzie of Gairloch died in childbirth, it was decided that her burial-place must be Beauly on the east coast. There were no roads for wheels, so word went round the parish commanding the attendance of all men between the ages of twenty and thirty. About a thousand, they say, came, of whom five hundred were chosen and divided into four companies. In the

Quartzite-topped heights of Beinn Eighe

first company every man was over six feet tall, but in the others, as Eric Linklater recounts the story, were little fellows of five foot nine or so. They took it in turns to carry the bier, eight men at a time, and on the first day they marched twenty miles, and on the second forty, leaving only nine miles for the day of the funeral. Food for the five hundred was carried in creels on led horses, and they found straw for their beds at night. They marched in silence, all in their Sunday-best clothes. And when they had carried the dead lady over the hills and buried her, they returned home again. Not a man, they say, fell out.

> *June 13:* Left Balharry in Dundonnell. Struck out for place on south-western shore of Loch Broom where he thought I ought to be able to pick up ferry for Ullapool. Arrived at dusk. The cliff-tops, the last reputed breeding-place of the sea-eagle looked like the edge of the world. Immense vista, crinkly sea, toothy-looking rocks and islands in a Wagnerian sunset. Lights of what I took to be the very best Ullapool restaurants just visible on the opposite shore, but they might as well be a thousand miles away as there's no bloody ferry. Local Charon seems to have gone on strike with that pal of his in Totaig. May their bowels bust! And all those who have to do with marine transport. Place deserted. Bathed feet. Two more toenails missing. But still got six. Mooched about, looking for somewhere to sleep. Came across partly-constructed dream house of man who was building it for his ailing wife. Hospitably received by them both and crossed the loch next morning in boat carrying their workmen.

Ullapool is a bright little port that has gone over to tourism, lock, stock and what used to be the fish-barrel. Nowadays the boats take visitors round the islands. Everyone seems to be doing fine. You can't see the quay for the cars, and there are queues for the boats and almost everything else.

Thurso in Viking country

OUTERMOST GAELDOM

Moir had advised me to start climbing out of the West Highlands at a hamlet about twenty-five miles away called Inchnadamph. Once there he recommended a route north-east, over the shoulder of Ben Mor Assynt and then down to the flat country beyond by Loch Shin. Everyone I talked to seemed to think that Assynt was by far the biggest obstacle I should be likely to encounter. Nasty country, they said. Solid rock for the most part. Uncharitable stuff. But when I got over the range there was absolutely nothing to 't. I asked them to say it again for, God knows, I needed a bit of comfort. I felt tired and depressed. The problem wasn't so much physical wear and tear as lack of drive. The main spring had gone slack. In a deck-chair on the beach at Ullapool the question was whether to get it over and done with by belting along to where the climb began. Or play it cool and hole up somewhere. At this point I went to sleep, for I felt extraordinarily tired.

I slept for three hours and then made for Inchnadamph. The route is across country, to Strath Kannaird and then up the main road north into Sutherland. You can't avoid the highway for it takes advantage of all the available gaps in the range. At Isle Martin it plunges down to the sea and then swings up again, up through the Cromalt Hills, always north, boring through a series of deep cuttings of rusty Torridonian sandstone. Skittering over bogs on

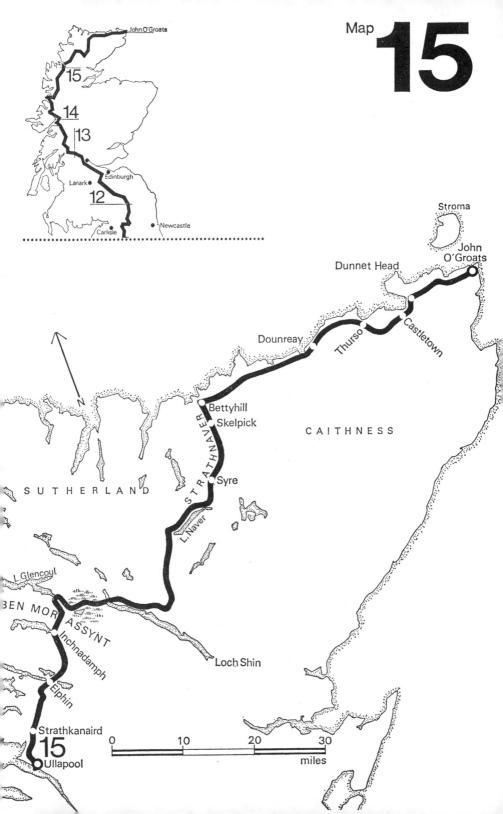

Map **15**

John O'Groats

15

14

13

Lanark •   • Edinburgh

12

Carlisle •   • Newcastle

Stroma

John O'Groats

Dunnet Head

Thurso   Castletown

Dounreay

Bettyhill

Skelpick

CAITHNESS

N

STRATHNAVER

SUTHERLAND

Syre

L. Naver

L. Glencoul

BEN MOR ASSYNT

Inchnadamph

Loch Shin

Elphin

Strathkanaird

15

Ullapool

0   10   20   30

miles

ferro-concrete stilts, the highway ignores mere depressions. It cuts through the death-grey Cambrian limestone, the silvery-white Moine schists and rocks which are as old as any in Europe. Here, bunched together, is the whole geological history of Scotland. And through it all goes the road, a good road as roads go. The traffic is tremendous. Coaches, cars and trailers roar past, often nose to tail, a curious sight in a country with enormous views and next to no resident population. Nobody stops until they reach the little shacks among the caravan sites where the cottagers sell tea and postcards.

'Got to get to Cape Wrath tonight,' said the man with the boiling radiator. I didn't ask why, because he might well have asked me the same question.

On the River Kannaird I got into strange argument about the sexuality of mayflies with three unusually masculine-looking women in waders who had been fishing the pool above Blughasary. 'Is this a female?' one of them asked, producing a specimen with three tails. And all I could say was that it looked that way although the sexes were sometimes a bit confused.

At dusk three V-shaped flights of grey lag geese honked across the sky in a formation that resembled sergeant's stripes. At Sassunaich you enter Sutherland, the southland of the Vikings where, due to the undulatory nature of the road in relation to the surrounding country, strange *things* begin to loom up ahead. Some resemble the heads of armed men. Or demons. They rise up and then seem to sink down again. These apparitions are the topmost peaks of distant hills. There is Suilven, which is a piece of the ground floor of Gaeldom, and Canisp, a curiously-shaped mountain that rises from a black bog, and Quinag with three peaks of white quartzite. They seem isolated, and all rather eerie.

At Elphin, a village only in name, the occupants of a few cars and caravans were whooping it up around the noisy light of a primus stove. They sang the *Cooper o' Fife* and the *Ball of Kirriemuir*, but without much enthusiasm. Two American girls detached themselves with some difficulty from amorous youths on motor-cycles. They were anxious that I should not think they were really complaining about the simple ardour of Gaels.

'Nothing *wrong* with them,' as one of them put it, 'but I guess your town boys are steadier.'

Late that night I got within five miles of Inchnadamph and looked for somewhere to sleep. A hillock beside a stream seemed pleasant enough, but the sight of a man putting up a tent drew first one caravan and then two more off the road. I had started yet another little colony.

Unfortunately, I had chosen a very bad site. It hummed, not only with mosquitoes, but black-flies, a little needle-point-sized creature said to be responsible for the Highland fling. Hoping that the caravanners wouldn't think it downright unsociability on my part, I packed up and went higher up the braeside. They watched me go. I turned round and waved my hands, violently, trying to give the impression that I was swotting at flies, but at that distance it probably looked like an abusive gesture.

Jimmie Mackenzie, a man with the imposing, the almost Oriental title of Keeper of Inchnadamph, said it was not, as he put it, 'the *very* best of days to cross Assynt'. What he meant was he couldn't see anything from his back garden, even with the aid of an enormous brass telescope. The hills were covered in a tablecloth of mist. 'Conditions,' as he put it, '*could* have been a wee bit better.' I dozed. He went out at intervals to look at the sky.

'Aye,' he kept saying. 'Aye, aye. Nae sae guid.' He even showed no noticeable surprise when, after a long period of silence, I drifted off into rude but quite irrepressible sleep. I had been on the go since five o'clock.

'Very tiring in the hills,' he observed.

Did he know of anybody who would be prepared to act as a guide? There'd be nobody about that day, he said. Should I go on by myself? Wait for a couple of hours, he advised. It was thundery weather. If the wind backed, it would probably rain, hard. But there was a chance, he thought, that the mist would be blown away by an easterly breeze.

If it shifted, he recommended a route up the gulley behind the Inchnadamph Hotel. He thought I should stick to the higher ground, avoiding the gorge, bearing north until, as he put it, I could get up to where there was something substantial to be seen.

He gave me the compass directions and names of corries and lochs in Gaelic. For those tempted to try this crossing on a wet day the way is by way of *Cnoc an Droighinn* to the head of *Allt Tarsuinn* towards *Loch nan Cuaran* and *Gorm Mor*, skirting *Cnoc an Fhurain Bhain* and *Creagan Reamhar* to Corrieakin. In plain English, the best thing to do is to keep pretty close to a line drawn between the Inchnadamph Hotel and the north-west corner of Loch Shin. In all about nine miles on the map, but three times that distance on foot.

In what seemed to be a nod of divine approval, a light breeze sprang up. One peak after another appeared mistily, as through a veil. Clearly, the time had come to go. With the assurance that with four hours of fine weather the worst ridge could be easily got over, I left the Mackenzies for the take-off point behind the hotel.

You climb up a sheep track for about two miles, mounting steadily, keeping to the contours of *Droighinn* to avoid the twists and turns of the stream in the gorge below. I sweated profusely. It felt sultry. The storm still hung about and though it was mistier there than I had anticipated I assumed hopefully that peaks hidden behind a distant bluff were still visible. At about twelve hundred feet it brightened up, and so did I. The top of the corrie appeared just where I had been told it would, and I looked out for the little lochan, *Cuaran*, on top of the ridge. To celebrate at what seemed at least Camp One, I sat down and had a drink, a remarkably untimely celebration as it turned out.

The track let me down disgracefully – or rather I disgraced myself by hurrying along, almost trotting at a time when I should have trodden more carefully on the loose stones underfoot. In fact, I was staring ahead at that most nebulous of opponents, a wall of mist or cloud. I could see it rolling down – not fast, but implacably, blotting out everything it touched. I reckoned, wrongly, that if I hurried I could get round the neck of the corrie and on to firmer ground before it enveloped me.

Something gave way underfoot. I lost my balance and slid down about thirty feet of scree. No damage. I was scarcely scratched. The rucksack acted as a toboggan, but there I was, on the banks of a stream that fell over the edge of a cliff. Frightened? I was terrified. But what do you do? Bawl for help? There wasn't a soul for miles. I don't know what the professional does on such an occasion. What I did was to collect and try to identify all the little plants within an arm's reach. I could make nothing of the mosses, grasses and liverworts, but the purple-flowered plants with heather-like leaves were clearly saxifrages. There was also moss campion, burnet rose, Alpine cinquefoil and some curious little things called spleenworts. A rich flora which has something to do with the limestone piled around the lower slopes. Further up, as I discovered, the rocks are composed of gneiss as bare as bone.

The mist still hung about. It can't go on like this for long, I thought. But it did. For perhaps two hours. And then some thrice-blessed visibility. Enough at least to see for about fifty yards. I couldn't move more than a few feet without starting a little avalanche of gravel, but there seemed no alternative but to go on, again, upwards, laboriously. Keeping an eye on the compass, I moved around the ridge, looking for the little loch that marked the divide.

Curious lightning effects caused the mist to flicker like a faulty fluorescent tube. This happened two or three times. I stopped, expecting a fearful crash of thunder. Instead, more flickers. The crags stood out, momentarily. And then from far, far away came a noise more like a groan than thunder.

The sole of one of my shoes became detached at the toe and I tried to sew it up with waxed thread, using a flat stone to push the needle into the sodden leather. The marvel is they had lasted so long. I scrambled on, uncomfortably, keeping to a strict compass course, swinging off only when the ground dipped or rose more steeply than I felt competent to tackle in the gloom. I reached what I took to be the little loch, following the western shore for about a quarter of a mile and then continued north-east until it looked as if I had got over the ridge.

A steep ridge. Not a *creag* I hoped, fervently. Rock everywhere. No vegetation. No sound. Still gloomy, but it looked brighter ahead. Down below, dimly, I saw the outlines of not one but innumerable lochs, irregular in shape, merging one with another. Nothing big enough to be Loch Shin as I imagined it, but they all seemed to be in the right direction.

Down I went into a deep gulley, a rift that swung first north-east and then north. Not the most encouraging direction, certainly, but there was no way out. I could go back or I could go on. There was no track of any sort to follow on those sloping plates of grey-black gneiss. On I went, still down into bleak uncertainty. The gulley led into a narrow valley with towering cliffs on both sides.

Both shoes by that time were in pretty poor shape. The sole of one flapped about and the stitching of the other had come loose in several places. To make things worse, a strap of the rucksack had broken in the fall. I had the feeling that the ex-pedition was dropping to bits.

What I needed for encouragement more than anything else was a glimpse of Loch Shin, the end of the difficult, path-finding part of the whole trip. But where was it? *Where*, in God's name, was it? Twice I saw what might have been water far ahead, but it may have been quartzite or a shaft of light on wet rock.

About six o'clock that night a loch loomed up far down in the gorge-like valley and I worked down to it, slowly. I felt ex-cessively tired. The water was far from where I expected to see it, but I imagined, hopefully, that I had swung round towards the eastern end of Shin. Hope changed to apprehension when the water appeared to curl away in the wrong direction, to the west.

I scrambled down to within two hundred yards of the shore. A flock of seabirds flapped off. I looked at them in utter dejection. Instead of Loch Shin, I had dropped down to the sea-loch Glencoul, on the coast. There was no way out, for the cliffs were precipitous, and I had no alternative but to go back.

A bad night that. The grey shawl of mist still hung round the top of the gorge. The rocks I scrambled down earlier, hope-fully, seemed twice as steep on the way back. I recall only a few landmarks: one, a prostrate pine, its bone-white roots sticking up in the air like a petrified octopus; another, an enormous water-fall, the famous *Chual Aluinn*, the biggest uninterrupted drop in Britain. It fell down with the noise of escaping steam. It seemed to fall out of the sky, for the crest was hidden in the mist.

How I had managed to stray down to Glencoul became compass-clear far too late for comfort. The sweep of the gorge had beguiled me away from harder going, over the wall of the valley. There, as in Glen Ling and elsewhere, a wrong decision at a critical point had led to hours of arduous and unnecessary scrambling. That particular point in the gorge isn't even graced with a Gaelic name, but for those who may stray there, the formal map reference of the point of decision is 305245. From there it took me another three hours to get down to Loch Shin.

Once down from those heights there are no *creags* or chasms. Only manure-coloured water and olive-grey bog gently rising and falling for miles and miles. I squelched along. Two more of my six remaining toe-nails fell off. Not painfully. New pink ones appear, miraculously, underneath.

The red ribbon of the northern night lay low along the west. Scarcely any mist, but almost dark now, the silence heavy and the sense of loneliness profound. No jubilation when the long-sought loch appeared, for in the dark I could scarcely see.

There, at Corriekin, after walking for fifty days, the most difficult part of the trip came to an end at midnight in the lodge of a good shepherd and his wife. The man had driven off down the valley to look at a prize-fight on a neighbour's television set and his wife had waited up for him. They treated me with heart-touching hospitality.

Little remains to be told. Most of the remaining hundred miles or so were walked either on or within sight of purposive tracks or roads. Only at one point on the two-day journey to Bettyhill, a little harbourage on the northernmost coast of Britain, is there need for serious navigation. This is among the luxurious bogs be-tween Shin and an isolated, angular mountain called Ben Kli-breck, the last I saw of Drum Albyn. For the rest I kept to the tracks above Strathnaver, where a famous salmon river flows through an infamous valley.

Here the Gordon Earls of Sutherland quadrupled their fortune by setting fire to the homes of established tenants who were reluctant to make way for sheep. The tale of the terrible evictions in the early part of the nineteenth century has been told with subtly-poisoned irony by Ian Grimble in *The Trial of Patrick Sellar.**

Donald Macleod, a local stone-mason and a contemporary witness, describes how 'strong parties for each district, furnished with faggots and other combustibles, rushed on the dwellings of this devoted people and immediately commenced setting fire to them, proceeding in their work with the greatest rapidity till about three hundred houses were in flames. The consternation and confusion were extreme; little or no time was given for removal of persons or property - the people striving to remove the sick and helpless before the fire should reach them - next, struggling to save the most valuable of their effects. The cries of the women and children - the roaring of the affrighted cattle hunted at the same time by the yelling dogs of the shepherds amid the smoke and fire - altogether presented a scene that completely baffles description.

'A dense cloud of smoke enveloped the whole country by day and even extended far on the sea; at night an awfully grand, but terrifying scene presented itself - all the houses in an extensive district in flames at once.' Donald Macleod said he ascended a height about eleven o'clock in the evening and counted two hundred and fifty blazing houses 'many of the owners of which were my relations, and all of whom I personally know; but whose present condition, whether in or out of the flames I could not tell. The conflagration lasted six days.'

Among those who died as a result of the fires started by Patrick Sellar, the Factor of the Gordon Earls of Sutherland, was an old bedridden woman of nearly 100 years of age. She was the mother-in-law of William Chisholm of Badinloskin and when they were on the point of putting torches to the thatch, she was alone.

*Routledge and Kegan Paul (1962)

In the report which has become part of the dreadful history of Strathnaver, Donald Macleod said: 'I informed the persons about to set fire to the house of this circumstance, and prevailed on them to wait till Mr. Sellar came. On his arrival I told him of the poor old woman being in a condition unfit for removal. He replied, "Damn her, the old witch, she has lived too long; let her burn." Fire was immediately set to the house, and the blankets in which she was carried out were in flames before she could be got out. She was placed in a little shed, and it was with great difficulty they were prevented from firing it also. The old woman's daughter arrived while the house was on fire, and assisted the neighbours in removing her mother out of the flames and smoke, presenting a picture of horror which I shall never forget, but cannot attempt to describe. She died within five days.'

Some people managed to escape by sea. 'While the burning was going on, a small sloop arrived, laden with quicklime, and when discharging her cargo the skipper agreed to take as many of the people to Caithness as he could carry. . . . about twenty families went on board, filling the deck, hold and every part of the vessel. They were childhood and age, male and female, sick and well, with a small portion of their effects saved from the flames, all huddled together in heaps. Many of these persons had never been on sea before . . . to add to their miseries, a storm and contrary winds prevailed, so that instead of a day or two, the usual time of passage, it was nine days before they reached Caithness.'

Of those who escaped, 'Robert Mackay, whose whole family were in a fever or otherwise ailing, had to carry his two daughters on his back, a distance of about twenty miles. He accomplished this by first carrying one, and laying her down in the open air, and returning, did the same with the other, till he reached the seashore and then went with them on board the lime vessel.'

All the foregoing was carefully set down on paper by Donald Macleod, the stone-mason of Strathnaver, the still-deserted valley that lies between Loch Naver and the sea. For his part in being one of the few people to resist the agents of the Great Lady of Sutherland, Macleod was driven out of the estate. In his absence, his home was wrecked and his wife, a young woman with a sucking infant at her breast, and three other children, were obliged to watch them wreck it. His wife later became incurably insane. But in driving the stone-mason to Edinburgh, the agents drew attention to themselves. For the outside world got a vivid picture of what was happening in distant Strathnaver: Donald Macleod published what he had seen, first in the *Edinburgh Weekly Chronicle* and then in his *History of the Destitution in Sutherland.*

The Strath is far from destitute today. A good road runs due north through miles of rolling country, much of it firm pasturage. But it still looks ominously deserted and those that farm it are mostly from the south.

The Altnaharra Hotel is filled with rich sportsmen. That morning, early, some tinkers on bicycles who said cautiously that they came from Dundee, were netting the outfall of the Naver with what looked like lace curtains. Later in the day, on the banks of the river at intervals were parked large, chauffeur-driven cars whose English owners, with a gillie at hand, cast flies into the coffee-coloured water. Nobody I saw caught anything. And on I walked to the windy sea at Bettyhill.

The village lies some thirty miles to the east of Cape Wrath, a corruption, they will tell you locally, of *Hvarf,* the turning-point, the place where the captains of the Norse ships pushed their helms hard over and turned to sail down the west coast of Scotland.

On that coast I turned east, towards John o' Groats. This is another corner of Norse Britain. Here it was that Earl Thorfinn the Mighty governed the Orkneys, the Shetlands, the Western Isles and nine provinces of Gaeldom. The place-names tell the story. There is Spyta, Skakker, Skirssa, Mireland, Brawl and Barrack. In Thorfinn's time there was gold in the rivers and pearls for barter.

> *17 June:* left Bettyhill at sunrise and scurried along the coast road with only fifty miles to go. Scenery bleak and windswept: undulating moors with worn-down outcrops of tortured rock. Granite churches with raised pine-wood pulpits in place of altars. At Melvick crossed into even flatter, windier Caithness which

apparently means wild cat country. Two pubs filled with local seamen getting drunk on strike pay, but less aggressively by far than in the Lowlands. Spent night in dismal lodgings in Dounreay where duralumin sphere of atomic station reactor looks like golf ball about to be driven off into North Atlantic.

Only thirty miles to go now. I strode on, faster. Past Lybster with enormous view of a crinkly sea, the home, one might think, of the Kraken. On I went. Past Thuster and Scrabster where, instead of hedges and walls, the rock-littered pastures are divided up by what look like long lines of gravestones. They are, in fact, Caithness flags, thin slabs of Devonian sandstone. Looking at them, I thought of far-away Devon and Cornwall. Similar moors, similar cliffs: John o' Groats resembles Land's End. On each headland a gaunt hotel and in front of each hotel a photographer with coat collar turned up and hands in his pockets. He stands next to a clever bit of salesmanship, a portable signpost with adjustable directions.

'Where are you from?' he asks. Manchester, Minneapolis? No matter where. He has a box of all the letters of the alphabet and you can be photographed against an arm of the post that points to your home town, together with the mileage. Price ten shillings for six, post free. The cliff-top concessions in Cornwall and Caithness are run by the same enterprising man.

Only twenty miles to go now. Down into the harbour quarter of new-built Thurso, a bright, attractive, angular place, like a bit of modern jewellery. And then on to Dunnet and Kirk o' Tang.

'Walked far?' asked the motorist, pulling up.

'Pretty far,' I said with carefully-contrived nonchalance. But when he asked how far and I told him, he drove off looking, I think, more saddened than surprised. Thank God, he didn't ask why.

Far out at sea rose Stroma. And then Hoy and Ronaldsay and the other isles of Orkney. Here is the very end of Britain. The wind blew hard. It blew me sideways, but, with the end in sight, a distant point of land narrowing mile by mile, I could have withstood a hurricane. Only ten miles to go.

Ten miles to *what*? To a mere name on a map? What had it all amounted to? Why hadn't I spent more time seeing fewer places more leisurely, using a car here and there? I finished the journey as I had started two months earlier, that is by asking myself a lot of questions. The difference was I could now answer some of those I had thought most about.

Part of the journey could certainly have been done more easily by car, but it would have been an entirely different journey. Roads are all more or less alike. Walking is intimate; it releases something unknown in any other form of travel and, arduous as it can be, the spring of the ground underfoot varies as much as the moods of the sky. By walking the whole way I got a sense of gradual transition from one place to another, a feeling of unity. The mosaic of my own country and its people had become a sensible pattern. Memory now acts like that little polished cylinder in the museum at Fort William which puts together the fragments of the portrait of the Bonny Prince. But this had been achieved at some cost.

Rain depressed me and mist I feared – mist on Dartmoor, on Kinder Scout, in the Cheviots above Redesdale and in at least three places in Scotland where, on the high tops, there is the additional hazard of drifting cloud. Cloud is impenetrable. It brought me to a stop. Through mist I went on, perhaps unwisely, but with caution and faith in a map and a bearing. I feared only a sudden drop, a *creag*. There are no unpredictable drops that I know of in England.

Only on Dartmoor are there bogs that I would not willingly venture near again, at least not in a mist. They seemed uniquely and deceptively deep, which, through a combination of ignorance and good fortune, I managed to get round rather than across. Those encountered elsewhere, especially in the southern Pennines and Scotland, could be easily avoided or occasionally walked through with no more than muddy knees. Probing showed that, marginally, at least, they were not deep.

During the trip I discovered that without making elaborate detours some of the country's most-talked-about bits of walking country are substantially impassable. This is particularly evident on the so-called cliff-top paths of Cornwall, on Dartmoor,

232

Offa's Dyke and, to a lesser extent, on sections of the Pennine Way where directions are, in places, miserably inadequate.

A walker expects hostility in the vicinity of military training grounds; it is understandable on the part of private landowners who, in places, have been obliged, reluctantly, to let pedestrians through ancient rights of way. But it is wholly intolerable on the part of Government agencies, such as the Nature Conservancy and the Forestry Commission, which, in areas such as Teesdale and the Border forest, have blocked the long-distance trail, north.

The walker is a convenient symbol for those who run cosy conferences on the importance of preserving the countryside. He is tolerated; he is ever encouraged if he keeps to a few well-trodden tracks from points of surveillance where he can be watched and warded. But the tracks are short and discontinuous. In the bits in between the walker is still to a great extent on his own.

He is the declared enemy of keepers, both private and those employed by municipalities, such as waterworks authorities. And landlords of most of the big public houses make it abundantly clear that a foot-borne man is as unwelcome among hard-drinking, wheel-carried customers as the gypsies are. This is nothing new. In 1782 a German pastor named Carl Philipp Moritz spent six weeks tramping from London to Derbyshire and back. In Britain, he says, the pedestrian seems to be

> considered as a sort of wild man or an out-of-the-way being who is stared at, pitied, suspected and shunned by everybody who meets him. . . . in England any person undertaking so long a journey on foot is sure to be looked upon and considered as either a beggar, or a vagabond, or some necessitous wretch, which is a character not more popular than that of a rogue. To what various, singular and unaccountable fatalities and adventures are not foot-travellers exposed in this land of carriages and horses?

Open country is diminishing rapidly. Those bits with any claim to distinction are protected, badly, by government agencies. The flooding of Upper Teesdale showed that the Nature Conservancy was not only powerless to save the place, but failed to realize its intrinsic importance until too late. The wrangle that ensued is wholly discreditable to government, local authority and industry.

> *How with this rage shall beauty hold a plea*
> *Whose action is no stronger than a flower?*

Yet many parts of Britain are still inexpressibly beautiful. The sense of airy suspension, the racing cloud shadows of the Brendons, the Quantocks and the Long Mynd, the sweep of the Pennine Way from Fountains Fell to Keld and the Border between Ettrick and Tweed contain content. No woods that I know of can match the Forest of Dean nor dales the limestone cliffs below Malham.

Those in search of the spectacular from a well-found track should walk across Glencoe by way of Rannoch Moor and look back on the pass from the Staircase. As to the rest of Scotland, Glen Dessary, Quoich, the hills above Loch Hourn and Wester Ross are more deserted, certainly more theatrical than I could have imagined. Assynt I am unlikely to tackle again.

The walk came to end at a craggy-looking place called Duncansby Head, a mile or two beyond John o' Groats. There, from the cliff tops, I looked down on the outermost tip of Gaeldom, a flurry of water and black rock. I turned round and walked back to the hotel in the greenish twilight. I ate supper, alone, wrote up a few notes and sat down on the edge of a small bed, flicking back through the pages of a diary filled with vigorous facts and names that already seemed rather strange and far-away.